Empire and the Animal Body

Empire and the Animal Body

Violence, Identity and Ecology in Victorian Adventure Fiction

John Miller

ANTHEM PRESS
LONDON · NEW YORK · DELHI

Anthem Press
An imprint of Wimbledon Publishing Company
www.anthempress.com

This edition first published in UK and USA 2014
by ANTHEM PRESS
75–76 Blackfriars Road, London SE1 8HA, UK
or PO Box 9779, London SW19 7ZG, UK
and
244 Madison Ave. #116, New York, NY 10016, USA

First published in hardback by Anthem Press in 2012

Copyright © John Miller 2014

The author asserts the moral right to be identified as the author of this work.

All rights reserved. Without limiting the rights under copyright reserved above,
no part of this publication may be reproduced, stored or introduced into
a retrieval system, or transmitted, in any form or by any means
(electronic, mechanical, photocopying, recording or otherwise),
without the prior written permission of both the copyright
owner and the above publisher of this book.

British Library Cataloguing-in-Publication Data
A catalogue record for this book is available from the British Library.

Library of Congress Cataloging-in-Publication Data
The Library of Congress has catalogued the hardcover edition as follows:
Miller, John, 1973–
Empire and the animal body : violence, identity and ecology in
Victorian adventure fiction / John Miller.
p. cm.
Includes bibliographical references and index.
ISBN 978-0-85728-534-8 (hardcover : alk. paper)
1. English fiction–19th century–History and criticism. 2.
Adventure stories, English–History and criticism. 3. Animals in
literature. 4. Ecocriticism. 5. Human-animal relationships in
literature. 6. Ecology in literature. I. Title.
PR878.A54M55 2012
823'.809362–dc23
2012031880

ISBN-13: 978 1 78308 317 6 (Pbk)
ISBN-10: 1 78308 317 4 (Pbk)

This title is also available as an ebook.

CONTENTS

List of Illustrations   vii

Acknowledgements   ix

Introduction   1

Chapter One: Otherness and Order   23

Chapter Two: Scientists and Specimens   57

Chapter Three: The Animal Within   97

Chapter Four: Wild Men and Wilderness   149

Conclusion   183

Notes   191

Bibliography   211

Index   229

LIST OF ILLUSTRATIONS

Figure 1	'Bathurst confronts the tiger'. G. A. Henty, *Rujub the Juggler* (New York: Mershon, 1901 [1893]), 12.	43
Figure 2	'The British Lion's Vengeance on the Bengal Tiger'. *Punch*, 22nd August 1857, 76–7.	44
Figure 3	'My First Gorilla'. Paul du Chaillu, *Explorations and Adventures in Equatorial Africa* (London: John Murray, 1861), 71.	106
Figure 4	'Skeletons of Man and the Gorilla, the latter drawn from a skeleton in my collection'. Paul du Chaillu, *Explorations and Adventures in Equatorial Africa* (London: John Murray, 1861), 370.	108
Figure 5	'The Lion of the Season'. *Punch*, 25th May 1861, 213.	118
Figure 6	'Death of a Male Gorilla'. Paul du Chaillu, *Wild Life Under the Equator* (London: Sampson Low, 1869), 195.	122
Figure 7	'Gambo's Friend Killed by a Gorilla'. Paul du Chaillu, *Lost in the Jungle* (London: Sampson Low, 1870), 131.	123
Figure 8	'Orang-Utan Attacked by Dyaks'. A. R. Wallace, *The Malay Archipelago* (London: Macmillan, 1877 [1869]), frontispiece.	128
Figure 9	'He was fascinated with horror'. R. M. Ballantyne, *Red Eric* (London: Nelson), 176.	136
Figure 10	'"Do you hear?" said Verkimier sternly.' R. M. Ballantyne, *Blown to Bits* (London: Nisbet and Co., 1889 [1885]), 187.	140

ACKNOWLEDGEMENTS

This book has been a long time in the making in Glasgow, Edinburgh, Norwich, Walmer and Prince George. Sincere thanks are due to the Bryce Bequest, the Arts and Humanities Research Council and the Department of English Literature at the University of Glasgow for initial funding for the project and assistance with library visits and conference attendance. A postdoctoral bursary at the Institute for Advanced Study in the Humanities in Edinburgh allowed me to continue research when unemployment was looming. A fellowship at the University of Northern British Columbia allowed me time and space to apply the finishing touches. A number of people have read part or all of the manuscript as it has developed in its various forms. Andrew Radford has been a meticulous and supportive editor and guide. Donald Mackenzie's knowledge, enthusiasm and scholarly generosity have been invaluable. Christine Ferguson and Erica Fudge have offered astute and detailed comments on an earlier incarnation of this work. The book's three anonymous reviewers provided insightful and diligent feedback, while Janka Romero at Anthem Press has been an ever reliable source of information. I'm grateful to friends and colleagues at ASLE-UK, especially Tom Bristow and Petra Hansson for expertise, encouragement and good company. Many thanks to Kevin Hutchings for giving me the opportunity to finish this book and to start my next in the beautiful surroundings of Northern British Columbia. Thanks also to Khlayre Mullin without whom I couldn't have started, to Mariangela Palladino for our ongoing collaborations, to Kelly Van Andel for keeping me going and to my family for sticking by me throughout my numerous peregrinations and misadventures.

    I am grateful for permission to reprint material that has appeared elsewhere in earlier versions. Some material from Chapter Three on R. M. Ballantyne's *Blown to Bits* appeared originally in the *Victorian Review*. Some of the material on gorillas from that chapter has appeared in *Popular Exhibitions, Science and Showmanship, 1840–1910* (ed. Joe Kember, John Plunket and Jill A. Sullivan). Many thanks to the editors of these publications for their kind permission. Similarly, substantially revised versions of sections of Chapter Two and

Chapter Four are published with the permission of Cambridge Scholars Publishing having appeared in earlier forms in two volumes of conference proceedings, *The Apothecary's Chest: Magic, Art and Medication* (ed. Konstantina Georganta, Fabienne Collignon and Anne-Marie Millim, 2009) and *Material Worlds* (ed. Rachel Moffat and Eugene de Klerk, 2007).

Lastly but not leastly, thanks to Ruth Hawthorn and our family of animals, Lily and Sophie, and Mildred, Milo and Marmaduke.

INTRODUCTION

In his 1861 bestselling tale of Africa, *The Gorilla Hunters*, the Scottish adventure writer R. M. Ballantyne describes a wounded elephant's final moments at the hands of the novel's heroes:

> Peterkin instantly sprang forward, but Jack laid his hand on his shoulder.
> 'It's my turn this time, lad,' he cried, and, leaping towards the monster, he placed the muzzle of his rifle close to its shoulder and sent a six ounce ball right through its heart.
> The effect was instantaneous. The elephant fell to the ground, a mountain of dead flesh.[1]

Ballantyne depicts the scene with evident relish. Peterkin and Jack, men in their early twenties, vicariously enact the author and his readers' pleasure in the hunt's successful climax. The untamed jungle the sportsmen traverse is a byword for adventure and excitement; the elephant's monstrosity emphasises their fortitude and prowess and forecloses any interest in its welfare. This mountain of flesh befits the 'rifle' and the 'six ounce ball', ontologically remote from the hunters; an object to be practiced on.

Ballantyne never himself visited the West-Central Africa of *The Gorilla Hunters*, but he was to travel to Southern Africa in 1876. In his nonfictional account of that journey, *Six Months at the Cape*, he delineates a different kind of 'animal' encounter when he comes across a hut on the veldt resembling a 'gigantic beehive':

> There was […] a hole in one side partially covered by a rickety door. Close beside it stood a little black creature which resembled a fat and hairless monkey. It might have been a baboon. The astonished gaze and grin with which it greeted me warranted such an assumption, but when it suddenly turned and bolted through the hole into the beehive, I observed that it had no tail – not even the vestige of such a creation, – and thus discovered that it was a 'Tottie', or Hottentot boy.[2]

Ballantyne's disdainful identification of the African with a monkey objectifies the boy as an ungendered 'it'; his simian 'gaze and grin' marking the absence of a human face. The 'beehive' he lives in then confuses Ballantyne's image with the suggestion of an even lowlier species. To this, Ballantyne adds an evolutionary joke. Without 'the vestige of such a creation' as a tail, the boy recalls for readers Robert Chambers' 1844 proto-Darwinian *Vestiges of the Natural History of Creation*. The boy is inserted into a supposed hierarchy of organisms in which the European is elevated far above such a debased, bestialised 'creature'. Yet if the Hottentot is like a baboon, he is also not like a baboon. The lack of a vestigial tail adds ambivalence to his position, affirming his division from the monkey so that even with his baboonish features he is neither one thing nor the other, neither fully animal nor fully human.

The representation of a resemblance between native and animal was a common trope of colonial discourse, forcefully asserting the supposed gulf between coloniser and colonised and opening a range of violent and repressive possibilities for colonial rulers as racial others are emptied of their human status. But as much as Ballantyne aims to separate himself from the object of his attention, his evolutionary allusion also expresses a relation between them: the intimation of an organic continuum between life-forms over time that connects as well as segregates. Accordingly, when in his 1877 novel of South Africa, *The Settler and the Savage*, Ballantyne portrays a young immigrant about to fire into a troop of baboons, the hero Charlie Considine is quick to intervene: 'Brute!' he exclaims, 'would you commit murder?'[3] The scene performs a complex philosophical manoeuvre that disturbs the easy polarity of the novel's title. As a 'brute' the ardent hunter is exiled from human civility, descending momentarily the evolutionary ladder; the baboons, on the other hand, are raised, albeit facetiously, to the moral rank of humans, or at least close enough to merit consideration. The 'brute's' planned act of violence confuses the straightforward split of human subjects from non-human objects. His position outside the animal world is questioned; the logical justification of colonial authority over bestialised savages falters. Specifically, in this instance, it is the uncanny likeness of baboons to humans that produces these rhetorical contortions, but the implications are far-reaching. The gorilla hunters' pleasure at the elephant's dispatch is not without its own hint of brutality. The '*muzzle* of [the] rifle' intrudes an animal presence into their victorious moment, identifying an emblem of human technological separation from the natural world with an image of an animal body: muzzle, an animal's snout from the old French. Even in this gory objectification of a savage beast, the human/animal divide seems uneasy; the most apparently self-evident and robust of biological categories appears under stress in Ballantyne's excited imagination.

These vignettes encapsulate two prominent issues in the emergent discipline of animal studies: the historical structuring of the human/animal interface as an opposition that facilitates violence and the figuring of animal being as an aspect of the human self. Or, to distil these two into one overarching concern, Ballantyne's colonial creatures lead us to interrogate the boundary of the categories human and animal; to investigate within this the knotted strands of kinship and difference. Adventure stories, as a genre often read for the determination of their dichotomies and for their intimacy to the material practices of empire, are key sites for interrogating the human/animal binary in a colonial context. In examining representations of exotic animal death and animal remains in Victorian and Edwardian boys' adventure fiction, this study argues that the polarity of human and animal is both central to imperial mythologies and a point at which these collapse. As the collaboration of British animal scholars the Animal Studies Group write, 'killing an animal is rarely simply a matter of animal death', but is 'surrounded by a host of attitudes, ideas, perceptions and assumptions'; encompassing, in the art historian Diana Donald's terms in the same volume, 'strange inconsistencies' and a 'compound of conflicting emotions'.[4] The boys' adventure was a significant element of hunting discourses in the nineteenth and early twentieth centuries and, as much as it appeared to celebrate and re-enact the pleasures of the chase, it was also a vehicle for numerous tensions, disturbances and complications that emerged around them, particularly in the constitution of ideals of masculine identity and in the complex and conflicted history and ideology of empire and environment.

As such, the animals in this study participate in three broad and separate, if overlapping, critical enterprises: not only animal studies, but also the longer established fields of postcolonial studies and ecocriticism. The investment of postcolonial studies in the themes evoked by Ballantyne's hunters hinges on the inter-implication of ideas of species and race in the nineteenth century and beyond and on the prominence of hunting as a point of colonial contact. For ecocriticism, Ballantyne's animals invoke the centrality of hunting in colonial environmental history and its importance as an expression of prevailing attitudes about human relations to ecologies. Despite some notable points of connection, these heterogeneous undertakings, postcolonial studies and ecocriticism, have often appeared theoretically divergent and even in conflict. Certainly, as Pablo Mukherjee writes in one of the several recent books to address this tension, between eco-/environmental and postcolonial positions 'there has been nothing like the degree and intensity of cross-fertilization that they potentially offer each other'.[5] As Susie O'Brien has pointed out, 1978, the year that Edward Said published his foundational work for postcolonial studies, *Orientalism*, also saw the coinage of the term ecocriticism in William

Rueckert's essay 'Literature and Ecology: An Experiment in Ecocriticism'.[6] This synchronicity is complemented, on a general level, by a degree of thematic continuity. If the aim of postcolonial studies is broadly to redress the legacies of colonial domination by re-empowering previously colonised peoples (the 'product', in postcolonial theorist Robert Young's words of 'resistance to colonialism and imperialism'),[7] then ecocriticism's privileging of the non-human in a world dominated by destructive anthropocentric attitudes offers a comparably politicised approach to reading: resistance to the catastrophic environmental abuse perpetrated by the industrial West. To O'Brien, 'both ecocriticism and postcolonialism are committed to locating the text in the world'.[8] Both, broadly, advance a connection of writing and materiality; questions of power and exploitation are central to each. Cheryl Glotfelty's description of ecocriticism as a critical practice that has 'one foot in literature and the other on land' might equally, though with a different range of investments, be applied to postcolonial studies, particularly in the light of Said's assertion that 'imperialism means thinking about, settling on, controlling land that you do not possess'.[9]

Yet, despite these common trajectories, clear disparities have emerged between postcolonial and environmentally focused criticism. Rob Nixon specifies the relation between them as one of 'reciprocal indifference and mistrust', informed by differing approaches to such questions as hybridity and purity, place, nationalism and history.[10] Additionally, the debt of some postcolonialists to poststructuralist theory was a source of disquiet among some early or first-wave ecocritics, who saw the realist position that ecological crisis seems to demand undermined by a postmodern overenthusiasm for textuality and the hyperreal. As Kate Soper famously remarked, 'it is not language that has a hole in its ozone layer; and the "real" thing continues to be polluted and degraded even as we refine our deconstructive insights at the level of the signifier'.[11] Other aspects of the development of these movements have also caused mutual misgivings. Ecocriticism's perceived interest, particularly in its early endeavours, in American nature writing to the near exclusion of other textual forms has a very real factual basis and supports Graham Huggan's 2004 conclusion that ecocriticism is at present 'a predominantly white movement'.[12]

Conversely, it is remarkable how few of the proliferating studies in postcolonialism since Said have accorded any space at all to consideration of environmental matters, giving rise to the supposition that postcolonial studies is determinedly anthropocentric. While as Richard Watts suggests, all areas of the *human*ities are by definition to some extent anthropocentric, postcolonialism has been perceived, even beyond this, to evince 'a tendency to isolate the humans at the centre of its analysis from the non-human universe that surrounds them'.[13] That postcolonial studies has shied away from ecological concerns indicates a degree of disconnection of the academic production of theories of the postcolonial from many on the front line of postcolonial struggles for whom, as Mukherjee reminds us, 'land, water, forests, crops, rivers, the sea' remain of central importance in the 'ongoing struggle of decolonization'.[14] Academic postcolonialism has been particularly marked by tension with ecocriticism's interest in non-human animals, and by extension, therefore, with animal studies. As the animals studies scholar Philip Armstrong summarises, 'In identifying the costs borne by non-European "others" in the pursuit of Western cultures' sense of privileged entitlement, post-colonialists have concentrated upon "other" humans, cultures and territories but seldom upon animals.'[15] Given the weight of colonial history, it is hardly surprising that a focus on animals in postcolonial analysis should seem at best narrow and at worst dangerously exclusionary. In a review of Huggan and Helen Tiffin's 2010 work on *Postcolonial Ecocriticism*, Erin James voices initial unease at 'attention paid to animals in postcolonial literature rather than the postcolonial subject and the larger postcolonial environment'.[16] This resolves, more explicitly, into a fear Armstrong identifies that 'pursuing an interest in the postcolonial animal risks trivialising the suffering of human beings under colonialism'.[17]

Although postcolonial studies' wariness of environmental and animal interests might at least imply something approaching harmony between ecocriticism and animal studies, they nonetheless also evince a different set of ethical priorities. While both animal studies and ecocriticism are broadly interested in disputing the terms of anthropocentrism, Greg Garrard turns to their historical origins to identify a stress between them:

> [E]nvironmentalism and animal liberation conflict in both theory and practice. Animal liberationists generally draw the line of moral consideration at the boundary of sentience and feeling [...] Environmental ethics, on the other hand, places far less emphasis on the individual organism, but demands moral consideration for inanimate things such as rivers and mountains.[18]

Animal studies, therefore, as a critical practice intimately connected with the politics of animal liberation inhabits a different ethical terrain to ecocriticism. This divergence is manifested, for example, as Garrard avers, in disparate views on culling as either a necessary aspect of ecosystem management or as a separate animal rights issue. An attention to wild animals in environmentalism, to the exclusion of domestic ones, is another perceived discontinuity, and, it is also worth pointing out, as Helen Tiffin does, that ecocriticism has, at least initially, focused less on animals than on other environmental themes.[19]

Added to this, despite its relative infancy as an explicitly demarcated discipline, animal studies has already resolved into distinct sub-disciplines. Animal studies itself has emerged as an umbrella term beneath which critical animal studies, animality studies and zoocriticism have announced different shadings of the interrogation of the human/animal binary. While critical animal studies is determined in its commitment to animal liberation, animality studies (as set out by Michael Lundblad) distances itself from direct animal advocacy to 'prioritize questions of human politics' (a central theme, of course, for postcolonial studies, to which this introduction will return).[20] Zoocriticism, a coinage of Huggan and Tiffin's, designates the specifically literary aspect of animal studies and forms a closer counterpart to ecocriticism than the broader disciplinary sweep of the other terms allows.

So, the relationship between animal studies, ecocriticism and postcolonial studies is marked by tension as much as by continuity. Unpacking the political, literary and ecological histories behind Ballantyne's animals, while setting out the scope of this study, enables a fuller sense of the strains and convergences across these uneasily intimate perspectives and marks out the possible ground for bringing them to a mutual accommodation, at least in so far as they apply to this discussion.

Historical Overview

Exotic animal death, often described in lurid detail, was a common component of Ballantyne's writing and did nothing to prevent him taking his place in the mainstream of Victorian juvenile fiction. Indeed, he was widely acclaimed, particularly by those who concerned themselves with the well-being of the young. Not long after *The Gorilla Hunters* had cemented its author's reputation, first established with the 1857 classic *The Coral Island*, Ballantyne's publisher Nisbet and Co. began concluding editions with several pages of advertisements for Ballantyne's prolific output, comprising glowing press reviews alongside appreciative letters from sympathetic clergy. The Rev. Aubrey C. Price of London commended Ballantyne for providing 'interesting and useful reading for the masses'. More pointedly, the Rev. Dr Andrew Thomson of Edinburgh identified a 'fine, manly moral tone [that] promotes the moral health of the community'.[21] Judging from such unstinting praise, it seems that big-game hunting rested comfortably with a wider ethical and educational agenda: part-and-parcel of connected conceptions of masculine decency and fitness that obsessed a generation troubled by the consequences, real and imagined, of aggressive industrialisation and urbanisation. Hunting came to be closely associated with Britain's imperial mission, especially in the post Berlin conference scramble for Africa of the 1880s and in the national anxiety generated by the Second Boer War at the turn of the century.

In *The Gorilla Hunters*, Ballantyne drew on an already established tradition of sporting travel narratives that had developed out of Britain's expanding colonial interests in preceding decades in other, more accessible regions of Africa, as well as in Canada, India and parts of the Far East. The most vaunted author of these was the old Etonian and erstwhile cavalry officer Roualeyn Gordon Cumming, whose 1850 *Five Years of a Hunter's Life in the Far Interior of South Africa* has attracted recent comment in environmental history and philosophy for the violence of its prose.[22] Yet, in his time, he was a figure of considerable public standing, delivering daily lectures in Piccadilly for a full eight years after his return to Britain.[23] Though notable for its popularity and visceral edge, Cumming's account was not breaking any literary ground. 1834, for example, had seen the Scottish borderer Thomas Pringle, a poet and emigrant to the Cape Colony, publish his *Narrative of a Residence in South Africa* in which he provided a chapter with the ideologically pointed title 'wars with wild beasts'.[24] Captain William Cornwallis Harris' 1839 *The Wild Sports of Southern Africa*, opened with an epigraph from Pringle's poetry and the author was able even at this early stage to comment in his introduction that tales of African sport had 'oftimes reached my ears'.[25] Pringle and Harris' texts illustrate two differing but complimentary strands of hunting literature: those of the settler and the soldier. Such narratives became increasingly common and the Indian Raj similarly saw a regular flow of sporting tales and treatises from the first years of the nineteenth century onwards.[26] A growing number of hunting journals and magazines provided an additional forum for the reflections of sporting travellers, as well as for articles on more widely practiced domestic field sports. The *Sportsman* was the first of these to go to press in 1836, followed by *The Field*, the 'country gentleman's newspaper', in 1853 and *Bailey's Magazine of Sports and Pastimes* in 1860.[27]

Ballantyne's fictional elephant, then, belongs to a growing body of work in which the virtues and successes of Britain's Nimrod adventurers were catalogued and eulogised. Although Ballantyne in *The Gorilla Hunters* does not name any of the works he evidently consulted, he later became assiduous in identifying his sources. A report of the death of a bull in the 1869 story *Hunting the Lions* is diligently referenced with a footnote:

> If the reader should desire fuller accounts of such battles, we recommend to him 'African Hunting', a very interesting work, by W. C. Baldwin, Esq., to whom with Dr Livingston, [sic] Du Chaillou, [sic] and others, I am indebted for most of the information contained in this Volume.[28]

Ballantyne's allusion to the missionary Livingstone, next to two authors more easily identified with colonial sport, illustrates the permeation of hunting discourse into other fields.[29] Killing animals appeared as a necessary element of most forms of exploration in the nineteenth century, whatever their central motivation. The representation of exotic animal death, accordingly, was not confined to specialised hunting narratives and Ballantyne's intertextual framework was not unitary and ideologically consistent. As a practice of the most ancient origins, hunting also carried a range of significations from classical antiquity and a more immediate British literary and historical past that add a broad and long-standing cultural overlay to the sporting enticements of the colonial moment.

Importantly, Ballantyne's œuvre not only drew on nonfictional sources, but also stimulated their production. Frederick Courteney Selous, later the inheritor of Cumming's mantle of Britain's most famous imperial hunter, described in tellingly visceral language in the 1900 *Sport and Travel East and West* how as a boy he used to 'devour ravenously the works of Ballantyne'.[30] Fictional accounts of hunting cannot, then, be divorced from the vast numbers of animal carcases that the British Empire generated. Ballantyne's figuring of the elephant as a 'mountain of dead flesh' might, with this in mind, be scrutinised as a metonymic evocation of the momentous effects of an enterprise that at first brooked few limits. Texts strewn with the remains of exotic fauna, often photographed or illustrated at the huntsman's feet or in the sights of his gun, both reflected and encouraged an undertaking of industrial proportions, remarkable to begin with as much for its indiscriminacy as for its sheer scale. The record 'bags' of fervent hunters uninhibited by any sense of ecological consequences soon became inscribed in sporting folklore. Cumming returned home from Africa in 1849 with an estimated thirty tons of trophies. In 1860 the party of Prince Alfred, the sixteen year old son of Queen Victoria, was said to have accounted for six hundred head of large game in one 'glorious day' in Orange Free State. Selous' personal tally came to more than two thousand between 1872 and 1874 in elephants alone.[31] Hunting narratives often featured appendices reckoning the totals of the different species killed as these monumental statistics became part of the cultural apparatus of sport.

The impact on animal populations and on biodiversity was unsurprisingly considerable. Mahesh Rangarajan in *India's Wildlife History* charts the disappearance of the rhino and wild buffalo from the 'north Bengal plains by the 1850s' and estimates that over '80,000 tigers, more than 150,000 leopards and 200,000 wolves were slaughtered in the fifty years from 1875 to 1925'.[32] In Southern Africa, the British (and also the Boers) demonstrated, at least initially, a cavalier attitude to the possibility of extinction. The quagga, a sub-species of zebra, was described as existing in huge herds by Cornwallis Harris in the 1830s and was even to be found in significant numbers in 1875, but was gone by the 1880s.[33] A rare antelope, the blaubok, was rendered extinct as early as 1799 through the first colonial excesses. This is not to say that hunting was the only factor in the decline of animal populations. Habitat loss, driven largely by the pressures of new forms of agriculture, particularly in India plantation agriculture, was also a key factor, as, in South Africa, was the spread of animal disease, particularly through the rinderpest epidemic of the 1890s, which saw the Cape warthog, already much reduced by over-hunting, pushed finally to extinction in 1900. Indigenous hunting also had an impact. The historian John M. MacKenzie notes that 'there were certainly pre-colonial species extinctions caused by hunting and, at times, profligate killing'.[34] The New Zealand moa, a large flightless bird wiped out by Maori hunting probably as early as the sixteenth century is one famous example of significant environmental impoverishment that predates the arrival of European guns.[35] In India, the Mughal Empire, especially in the seventeenth century, took an extraordinarily heavy toll on animals and some independent princes in the period of British rule were every bit as uninhibited as their European contemporaries.[36] It should not be supposed either that Britons' evident appetite for violence was entirely untroubled by misgivings about cruelty towards animals during the years of colonial expansion. In fact, despite the popularity of Ballantyne and Cumming's bloodthirsty prose, the Victorian age saw something of a flowering of considerations of animal welfare, although these concerns were rather uneven in their scope both in terms of species and geography.[37]

Ultimately, colonists and adventurers could not ignore the unprecedented results of their sporting enterprises overseas and towards the end of the nineteenth century a wistful note commonly emerges in hunting literature. In the dedication to his 1889 tale *Allan's Wife*, H. Rider Haggard, a noted exponent of the fictional hunting narrative, bluntly declares of Transvaal 'the game is gone';[38] a conclusion echoed in another setting by one Captain Harry Storey, who in the 1907 *Hunting and Shooting in Ceylon* sadly reflects that 'localities which ten years ago teemed with game are now almost void of life'.[39] John Buchan, in his 1903 work of nonfiction *The African Colony*, correspondingly regretted that 'the great days of South African sport are over'[40] and gloomily anticipated a dreary future for the keen sportsman:

> [F]or the big game hunter, in the old African sense, there is little or nothing left. The day of small things has arisen, and we must be content to record tamely our sport in braces of birds and heads of small buck, where our grandfathers recorded theirs in lion-skins and tusks and broken limbs.[41]

Buchan's lament not only charts the ecological decline of imperial territories, but also reveals one of the most prominent ideological trajectories of big-game hunting. The Industrial Revolution, while providing the economic impetus for imperialism, had also generated social and environmental problems that the

Empire, it was hoped, might to some degree alleviate, offering new homes for the urban poor and, more pertinently to hunting, a healthier vista to the enervated wealthy. Increasing industrialisation altered both the natural world and man's relation to it, instituting a segregation of humanity from wild non-humanity construed by some to have sapped the nation's strength.[42] Empire offered the possibility of forgetting an urbanised homeland for a while in invigorating hunting grounds overseas in which the nation's men could be rejuvenated before returning to the drawing rooms and theatres of civilisation. Colonial discourse, paradoxically then, retained a substantial investment in the wilds it intended to tame and cultivate so that in the decline of the wilderness, Buchan divines a diminution of the self: a disconcerting lack that emerges from the aboriginal plenitude. Where hides and broken limbs had marked the extrovert virility of the hunter, the tameness of inferior prey now illustrates his potential regression, restricting his opportunity to assert his mastery and rediscover the crusading manhood fading from Britain's developed landscape.

Consequently, colonial attitudes toward animals, and the natural world more generally, gradually underwent a change in the decades after Ballantyne's elephant met its grisly end and might be seen (problematically) to constitute part of the dawning of a global environmental consciousness. While Captain H. Shakespear, the 'commandant of the Nagpore irregular force' referred rather dismissively in his 1860 account of *The Wild Sports of India* to the 'wild beasts of the forest, which God has ordered us to destroy'[43] by the end of the century determined efforts were underway to ensure the protection of colonial animals for the next generation and beyond. Acts granting legal protections to wildlife were passed in India in 1873 and 1879 and in Southern Africa in 1866 and again in 1886, when the quagga was finally granted protected status three years after the last individual had died in the Amsterdam zoo.[44] Storey in *A Ceylon Sportsman's Diary* records the foundation of the 'Ceylon Game Protection Society' in 1894, in response to the 'unlimited destruction of game' that threatened to finish the colony as a sporting destination.[45] On a larger scale, the Convention for the Preservation of Wild Animals, Birds and Fish in Africa was signed by several European powers in 1900, followed shortly by the establishment of the more widely active 'Society for the Preservation of the Wild Fauna of the Empire' in 1903, a year in which Buchan urgently pleaded for the strict observation of the new game laws in South Africa to reprieve 'vanishing species' and to rescue the national conscience from 'one of the most heinous sins of civilisation'.[46] Hunting, then, segued into an early, rather questionable, form of conservation. Importantly, the game reserves established in these years were the sites of many of today's national parks, key locations of biodiversity in many former colonies.[47]

Evidently, these histories of colonial hunting are tied closely to both postcolonial and ecocritical interests. While the scale of carnage is a striking illustration of the impetus of environmental degradation since the Industrial Revolution, the centrality of hunting in colonial discourse and its consequences for the indigenous human populations of imperial hunting grounds identify its signal relevance to a postcolonial analysis of the effects and strategies of empire. In the African context, for example, MacKenzie divides imperial hunting into three stages, each of which, in a different but related way, is inextricably linked with imperial politics.[48] The first phase, the commercial hunt, in which animal 'resources' were plundered for Britain's financial gain constituted to a large extent the frontier of colonial incursion. The second, hunting as subsidy, evinces the wider implication of hunting in a range of imperial and proto-imperial practices. Animal bodies supplied food for missionaries, traders, prospectors, natural historians and geographers as well as a means of paying their guides and bearers. Finally, MacKenzie identifies the emergence of 'The Hunt' as a ritualised demonstration of mastery of colonial space involved closely with imperial militarism and completing the transition, as MacKenzie explains elsewhere, of hunting 'from economic necessity to ethical luxury'.[49] In this guise as a 'symbolic act of global dominance',[50] 'The Hunt' also incorporated the collection of natural history specimens, an important prop of empire's ideological framework and a significant element of hunting discourse.

If MacKenzie's research adumbrates a natural convergence of postcolonial and environmental agendas in an analysis of hunting, increasing British control over colonial hunting grounds in the name of conservation illustrates a source of conflict between them. Hunting came to be practiced within a forest of legislation. Licences and boundaries constrained the free-ranging overindulgence of the early Victorians and the ambitions of the colonial hunter shifted from the sheer volume of slaughter to the less easily quantifiable virtues of self-restraint, superior marksmanship and *veldtcraft*. Organisations such as the Shikar Club in India added informal codes of conduct to government commands; it became anathema to shoot at females or young males and to fire indiscriminately into a herd was most definitely 'bad form'. This development might be read as the kind of combination of state intervention and voluntary action often welcomed today by environmentalists; yet, as a bureaucratisation of natural resources, it also comprised a disciplinary supervision of colonised peoples. Imperial hunting was a forceful marker of social status, recalling a feudal system of land access, power, patronage and privilege. Most noticeably, game laws operated as an integral element of the racial politics of imperial hegemony, denying or restricting indigenous access to an important, traditional food source in order to safeguard the white man's hobby. In a recent work of colonial environmental history, Beinart and Hughes summarise how 'Conservationist controls […] exacerbated political tensions over dispossession' and evictions in the name of the environment were commonplace.⁵¹ With remarkable consistency, the blame for the decline of beasts of prey is assigned in hunting narratives to the improvidence of 'natives' whose unrestrained use of firearms and appetite for trade is held up as an exemplar of a congenital irresponsibility that demands British rule. As Captain C. H. Stigand and D. D. Lyell contend in their 1906 *Central African Game and its Spoor*, 'game suffers more at the hands of the native than of the white man'.⁵² Conservation in the context of hunting, then, enabled an intensification of racist identity politics: the more responsible the British imagined themselves, the more reckless they imagined 'the native'.⁵³

Opposing Interests

The relationship between conservation management and the rights of indigenous peoples remains a vexed issue to this day, as, more broadly, do the manifold intersections of environmental responsibility and global social justice. These are large questions that it is perhaps not helpful to generalise about; particular historical forces in distinct geographical regions require specific analysis. That said, the exclusionary politics behind the foundation of game reserves and the origins of colonial environmentalisms are still widely apparent. O'Brien cites the 'forcible removal of humans living on the borders of Kruger Park in South Africa' as an example of the enduring significance of this history.⁵⁴ In another geographical context, the Indian conservation enterprise Project Tiger established in 1973 and generally considered an environmental success story, 'sharply posits', in the words of Ramachandra Guha, 'the interests of the tiger against those of poor peasants living in and around the reserve'.⁵⁵ Indeed, as William M. Adams writes, 'Until the 1990s the establishment of national parks conventionally meant the suppression of resource use by local people and the forced abandonment of established rights.'⁵⁶ Accordingly, Graham Huggan in '"Greening" Postcolonialism' identifies a suspicion, particularly among 'Third World scholars' that 'First World environmentalism […] runs the risk of turning itself into another, late-capitalist form of "ecological imperialism".'⁵⁷ High profile debates on carbon trading and biofuels are clear grounds for such concerns and illustrate the potential for a new environmental era (should it ever arrive) to renew old inequalities. This is not, of course, to assert that there have not been numerous and pointed environmental interventions among previously colonised peoples. Ken Saro-Wiwa and the Ogoni opposition to multinational oil interests in Nigeria would be one famous example; the Nobel Prize–winning Kenyan environmentalist Wangari Maathai another. Nonetheless, on the international stage there remains a sense of diverging, perhaps even in some cases directly opposed, material interests between postcolonial peoples and first world environmentalists. Postcolonial ecocriticism in this context seems a deeply troubled critical enterprise.

But to insist on the separation of human, animal and environmental ethics is to miss the crucial connections between them. The potentially rival claims of human and animal interests (to start with this) are more than a simple choice that excludes one as it selects the other, but rather an inextricably entangled web of exploitation and injustice in which both are inseparably joined. When in their introduction to *Killing Animals* the Animal Studies Group identifies the variety and scale of animal slaughter as 'a holocaust of immense proportions', their choice of language seems deliberately inflammatory.[58] Are the myriad abuses of animals in the industrial West, however grotesque, really appropriately considered within the same terminology as the Jewish holocaust or the holocaust of slavery? In approaching this most contentious and emotive of questions, many animals scholars have seized on the idea of speciesism, a neologism coined in 1973 by the psychologist Richard Ryder and developed subsequently by animal ethicists Tom Regan and Peter Singer.[59] Conceived to take its place alongside racism, sexism and anti-Semitism (among others), speciesism self-evidently describes the oppression of organisms based solely on their species and represents an aspiration to move beyond the attribution of meaningful moral status to *Homo sapiens* alone.

To Ryder, the connection of speciesism and racism is explicit; both are 'forms of prejudice that are based upon appearances – if the other individual looks different then he is rated as being beyond the moral pale'.[60] The problems with this position are numerous – not least regarding the question of where to draw the ethical line in speciesism. Are rights to be accorded to single-celled organisms (harmful bacteria and viruses are often cited), or should they be reserved for invertebrates, crustaceans, mammals? Such finicky philosophical questioning might evoke speciesism as a bleeding-heart hyper-liberalism that is a legitimate object of moral outrage for those engaged in more urgent and momentous political campaigns. Added to this, Ryder's insistence on the priority of 'appearances' in determining violent possibilities also seems an oversimplified way of thinking about complex varieties of difference.

Yet the significance of the philosophical category of 'the animal' (a problematic term in itself to which I will return) to the most vicious episodes of human history has emerged forcefully in the work of a number of the twentieth century's most prominent thinkers. Theodor Adorno writes that:

> The constantly encountered assertion that savages, blacks, Japanese are like animals, monkeys for example, is the key to the pogrom. The possibility of the pogroms is decided in the moment when the gaze of a fatally-wounded animal falls on a human being. The defiance with which he repels this gaze – 'after all,

it's only an animal' – reappears irresistibly in cruelties done to human beings, the perpetrators having again and again to reassure themselves that it is 'only an animal'.[61]

To Adorno, the interdependence of human and animal suffering is constituted through a rhetorical strategy that legitimates violence against humans by naming them as animals. Next to this we might also cite Jacques Derrida's identification in his essay 'Eating Well' of a place that remains open through violence against animals for 'a noncriminal putting to death' that implicitly permits the kind of atrocities to which Adorno alludes.[62] Comparably, Jean Baudrillard in an analysis of the 'industrial organisation of death' in contemporary agri-business reflects with similar emphasis on the intimacy of human and animal suffering that, 'Everything has happened to them that has happened to us. Our destiny has never been separated from theirs.'[63] These analogies are uncomfortable; Baudrillard's 'us' perhaps especially so, aligning the European intellectual with the victim without due acknowledgement of the historical particularities of vulnerability.

Marjorie Spiegel's influential study of the correspondences between human and animal slavery *The Dreaded Comparison* spells out the discomfort of linking violence against humans and animals in its title. The topic is 'dreaded' because slavery's dehumanisation of millions of Africans surely necessitates a vigorous restatement of human status rather than its apparent, continuing erosion through association with the suffering of animals. Spiegel's analysis has proved compelling, however, and it has the virtue at least of optimism, if not naïve utopianism. She argues that:

> By eliminating the oppression of animals from the fabric of our culture, we begin to undermine some of the psychological structures inherent in a society which seems to foster and create 'masters'. With a philosophy of universal respect for others' lives, treating anyone – human or non-human – in a cruel manner begins to be unthinkable.[64]

At root, then, for Spiegel species-based moral hierarchies enable violence; it is because it is possible to harm animals that it is possible to harm humans, a theme which aside from these theoretical interventions has long been a staple of vegetarian philosophy.[65] This conclusion is encapsulated by the concept 'intersectionalism', a term prominent in social sciences but less so in the humanities, originating in 1980s feminism and denoting a concern with, as Richard Twine summarises, 'the interplay of *multiple* differences' (original emphasis).[66] Pursuing the connections between discourses of race, species, gender and environment should not, of course, constitute an erasure of specificity. Neel Ahuja, for example, bemoans 'simplistic comparisons of racial and species violence that continue to abound in "animal studies" and mainstream animal activism'.[67] The key for Ahuja is to hold 'race and species as intersecting yet discrete aspects of identity'.[68] Taking this warning on board, human, animal and environmental politics can be seen to participate in one another in a multiplicity of ways which reveal them as mutually indispensable. 'Considering the question of animals', as Tiffin explains, is to return to 'the very basis of issues such as otherness, racism and colonialism with which postcolonial discourse has been concerned for the last few decades'.[69] Thinking about the operation of the category 'animal' in colonial discourse is not a distraction from or evasion of consideration of the human costs of empire, but an integral part of challenging the network of violently hierarchical Manichean opposites (self/other, coloniser/colonised, human/animal) that underpin the 'master' narratives Spiegel describes.

Some Problems of Intersectionalism

If this provides a basis for reconsidering representations of non-humans within the cusp of postcolonial studies, ecocriticism and animal studies, there are still some problems with this kind of intersectionalist thinking from animal studies and environmentalist perspectives, fostered by the suspicion that it is ultimately the human side of the equation that validates the non-human. To care for animals *only* because of what that care yields for human well-being, (however vital this may be) is not, perhaps, to care for animals at all, but rather to exemplify a position set out in Kant's *Lectures on Ethics* that '[o]ur duties towards animals are merely indirect duties towards humanity'.[70] Indeed, environmental concerns are often framed within questions of human welfare that reinvigorate rather than contest dominant anthropocentric attitudes. A key question in this context (although it may well be the wrong question) is, what really is biodiversity *for*? One commonly reproduced argument for the vital environmental cause of halting Amazonian deforestation, for example, is the suggestion that the forest, among the world's most biodiverse locations, may contain compounds of pharmaceutical or some other utilitarian significance. While any effective justification for conservation might seem a good one, preservation for medicine is haunted by the logical possibility that were some miraculous panacea discovered elsewhere we could then with a clear conscience turn it all into furniture. The forest in this scenario has no intrinsic value. Even the website of Friends of the Earth states with functional emphasis under the heading biodiversity that '*We* depend on biodiversity for food and materials, clean water and air' (my italics).[71]

This dilemma embodies a wider debate between shallow and deep ecologists, or light and dark green political positions. On the one hand, 'shallow ecologists', in the term of the Norwegian philosopher Arne Naess, consider the non-human largely for what it contributes to the human. Against this, deep ecologists like Naess contend that non-human life has value in itself and that humans have 'no right to reduce [its] richness and diversity except to satisfy vital needs'.[72] Here postcolonialists may once again perceive elements of environmentalism as a suspiciously hierarchical structuring of environmental and human interests with deep ecology as a hole into which the world's disenfranchised will inevitably tumble first. Whose needs will history decide are most vital? Indeed, hierarchical colonial relations may ultimately be revivified by what Cilano and DeLoughrey stress as deep ecology's tendency to depict the global south as 'hapless victims of an industrial north which is simultaneously their source of exploitation and, through the intervention of deep ecologists, their salvation'.[73] The apparent extension of deep ecological thinking beyond matters of clearly immediate environmental significance accentuates these concerns. Global warming may be a crisis of the most pressing dimensions that demands action as much as a humanitarian as an environmental imperative, but why worry about the Cape warthog?

Ultimately, the danger of these negotiations of priority between human and non-human is that they might merely add another set of pairs to colonial Manicheanism (deep ecology/shallow ecology, biocentric/anthropocentric, ecocritic/postcolonial critic) and re-energise, rather than transcend, the reductive binarism behind Spiegel's psychological structures of mastery. Furthermore, a hierarchical structuring of human and environmental issues replicates a concern among postcolonialists about a potential pitfall of postcolonial analysis of imperial dualisms. As Ania Loomba proposes, 'many critics are beginning to ask whether, in the process of exposing the ideological and historical functioning of […] binaries, we are in danger of reproducing them'.[74] Here, a closer engagement with ecology may be beneficial. Ecology, in its initial formulation by the German biologist Ernst Haeckel in 1866, concerns the complex relationships between organisms and their environment. Accordingly, ecological thinking by definition emphasises connectedness and interdependence, themes that have found particularly influential expression in James Lovelock's Gaia hypothesis that the earth represents a single system of life. Importantly, the assumption of interconnectedness (or what Timothy Morton calls the 'mesh') should not be considered mainly as a product of Western scientific ecology. Mukherjee cites the example of the Senegalese poet and politician Leopold Senghor whose formulation of the 'oneness of the human and the non-human' identifies 'quantum developments in European science' with the 'very basis of African philosophies and sciences'.[75] Dualistic worldviews, then, are directly antithetical to ecology's central premise. As Morton explains, 'Really thinking the mesh means letting go of the idea that it has a center' so that any hierarchical or dualistic ideology is immediately antithetical to what ecology tells us about the world.[76] In the end, nothing can live outside the ecosphere and the intricate, mutual entanglement of everything in it is profound and still, as climate scientists are discovering, somewhat mysterious.

Ecological and human interests are better conceived, then, as community rather than opposition, a mutual involvement that vouchsafes the basis for both a more accurate appreciation of the realities of our ecological situation and also a more inclusive ethical commitment that imagines no being as the disempowered, passive side of an imperial either/or. The contact of the postcolonial and the ecological can be seen as salutary to both. Firstly, it offers the possibility of the decolonisation of environmentalism, defined as the political suppositions and practices that emerge from an appreciation of the vital significance of our relationships with ecosystems and the organisms that comprise them. As Adams suggests:

> [C]onservationists need to re-think their dependence on standard Western assumptions about the 'divide' between people and non-human nature. They need a more pluralist understanding of different understandings, meanings and values of biodiversity. There is already widespread acceptance that indigenous or traditional knowledge is highly relevant to ecosystem conservation. Compared to modern science, such knowledge may be holistic and adaptive, gathered over generations by observers whose lives depended on its use.[77]

The movement towards a postcolonial environmentalism is thus a matter of praxis as much as ethics: an enrichment of conservation strategies through a revival of repressed indigenous knowledge, all the more urgent for the nagging inkling among many in the green movement that if industrial capitalism has got us into this mess it is probably quite unlikely to get us back out. Conversely, a postcolonialism without an environmental consciousness both neglects the importance of the environment in the colonial past and provides a perilous blueprint for the postcolonial future.

To return to the central interest of this study, consideration of the representations of 'colonised' animals in imperial adventures contributes to the large practical task of exploring the specific historical interdependences of human, animal and ecological concerns. This is not to say that there are not still many issues to be resolved in balancing ecocritical, postcolonial and animal studies perspectives. In dealing mainly with wild animals in wilderness areas, for instance, I skirt round the tension between animal studies and ecocriticism concerning the rival claims of individual animal rights and ecosystem preservation, although the emergence of a form of environmentalism that accepts violence against animals is very much a part of this study. Clearly, there is a lot more to be said about the relative merits of deep and social ecological positions than I have outlined here.[78] Also, the growth of ecocriticism beyond its early limited and theoretically naïve interests in nature writing to something that, in Lawrence Buell's words, brings theory and ecology together in a 'fruitful, energizing collaboration' is worthy of further detailed thought to situate it more thoroughly in relation to postcolonial and animal studies.[79]

Notwithstanding the emphasis on connectedness, following Ahuja's warning, my aim is also to remain attentive to differences, although, it should be noted, in analysing a genre that can often be negligent of cultural and ecological specificity. It is for this reason that I offer the problematically homogenising *Empire and the Animal Body* as my title. As many scholars have insisted, the neat formulation '*the* animal' reduces myriads of entities into a transcendental singular that compresses biodiversity into generality. Derrida's eloquent exposition of this theme has been particularly important:

> Confined within this catch-all concept, within this vast encampment of the animal, in this general singular, within the strict enclosure of this definite article ('the Animal' and not 'animals'), as in a virgin forest, a zoo, a hunting or fishing ground, a paddock or an abattoir, a space of domestication, are *all the living things* that man does not recognize as his fellows, his neighbours or his brothers.[80]

Derrida's metaphors pointedly locate such crude erasure of heterogeneity in relation to violent histories. His inventory of spaces of domestication,[81] from the fantasy of the 'virgin forest' to the gruesome reality of the 'abattoir', transposes the linguistic commonplace 'the animal' to sites of bodily objectification. The imperial figuring of a generic animality that emerges at points in this study is likewise implicated in forms of violence and reaffirms a key topic in animal (and also postcolonial) studies: how 'we' write, think and talk about 'others' is inseparable from how we treat them. Based on this association, I use the plural 'animals' rather than the singular throughout this study, although to signal the overarching context of objectification I retain the problematic 'the' in the title.[82] It is also worth noting here that the empire referred to in the title is restrictedly the British Empire: interesting and important comparative work on how the concerns of this study are apparent in different imperial contexts remains to be done.

Chapter Summary

My primary texts are selected from six prolific, but to varying degrees neglected authors, intimately associated at various points and through various means with the British Empire between the mid-nineteenth and early twentieth centuries. G. A. Henty (1832–1902) was a war correspondent and popular boys' adventure novelist publishing over a hundred works of fiction while also contributing to a number of boys' magazines. John Buchan (1875–1940) was an eminent statesman, wartime propagandist and man of letters involved as a colonial administrator in South Africa in the first years of the twentieth century. The schoolmaster G. M. Fenn (1839–1909), a friend and biographer of Henty, was also distinguished by a remarkably prolific literary career but never quite achieved Henty's popularity, nor had the personal opportunity for involvement in the Empire except through his writing. H. Rider Haggard (1856–1925), the son of a Norfolk squire, and like Buchan employed for a time in South Africa, produced well over fifty volumes mainly of fiction as did the Scottish writer and church elder R. M. Ballantyne (1825–1894). A distinct figure to these British authors and adventurers is the French-American travel writer and naturalist Paul du Chaillu (1831–1903), whose handful of texts offers an intriguing contribution to representations of exotic animals in Victorian natural history and to the, at times, uncertain boundary between scientific and adventure writing.

The value of this selection of authors exists both in their commonalities as practitioners of adventure writing and in the degree of variety between them. This enables differing perspectives on the adventure mode and permits both an appreciation of the relevance of adventure to other textual fields and an engagement with the distinct significations of animal death in discrete components of colonial discourse. Geographically, for the sake of cohesion, the choice of novels is confined to those that engage with the tropics, with the bulk addressing regions of Africa with the addition of one located in India and another in what is now Indonesia. Although adventure fiction ranged widely in its choice of settings, questions of animal otherness and species hierarchy are addressed most consistently in the particularly high volume of such texts that obsess on the savage denizens of the 'Dark Continent'. My privileging of this location over alternative regions thus adopts adventure fiction's own fascination with Africa. In terms of chronology, the earliest text considered was published in 1861, the latest 1906 so my analysis encompasses distinct moments in environmental and colonial history, both during aggressive periods of colonisation and later stages of administration, or, in environmental terms, phases of depredation and preservation. Rather than offering a sequential narrative literary history of animals in colonial adventures, the organising principle of the study is thematic, focusing on how various aspects of colonialism extracted ideological and material value from their engagements with animals across this historical continuum. This approach allows for a fuller sense of the intersections, tensions and discontinuities of animal representation within political, scientific and psychological discourses.

The relation of adventure fiction to ecology and colonialism is riven with contradictions; informed by energies that lead simultaneously in different directions, both extolling the necessity of conservation and facilitating the recruitment of land into profit. Imperial romance (a common synonym for adventure fiction discussed in detail in Chapter One) is not unitary or consistent either in ideological or textual terms; it embodies both an internally conflicted political ecology and contrasting, even contradictory, narrative traditions. Animals in this confused domain appear in several guises; as the 'other' in a well-established, pre-existent narrative tradition that emphasises confrontation and conquest; as the symbolically resonant victims of colonial power; as objects of scientific scrutiny in a discourse of knowledge; as emblems of an ecological purity beyond the reach of industrial contamination that invites the untrammelled aggression of the 'natural man'; and also as economic resources for an acquisitive empire. Animals are also, of course, simply 'themselves', living entities beyond these symbolic economies. Far from a set of self-enclosed compartments, this deathly spectrum of animal significance constitutes a blurred and fluctuating picture that illuminates the complexity of human/animal relations in this context.

In Chapter One, I begin with an overview of the situation of Victorian and Edwardian adventure fiction in current and contemporary critical debates, leading to a calibration of the relation of the genre, and the intertextual heritage it draws upon, to imperial history and to questions of environment and animality. An insistence on the naturalness of hunting (a theme again considered in detail in Chapter Four) is central to its function in imperial romance. Violence is construed as a rapt immersion in nature rather than a separation from it, a construction that in a wider schema serves to naturalise colonial domination at the same time as it bemoans the impact of the nexus of imperialism and capitalism on wild space. I gauge how the domestication of animal otherness contributes both materially and symbolically to the development and maintenance of colonial order with close reference to two contrasting approaches to imperial romance. Buchan's 1906 African symposium on the future of British imperialism *A Lodge in the Wilderness* and G. A. Henty's 1895 narrative of the Indian 'Mutiny', *Rujub the Juggler*, demonstrate, in contrasting geographical settings, firstly, the political value of hunting as a tool for administering colonial space and secondly, the value of animal bodies to the economics of imperialism. Each of these modes of signifying encounters with exotic animals also in turn contributes powerfully to the symbolisation of Britain's domination of these territories; yet despite the emphasis on control and assimilation of animals, the continuing sense of animals as 'other' to a regime of human civility paradoxically emerges as an essential aspect of their ideological recruitment into the Empire, particularly in the deployment of animal remains in domestic furnishings.

Chapter Two elaborates the theme of order in an analysis of the violent contribution of natural history to Britain's colonial interests. Focusing on two texts that emerged as part of the development of 'boy's own' fiction in the 1870s and 80s, I appraise the meaning of violence in relation to natural history's role in Victorian pedagogy and the reflection of this role in ideas of genre and masculinity. Henty's 1884 tale of the Ashanti War in West Africa, *By Sheer Pluck*, and Fenn's 1882 novel of an Indonesian specimen collecting trip, *Nat the Naturalist*, illustrate the slippage between legitimate categories of masculine violence and degenerate acts of aggression in colonial hunting and question the very masculinities (and, indeed, the humanity) they seem to encourage. Issues of technology, especially through the novels' depiction of taxidermy, and of hygiene, both at home in Britain and away in the tropics, depict the racist undercurrents of animal representation, but also destabilise the ascendancy of the natural historian through insistent imaging of the scientist as outsider.

Taking up these themes of race, hygiene and natural history, Chapter Three examines in detail the early cultural history of gorillas and the blurring of boundaries of species and genre that it stimulated. Addressing the texts of the French-American naturalist Paul du Chaillu and their reception in the scientific and popular press, I chart the anxieties and fixations that gathered around the 1861 'great gorilla controversy', most notably the contamination of science by romance and of humanity by animality. Ballantyne's 1861 novels of great apes, *The Gorilla Hunters* and *Red Eric*, heavily indebted to du Chaillu, illustrate particularly forcefully the relation of ideas of species, and especially degeneration, to concerns about sanitation, and promote a questioning of the hierarchies that situate the coloniser above and inherently separate from animal others.

Chapter Four develops the problematising of species boundaries with reference to degenerationist discourse at the *fin-de-siècle* and especially the bestialised human creatures that many Victorians imagined evolving in Britain's depressed metropoles. Crucially, the escape from this animalising environment is imagined through the assumption of another form of animal identity: the savage and belligerent fitness of the wild-born man. This theme of animal transformation and its relation to human aggression, already a context for the discussion of gorillas, is explored in connection with Haggard's 1892 *Nada the Lily* and by returning to *A Lodge in the Wilderness*. While environmental violence is often rightly identified, most notably in eco-feminist evocations of masculine engagements with animals, as a form of domination that draws on psycho-sexual as well as political imperatives, I propose through further analysis of Ballantyne's *The Gorilla Hunters* that colonial romance's depiction of human power over animals is more complex than has been previously allowed. The interplay of subject positions produced through fantasies of transformation and by subtle depictions of the coloniser's disempowerment in the colonial situation ultimately configure a humanity always intimately involved with the object of aggression, a pattern that again questions imperial boundaries and hierarchies and provides the basis, in conclusion, for a final consideration of the inter-implication of human, ecological and animal ethics.

Chapter One

OTHERNESS AND ORDER

Imperial Adventures

At the outset of his 1980 *Dreams of Adventure, Deeds of Empire*, Martin Green summarises the political investments of adventure fiction:

> [T]he adventure tales that formed the light reading of Englishmen for two hundred years and more after *Robinson Crusoe* were, in fact, the energising myth of English imperialism. They were, collectively, the story England told itself as it went to sleep at night; and, in the form of its dreams, they charged England's will with the energy to go out into the world and explore, conquer and rule.[1]

To Green, adventure constitutes a meeting point of literature and politics. Tales of derring-do in foreign lands reflected and promoted Britain's developing colonial interests and burdened the 'light reading of Englishmen' with some heavy ideological baggage. Far from a discovery of the postcolonial moment, this textual politics was an overt and self-conscious commitment for many practitioners of adventure fiction, most notably in the second half of the nineteenth century when the height of the British Empire saw a proliferation not only of sporting texts, but, connectedly, of imperial adventures. The poet and distinguished Indian civil servant Alfred C. Lyall, writing in 1894 of the 'expansion of British enterprise' across Africa, the South Sea Islands and India, commented that 'the Novel of Adventure [...] is drawing copious sustenance from these outlying regions'.[2] Comparably, in a survey of *Literature of the Empire* (1924), the literary historian E. G. Salmon anticipated Green's conclusion as he addressed the political undercurrents of adventure, rather more flamboyantly, in a rhetorical question: 'How far have action and thought been inter-related? To what extent have the pen and the printed page fostered or supplemented the daring of the sailor, the soldier, the statesman, the settler?'[3]

Central to this relation of thought and action was an emphasis on the association of national destiny and character formation, especially with a view to encouraging the kind of virtues and disciplines necessary to success in Salmon's inventory of imperial vocations. Commonly mixed in with this in adventure fiction are depictions of evangelical Christianity as a vital component of Britons' sense of their empire's civilising mission and an aspect of the wider schooling of a predominantly male readership. As Salmon expressed it, boys 'gain most of their information, apart from what they are taught at school, from the stories which they read; and this fact lends a new responsibility for the fiction which is produced for them'.[4] The genre was understood, therefore, as more than just fictional entertainment. Andrea White in her analysis of Joseph Conrad's engagement with the 'adventure tradition' maintains that 'adventure fiction, like travel writing, was perceived as primarily factual, reliable reporting within a narrative enacted by fictional or semi-historical characters'.[5] Geographical and historical details as well as more specifically vocational information on the practicalities of life overseas emphasised these stories' ideological importance; the sense that they are somehow 'true to life' lending authority to their pro-imperial didacticism.

Consequently, adventure fiction is a key site for investigating the strategic formations of colonial discourse. Nonetheless, studies of the genre have been few and far between with critical works generally confined to the same handful of 'classic' texts (and, indeed, considering the variable literary quality and sheer quantity of nineteenth- and early twentieth-century adventure fiction, a measure of neglect is hardly surprising). Such prolific and popular figures as Henty and Ballantyne have received scant academic attention and Fenn none at all; Paul du Chaillu, a figure widely celebrated and vituperated in his lifetime, has stimulated just three recent full-length articles and a sprinkling of brief paragraphs and occasional footnotes in longer works on Victorian exploration.[6] Haggard studies in comparison have been relatively abundant if rather limited in range: *King Solomon's Mines* and *She* in particular attracting a steady flow of scholarly articles from a range of theoretical positions, most regularly gender and postcolonial studies.[7] But although Gerald Monsman's monograph *H. Rider Haggard on the Imperial Frontier* (2006) has to some degree extended the scope of Haggard research beyond these core texts, the vast majority of his more than sixty works remain entirely untouched by scholarship. Buchan, the most accomplished literary craftsman of these authors, has suffered a similar fate to Haggard. *The Thirty-Nine Steps* and *Prester John*, for example, have remained consistently on the academic radar while the majority of his texts have slipped off screen, although an edited collection *John Buchan Reassessed* (2009) has expanded Buchan scholarship considerably.[8] Joseph A. Kestner's *Masculinities in British Adventure Fiction, 1880–1915* (2010) meanwhile has added a welcome theoretical gloss to reflections on the form as a whole, but for the most part with attention restricted to the same narrow corpus of texts: Ballantyne's *The Coral Island*, Stevenson's and Conrad's romances and the usual Haggard suspects.

In approaching a literary form that seems to correlate directly with Britain's imperial interests, there has also emerged a tendency among some scholars to stress an overarching simplicity that serves to remove the necessity for close textual analysis. Linda Dryden, for instance, claims that:

> Imperial romances represented simple escapism: its appeal lay in the ability to transport its readers away from everyday concerns and to immerse them in uncomplicated exotic romance. It was pure escapism, laced with patriotic overtones and a zeal for imperial adventures.[9]

Dryden's insistence on the escapist appeal of the romance, at first 'simple', then 'pure', leads her to speculate an 'uncomplicated' exoticism that jars with many of postcolonial theory's most influential and perspicacious readings of colonial discourse.[10] Colonial engagement with the exotic through encounters with the stereotyped racial other, for example, surface as anything but uncomplicated in Homi Bhabha's Lacanian analyses of the fault lines in colonial orthodoxy.[11] The zeal for escapism that Dryden identifies in the imperial romance in this light evokes a far more complex experience than she appears to realise and one that raises a number of important questions concerning the relation of romance and colonial power.

Clearly, adventure fiction serves not only to recruit its readers into their imperial duty, but also offers them, Dryden's view reminds us, a readerly satisfaction, the chance to escape momentarily into a more exciting world. The ideological imperatives ('patriotic overtones') of the texts coexist, despite pretensions to factual veracity, with a deliberate fictionality that hinges on a psycho-geographical dichotomy: the escape from here to there, from drab domestic confines to exotic expanses. As such, romance is the locus of a series of fantasies that merge, at least to some degree, with questions of environment: a sense of the opposition of places, usually the urban homeland and the wild colonial frontier. Indeed, the journey from the one to the other, and often back again, is commonly (though not always) the structuring movement of the imperial adventure. Necessary to a full appreciation of the literary tradition behind this spatial duality is a brief consideration of the different terms that Green and Dryden deploy to refer to largely the same group of texts, the explosion of frequently (but not restrictedly) empire-themed adventures for boys that began in the 1830s with the novels of Captain Marryat and developed through the remainder of the century and into the next in the work of such figures as Mayne Reid and W. H. G. Kingston, in addition to the figures central to this study.[12]

'Adventure' and 'romance' have often been used interchangeably by practitioners and critics. The overlap between the terms is clearly substantial, although there is also a tension between them that illuminates some of the form's complexities. As one of romance's most important theorists, Northrop Frye, remarked, the 'essential element of plot in romance is adventure'.[13] 'Adventure', then, describes the fundamental characteristics of 'romance' and suggests a synergy between them that may be sustained through comparison of Frye's précis of the formula of romance with Green's outline of adventure. To Frye, romance consists of three stages, a 'perilous journey', a 'crucial struggle' and the 'exaltation of the hero', a structure which evokes the key ingredients of Green's somewhat dryer résumé of adventure: 'In general, adventure seems to mean a series of events, partly but not wholly accidental, in settings remote from the domestic and probably from the civilised [...] which constitute a challenge to the central character.'[14] From these synopses, it is clear that imperial expansion is perfectly suited to depiction as romance/adventure. The sense of departure, struggle and the ultimate glorification of the hero provided imperialists with a readymade imaginative representation of themselves as virile, virtuous and victorious: as Green suggests, 'To celebrate adventure was to celebrate empire and vice versa.'[15]

A notable dissenting voice from the critical association of the terms 'romance' and 'adventure', however, is that of C. S. Lewis, an embattled defender of romance in an era he felt was hostile to it. In an essay 'On Stories', Lewis expresses dissatisfaction with novels with too great a stress on 'excitement'. Taking Dumas' *The Three Musketeers* as his example, he bemoans the absence of 'atmosphere' and 'weather', concluding '[t]here is not a moment's rest from the "adventures": one's nose is kept ruthlessly to the grindstone. It all means nothing to me.'[16] But while the plural 'adventures' may well indicate an overemphasis on fluctuations in plot, adventure in the singular, as a mode of writing represented here in imperial adventures, often (though not always – Henty being a notable exception) relies equally on the kind of atmosphere Lewis finds lacking in Dumas. To further complicate matters, both 'romance' and 'adventure', and the tropes and conventions they describe, extend well beyond the output of Victorian and Edwardian adventure novelists. Green's study of adventure considers such canonical figures as Defoe, Scott and Tolstoy in contrast to which boy's own adventures work, he suggest, 'at a lower artistic and cultural level'.[17] Similarly, while romance is commonly applied to the works of Haggard, Ballantyne et al. it also refers to an extensive and longstanding body of literary endeavours, of which the imperial romance is only one, relatively critically marginal facet. Indeed, Barbara Fuchs' introduction to the critical idiom *Romance* makes no mention of the nineteenth-century colonial fiction that concerns Dryden, charting instead the more culturally central forms of the genre in classical, medieval and Renaissance romance. In agreement with Green's summation of the literary deficiencies of imperial adventure fiction, Fuchs is also keen to underscore a conception of romance as an artistically inferior form, beginning her study with an epigraph from Margaret Doody in which romance is described as a term used to 'allude to forms conveying literary pleasure the critic thinks readers would be better off without'.[18] Frye asserts in similar vein that 'Romance is older than the novel, a fact which has developed the historical illusion that it is something to be outgrown, a juvenile and undeveloped form.'[19] Rather than a discouragement to imperial romancers, this apparent, and to Frye illusory, literary naivety is a key part of its appeal, announcing the suitability of romance for the youthful readership that constituted the next generation of imperialists. It also evokes an ostensibly straightforward, uncomplicated masculinity that emerges, though as we shall see in following chapters problematically, as a core theme of imperial romance.

Importantly, 'adventure' has etymological associations that resonate with empire and particularly with an economic discourse of financial speculation. As Peter Hulme explains:

> In one form or another the term has had a continuous existence from the twelfth century to the present day to refer to certain kinds of investor, originally 'merchant adventurer' – anyone investing in overseas trade – more recently 'adventure capitalist', the asset stripper who occupies in contemporary populist demonology the place of the early eighteenth-century stock-jobber. Yet the interest of the word obviously lies in its overlap of the financial and the colonial, the worlds of Lloyd's lists and John Buchan, the common element being risk. It might be said that the 'pure' adventure story, which has to take place outside metropolitan Europe and preferably in as remote an area as possible, reached its apogee as the tentacles of European colonisation were at their greatest reach in the late nineteenth century.[20]

With capitalism, in Robert Young's words, as the 'determining motor of colonialism', adventure's twin significance as romantic narrative and entrepreneurial endeavour highlights the literary form's expression of imperialist ideology.[21] Trade often features as a background to and at times as a driving force of adventure narratives, from Haggard's gruesome tales of the professional ivory trader Allan Quartermain to the gentler speculations of sandalwood traders in Ballantyne's South Seas.[22] More far-fetched depictions of colonial riches in *King Solomon's Mines* or Buchan's *Prester John*, for example, have often been read in reference to imperial economics as vindications and celebrations of the profit motive that make use of romance with one eye on revenue.[23] The geographical structure of romance/adventure is a movement into a space of opportunity, of untapped resources available for settlers and speculators. Adventure's educational purpose, then, is in part to provide a framework for exploitation of foreign lands; a function that relies as much on the dissemination of factual information as on a broader and at times fantastically imagined sense of economic possibility.

This emphasis on the factual, however, adds a degree of stress to the apparent congruence of 'adventure' and 'romance' and indicates a paradox at the form's core. While the addition of a didactic educational agenda to the literary structures of romance is vital to the ideological function of such writing, it also produces a disjunction that White seizes on as she develops her analysis of the relation of travel writing and the adventure tradition. 'Because of this association,' she writes, 'the credibility and respectability of the one was also attributed to the other, thus gaining for adventure fiction an influential power that [...] the Romance lacked.'[24] Imperial adventure, then, is reinforced by its connection with travel writing, a textual form that is founded, broadly speaking, on mimetic realism: the collation and representation of ethnographic, geographical and natural historical details in the spirit of a strictly scientific commitment to factual veracity. To enthusiasts for romance, this was far from a pleasing development. Lyall, for example, looking back toward the beginning of the nineteenth century, described the origins of a 'practice, so entirely alien to the spirit of true romance, of verifying by documentary evidence the details of a story'.[25] Later in the same article, he gives a blunter depiction of this trend: 'Realism wages war against romance.'[26] The opposition of these two textual modes is enshrined in dictionary definitions of romance: Dr Johnson glosses the verb to 'romance' as 'to lie or forge', while the OED defines 'romancing' as 'extravagant fictional invention'. 'Romance' by these definitions is a concept fundamentally incompatible with the (supposed) literal truthfulness that constituted an element of colonial versions of the form.

To look at this internal contradiction another way, the documentary candour required by colonial discourse in its romances finds itself haunted by elements of fantasy that combine uncomfortably with these sober intentions. Magic and the supernatural are traditional components of romance and Frye, significantly, diagnoses it as the 'nearest of all literary forms to the wish-fulfilment dream', signalling a potential for psychoanalytic excavations that, rather than going against the grain of authorial intention, are in fact very much in the spirit of some, if certainly not all, authors of imperial romance.[27] Psychoanalytic approaches to Haggard, for example, are particularly encouraged by his preference for an artistic technique that disdained editorial refinements in favour of a swift and spontaneous prose that displays, as Monsman argues, 'powerful affinities with dreams or with such early psychoanalytic devices [...] as Rorschach tests'.[28] Accordingly, describing his approach to romance in his autobiography, Haggard wrote that 'such work should be written rapidly and, if possible, not rewritten, since wine of this character loses its bouquet when it is poured from glass to glass'.²⁹ While Haggard's work is particularly open, therefore, to interpretations that privilege unconscious longings over conscious intentions, his *modus operandi* is part of an aesthetic that deliberately proposes, in his argument from 'About Fiction', to 'cross the bounds of the known, and, hanging between earth and heaven, gaze with curious eyes into the great profound beyond'³⁰ so that the romance may finally emerge, as he was to phrase it in his diaries, as 'the vehicle of much that does not appear to the casual reader'.³¹

Scornful of what he sees as a banal and emasculating urban culture and fascinated by spiritualism, myth and the primitive, Haggard knowingly seeks out an 'other' world 'beyond' the conscious that allows us to identify the apparently subtextual trajectories of Haggard's novels not just in terms of the repressed libidinal energies of the Freudian unconscious, but also as a wilful reference to a comparable, atavistic residue that inheres in the self and the world at large: what the Victorian anthropologist E. B. Tylor termed a 'survival'. Indeed, referring explicitly to Tylor's work, Haggard's friend, the novelist, folklorist and anthropologist, Andrew Lang praised 'our few modern romances of adventure' as 'savage survivals' that appeal 'to the natural man within me, the survival of some blue-painted Briton or some gypsy'.³² Consequently, the journey of the romance takes its heroes not just across space but also, effectively, back in time to a pre-modern, pre-industrial society, often to be found in Haggard's work in remote African wilderness. Here the frequently violent engagement with the exotic fulfils both empire's civilising mission and romance's interest in confrontation and the testing of the hero. It also constitutes a complex reimagining of the colonial self as akin to the colonial other, notably more akin than colonial orthodoxy would like to think. Lang in delineating the pleasures of the romance observes that, 'Not for nothing did Nature leave us all savages under our white skins; she has wrought thus that we might have many delights, among others the joy of "adventurous living", and of reading about adventurous living.'³³ In terms that similarly blur imperial segregations between self and other, Buchan begins the African story the 'Green Wilderbeest' from *The Runagates Club* (1928) with a line from Thomas Browne: 'We carry with us the wonders we seek without us; there is all Africa and her prodigies in us.'³⁴ Imperial romance aims, nostalgically, to visit this interior, to look below layers of civilisation to discover the 'savage' beneath. Romance in the imperial context might be about opposition, confrontation and ultimately victory, but it also about liminality, ambivalence and regression.

Consequently, the dreams of adventure that Green bridles onto the deeds of empire may be construed as far more than mere aspirations. In place of Dryden's 'simple escapism [...] laced with patriotic overtones', imperial romance, on the contrary, would be better distilled as a complex negotiation of space, identity, literary form and colonial power. The exotic, rather than 'uncomplicated' evolves through a fluctuating interplay of scientific (or pseudo-scientific) discourse and fantasy that is key in postcolonial readings of colonial discourse. As Gail Low expresses it in a work on Haggard and Kipling, the racial (exotic) other provides 'both an object of knowledge and surveillance and an object of libidinous impulse'.[35] Significantly, these complexities articulate, illumine and to extent hinge on, questions of environment. Lang's rediscovery of the 'natural man' in romance, a theme that will be appraised in more detail in Chapter Four (along with romance's ripeness for psychoanalytic interpretations), evokes the movement from home to the far-flung colonial outpost, as, ironically, a kind of homecoming that refers disapprovingly to post–Industrial Revolution Britain as, with a few exceptions north and west, a landscape shorn of romantic possibility. Robert Louis Stevenson's description of his pleasure in 'brute incident' in his 'Gossip on Romance' adds an animal hint to the natural aura of the romance mode, inscribing the non-human world in its generic expectations.[36]

Haggard's and Buchan's works, in particular, not uncommonly include reflections that might today be characterised as pointedly environmentalist. In the introduction to Haggard's *Allan Quartermain* (1885), the eponymous narrator declares a 'thirst for the wilderness' and a sense of Western civilisation as 'vainglory'.[37] Buchan, comparably, begins his autobiography, *Memory Hold-the-Door* (1940), with an impassioned comment on the industrial defilement of Britain through a depiction of the condition of the streams in the Fifeshire home of his childhood:

> [O]ne was foul with the discards of the bleaching-works. There must have been a time when sea-trout in a spate ran up them from the Firth, but now in their lower courses they were like sewers and finished their degraded life in a drain in the town harbour. There was no beauty in those perverted valleys.[38]

The modern environmental movement considered through Haggard's and Buchan's ecological sensibilities might be perceived as (among, of course, many other things) an attempt to reinvest landscape with beauty and mystery, with the kind of otherness that makes wilderness vital to romance and which is far harder imagined in intensively managed, charted and cultivated land. As the environmental philosopher Neil Evernden comments, 'Environmentalism without aesthetics is merely regional planning.'[39] Arthur Conan Doyle's 1912 *The Lost World*, in which an extraordinary range of previously supposed extinct reptiles are discovered alive on a distant South American plateau, dramatically illustrates an environmental point present in less exaggerated guise in numerous imperial romances. Real wildness and thriving biodiversity now only exist far away, at the end of a long and punishing journey. The escapism Dryden insists on is in part the quest for this. To underline this environmentalist agenda, in *Memory Hold-the-Door* Buchan extends his description of an earth denuded of secrecy into an imagination of a dystopian future that provides a remarkably prescient account of globalised economies, the power of oil industries and the problems of eco-tourism:

> There was no corner of the globe left unexplored and unexploited, no geographical mysteries to fire the imagination. Broad highways crowded with automobiles threaded the remotest lands, and overhead great air-liners carried week-end tourists to the wilds of Africa and Asia. Everywhere there were guest-houses and luxury hotels and wayside camps and filling-stations. What once were the savage tribes of Equatoria and Polynesia were now in reserves as an attraction to trippers, who bought from them curios and holiday mementoes.[40]

While undeniably related to empire's rapacity for profit, imperial romance also, therefore, contains a marked strand of anti-materialism as it laments the impact of colonial development and fantasises lands beyond the reach of imperial capital.[41]

Ecocriticism and animal studies may justly, then, look to imperial romance at least on one level as an early and, considering the wider colonial context, politically awkward form of literary environmentalism that consistently addresses questions of landscape and land use. As such, adventure fiction forms an important part of what might be called the Victorian and Edwardian ecological imagination, a culturally prominent ideal of human/environmental involvement and, connectedly, of human interactions with non-human animals. Engagement with wild beasts is an inevitable part of the hero's sojourn in far-flung, flourishing bio-regions and an aspect of the generic savagery that so appealed to Lang. Yet, problematically for environmentalist assessments of imperial romance, the hero's encounter with animals is generally structured around violence: Africa's formerly substantial populations of spectacular and aggressive megafauna, especially, providing perfect exemplars of hostile otherness and an ideal opportunity for the heroic self-assertion central to romance. Indeed, violence against animals appears inscribed in the narrative expectations of the form. Lang commented on Haggard's style that he 'writes like a sportsman of genius', a curious critical judgement that nonetheless clearly promulgates an intimacy between literary form, colonial masculinity and environmental carnage.[42] This violent domination of the natural world is a vital component, both symbolically and materially, of the colonial appropriation and transformation of land and is antithetical to most twenty-first century streams of environmental politics. In this context, another way to gloss the real wildness and thriving biodiversity besought at the colonial frontier, then, would be as simply good sport, a theme which reflects the continuing, and problematic, involvement of the pro-hunting lobby in the environmental movement, particularly in the USA.

Political Animals

The relation of Buchan's *A Lodge in the Wilderness* (1906) and Henty's *Rujub the Juggler* (1895) to the traditions of romance and adventure is perhaps less straightforward than others of these authors' texts. Comprised of a series of set piece discussions on imperial themes, Buchan's *Lodge* is a fictional symposium without a unifying narrative dynamic or a single hero. Nonetheless, its reflections on empire and the depiction of the land around Musuru, the luxury East African estate of the millionaire Sir Francis Carey in which the conference occurs, constitute a valuable resource for understanding the nexus of empire, literary form and the non-human. Buchan's cast of the colonial great and good encompasses divergent aspects of the imperial whole and demonstrates eagerness to address the subject of imperial administration (rather by this time than conquest) broadly and thoroughly, reflecting Buchan's own experience as an enthusiastic and ambitious civil servant under Lord Alfred Milner in the Cape.[43] A financier, a soldier and a hunter take their place alongside Liberal and Tory parliamentarians, while a Canadian statesman appears next to British women who pointedly include the wives of high-ranking servicemen in India and the Cape and of the high commissioner of East Africa. This elite and geographically diverse company's engagement with empire begins as they trade opinions and definitions of imperialism. Carey's judgement that it is 'a spirit, an attitude of mind, an unconquerable hope […] a sense of the destiny of England' (33) introduces the fervent idealism that characterises the *Lodge*'s pro-imperial stance.[44] Its reissue in 1916, after initially anonymous publication, with a new preface emphasises this patriotic intent as Buchan, writing from 'the British army in France', summarises in lofty, biblically resonant language the value of empire in a turbulent era: 'We understand, as we have never understood before, that our Empire is a mystic whole that no enemy may part asunder' (x). In the ensuing chapters Buchan moves these rather nebulous valuations of empire into the more concrete domains of economics and political policy, but retains throughout a sense of the other-worldly or the transcendental that ostensibly complements (and also mystifies) these more pragmatic discourses.

Following Carey's avowal, the turn passes to Mrs Deloraine, a religious poet and 'the most beautiful woman in England' (25) who identifies imperialism as 'an enlarged sense of the beauty and the mystery of the world' (34). Although the Canadian statesman Mr Wakefield then changes the tone with the outburst, 'For Heaven's sake let us keep out of mysticism' and the dryer assertion that imperialism means the 'organic connection under one Crown of a number of autonomous nations of the same blood' (34), the hunter Considine returns to more speculative mode with his contribution: 'And I [...] call it romance [...] It is what made the Elizabethans, and all ages of adventure' (35).[45] Imperialism, then, develops for its agents as a combination of political practicalities with a less easily quantified aesthetic, even spiritual, experience that illuminates the twin sense of adventure as both an economic and a romantic narrative undertaking. Musuru, accordingly, as a site of notable extravagance is both testimony to the material triumphs of imperialism in raising profit from previously, in European terms, 'derelict' land, and also the manifestation of a romantic ideal. Carey's home has 'the airy perfection of a house seen in a dream' and when the journalist Astbury imagines a group of hunters stumbling upon the estate by chance, he concludes that it 'would take a long time to persuade them that it was not an Aladdin's palace' (148). Carey himself describes his first discovery of the land on which he was to erect Musuru as the apprehension of 'a kind of fairyland' (38). If Buchan's *Lodge* is not, then, itself a romance, it is clearly in part *about* the sentimental and generic expectations that romance cultivates and what they contribute to and borrow from the administration of colonial Africa. Indeed, as part fiction and part politics, it constitutes an intriguingly transitional point between Buchan's first African text, the substantial and serious nonfictional account of his work as a colonial administrator in the Cape, *The African Colony* (1903), and the boys' adventure *Prester John* (1910), indicating the clear interpenetration of these politically charged forms of writing.[46]

Henty's *Rujub the Juggler*, meanwhile, is identified by his biographer Guy Arnold not as one of his romances but as one of Henty's 'adult novels'.[47] More openly, though still distinctly, the publisher's introduction to *Rujub* describes it as 'an historical tale for young and old' (iii). Such division of Henty's output into discrete categories is tenuous and *Rujub*'s points of difference from other of his novels categorised unproblematically by readers and publishers as 'romances' are minute matters of character and setting rather than of a substantial stylistic and generic divergence. Principally, *Rujub* differs from Henty's other work in colonial settings in the age and character of the hero (a mature, somewhat introspective man rather than a daredevil adolescent), and perhaps also in the unusual degree of interest in female characters and domestic arrangements. Beyond this, the novel provides the kind of staple Henty diet of military adventure that prompted Joseph Bristow to write that, for Henty, fiction 'seems to serve as an alibi for relating the precise movements of the army'.[48] Henty's military enthusiasm is not surprising given his long career as war correspondent for the *London Standard*, and *Rujub*'s coherence with this strand is apparent in its later renaming to *In the Days of the Mutiny: A Military Tale*, though it is important to note that the novel's hero Bathurst is, as we shall see, a rather unusual military hero.

But while *Rujub* need not be considered as significantly divergent from Henty's 'romances', it, and indeed all Henty's work, clearly offers a markedly different form of romance from Buchan's. C. S. Lewis' criticism of adventures that in opposition to the romance tradition they offer excitement without atmosphere is easily applied to Henty's bald recitations of military history.[49] Henty's fictional world does not witness Buchan's breadth of cultural reference, ideological nuance or literary sophistication and consequently lacks a deliberate, knowing deployment of romance in his imaginative recreation of empire. Yet the interest in the heroic and the encounter with the other in distant colonial spaces in Henty's works adheres to the fundamental patterns of romance. Furthermore, *Rujub*'s eponymous juggler is surrounded by a supernatural ambience that gestures, in characteristic romance fashion, towards a mystical, dreamlike realm that offsets and envelopes the determinations of imperial conquest and administration.

Like Buchan's *Lodge* with its enthusiasm for the 'destiny' of England, Henty's novel, and his œuvre in general, is unashamedly imperialist. In a 1902 article in the *Boy's Own Paper*, Henty summarised one of the chief motivating forces behind his literary career:

> To endeavour to inculcate patriotism in my books has been one of my main objects, and so far as it is possible to know I have not been unsuccessful in that respect. I know that very many boys have joined the cadets and afterwards gone into the Army through reading my stories and at many of the meetings at which I have spoken officers of the Army and Volunteers have assured me that my books have been effectual in bringing young fellows into the Army.[50]

E. G. Salmon's suggestion of a connection between the 'pen and the printed page' and the daring of the soldier is powerfully evinced by Henty's jingoistic militarism. Yet crucially, both Buchan and Henty are dealing in their texts with an imperilled empire. *A Lodge in the Wilderness* is associated in its second edition with the threat to Britain's global position of the First World War. More pertinently in its original form, the *Lodge*'s idealised enclave of East African harmony pointedly commentates on the significant upheavals of the Second Boer War of 1899–1902 in South Africa. By comparison, *Rujub* is a tale of the most noted and bloody nineteenth-century assault on the British Empire, the unsuccessful 1857 Indian war of independence, commonly described in the imperial context as the 'Mutiny'. Although Henty is writing at a distance of almost forty years, campaigns in India against insurgent elements were still ongoing at the end of the century, especially along the North-West Frontier, so a sense of the Raj as at least intermittently embattled would have been fresh for his readers.

The political and historical background for both the *Lodge* and *Rujub*, then, is colonial administration beset by potential and very real insecurities. Each text is engaged in the narration of the interplay between a sought-after stability and order and forces oppositional to or simply outside the stable, successfully administrated colony. This dichotomy facilitates what Frye describes as the essentially 'dialectical' form of romance, with its emphasis on contest, testing and the adversarial.[51] For Henty, the most pressing dialectic, in the broad sense of a conflict moving ostensibly towards resolution, and his novel's racing excitement consists in the battle for control of India between the sepoys and the British army. Buchan's text, meanwhile, gives more emphasis to an environmental dichotomy of managed land and the African wilderness beyond the pale of Carey's estate. In each of these differently oriented scenarios, the relationship with animals appears as a prominent part of the articulation of a colonial power dynamic. To return to MacKenzie's model of the three stages of colonial hunting, Henty and Buchan are dealing with the final, ideologically laden phase of 'The Hunt' as sport rather than as subsidy, a means of food acquisition or a commercial enterprise (though as we shall see in the following section the commodification of animal bodies is an important element of these texts). Killing animals in this context emerges as an integral part, both practically and symbolically, of managing both humans and the land as well as providing the narrative satisfactions of heroic conquest.

The boundary between colonised and unreconstructed space is marked at the beginning of both *Rujub* and the *Lodge* by the territory of wild animals. Buchan describes in his opening chapter the rather awed experience of the recently arrived guests in their unfamiliar surrounds:

> The place and time were so strange – there among delicate furniture and all the trappings of a high civilisation, looking out over the primeval wilds. Savage beasts roamed a mile off in that untamed heart of the continent. The most sophisticated members of the company felt the glamour of the unknown around them. (37)

The frontier between sophistication and the 'untamed', 'unknown' exterior is reached with the apprehension of the 'savage beasts', providing a metonym of space which has as yet evaded the ordering hand of colonial incursion. Such contrasts, between the wild and the civilised, are a favourite theme of Buchan's and the key to Musuru's romantic frisson.[52] Carey finds romance in his life 'by the device of importing the fine flower of civilisation into the stronghold of savagery' (13), a metaphor of cultured, horticultural accomplishment that juxtaposes the 'primeval wilds' the company survey from their urbane vantage point. The title *A Lodge in the Wilderness* encapsulates this antithesis of civilisation and savagery in terms subtly evocative for animal studies: the house amid the 'wilddeoren' or abode of beasts, to cite the Anglo-Saxon etymology of wilderness, frames Buchan's romantic imperialism within the contact of human and non-human domains. Savage animals thus constitute both an emblematic otherness that embodies the point at which colonial authority loses its grip and also a key compositional feature of the *mise-en-scène* that exemplifies Mrs Deloraine's enthusiasm for the 'beauty and the mystery of the world'.

For Carey's more vigorous guests, the sound of these beasts across the untamed landscape is an enticing invitation to sport. As the youthful enthusiast Hugh Somerville remarks later after a successful lion hunt: 'there is no satisfaction so intense as victory over some one of the savage forces of nature' (126). This emphasis on the reform of the wild environment through the destruction of its most aggressive denizens, emblematic here of the very idea of nature's savage force, is central to the colonial politics of hunting and the background to an ominous roar that Henty describes in the first moments of *Rujub*. As the civil servant Bathurst goes about his business in his administrative district he meets with an alarmed villager:

> 'My lord sahib has seen nothing of the tiger?' the head man said; 'our hearts were melted with fear, for the evil beast was heard roaring in the jungle not far from the road early this morning.'
> 'I never gave it a thought, one way or the other,' Bathurst said, as he dismounted. (9–10)

In this exchange between administrator and head man, their differing approaches to the man-eating tiger that has for some time been ravaging the neighbourhood announces the hierarchical structure of their relations. The Englishman's complacency identifies Bathurst as the natural master of this terrain and highlights the ongoing task of British rule in bringing this dangerous region into the safety of colonial administration. By comparison, the native is anxious and afraid; 'Hindoos', Henty's narrator determines later, 'have no more heart than a mouse' (62). An analogous expression of an imperial racial hierarchy through contact with wild beasts occurs in the *Lodge* when Hugh notes with 'huge pleasure' that of the two lions killed on their expedition, one by himself, the other by the chief shikari Akhub, that his was 'the finer and the bigger of the two' (126). Necessarily for Buchan's imperial agenda, the Englishman's prowess is magnified above his employee's by the relative dimensions of the beasts.

This demonstration of imagined British superiority through encounters (or in Bathurst's case a near encounter) with large mammals is intensified by the adjectives Buchan and Henty attach to colonial fauna. The 'savagery' of the East African beasts automatically casts their European opponents as civilisers while the roaring of the 'evil beast' in Henty's India similarly portrays the white hunters by extension as forces for good. Behind these designations of animal 'savagery' and 'evil' lays a long-standing representational tradition in which carnivorous mammals are imagined as supreme exemplars of an animal otherness powerfully antithetical to human interests. The predatory aggression of big cats suggests an extremity of wildness that ultimately carries theological connotations. Reflecting on the place of animals in the biblical narrative of the fall, Diana Donald argues that since animal antipathy to man was a part of 'God's curse on disobedient humanity', the distinction 'between "wild" and "tame"' may be considered 'at bottom religious rather than zoological'.[53] This religious agenda enjoins mankind, even in the prelapsarian chapters of Genesis, to subdue the earth and 'every living thing that moveth upon' it, an injunction that is consistently reprised in imaginings of colonial contact.

The destruction of lions and tigers, then, provides a potent exhibition of man bringing the earth into his divinely sanctioned order. Tigers, especially, suffer from a cultural identification as the most recalcitrant of animals, inviting destruction by the unremitting violence of their otherness and their complete exteriority to human harmony. Donald argues that they are described by 'every eighteenth-century writer on zoology [...] as the cruellest, bloodiest, least tractable of creatures'.[54] Literary and philosophical deployments of tigers have often confirmed and exacerbated this exaggerated brutality. Martin Danahay remarks that 'Nietzsche uses the tiger as the symbol of the most extreme violence imaginable', while the fiery rhetoric of Blake's 'Tyger' conveys a similarly fearsome image, reinforced in different terms by Kipling's cowardly Shere Khan.[55] Indeed, Blake's feline sublime and Shere Khan's degeneracy comprise two intertwining traditions of tiger representation that equally encouraged the ecocidal enthusiasm often apparent in British colonial representations of big cats. Hinging on the distinction of game-eating and man-eating animals, the British, in MacKenzie's words, 'saw the tiger as a magnificent beast [...] but also defined it as vermin'.[56] Similarly, lions were both an emblem of British colonial might and the most regal embodiment of animality (perhaps most famously illustrated by Edwin Landseer's lions in Trafalgar Square), and simultaneously, like tigers, legally vermin.[57] In each guise these animals attracted violence, promising the supreme contest for the hunter or an act of zoological hygiene. The obsessive interest of British colonists in India's largest predator produced the effect, to MacKenzie, that the 'British and the tiger seemed […] to be locked in conflict for control of the Indian environment'.[58] Many imperialists, indeed, were unabashed about the possibility of a final solution for the tiger problem (and for the vexing persistence of savage beasts in general) unfolding as a desirable collateral benefit of the march of European civilisation. Edward Bennett, assistant secretary of the Zoological Society London, wrote in 1829 that civilisation involves 'as a necessary consequence, either the complete extinction or, at least, the gradual diminution and dispersion […] of all the more savage and obnoxious beasts'.[59] The lack of legal protection for tigers until the 1930s confirms their position in colonial India as the antithesis of human authority. In the heyday of the Raj, conservation of such a symbolically resonant animal appeared unthinkable.[60]

The performance of imperial order in engagements with predatory mammals is informed, therefore, by a deep-rooted cultural tradition that develops and re-enacts foundational theological imperatives in the colonial situation. While there were clearly also practical benefits, especially for animal husbandry, of controlling populations of large predators around human settlements, these concerns, perhaps most significantly, formed a part of hunting's wider symbolic dimension. To Anand S. Pandian, writing on the importance of hunting within both the British and Mughal Empires in India, the 'imperial hunt constituted a culture of rule through both its symbology of power – the representations and rituals expressing authority – and the power of its symbology – the deployment of these cultural forms in political practice as a means of subjection'.[61] As *Rujub* and the *Lodge* dramatise the diverse connections of 'The Hunt' with the imperial themes of command and subjugation, they exemplify Pandian's analysis of the political centrality of large scale big-game hunting. Hunting emerges as both a paramilitary and administrative intervention that flourishes through inscribing dominion on the bodies of its prey, in the process illustrating a particular kind of masculine subjectivity. The qualities required and encouraged by hunting serve as a badge of good character and imperial usefulness throughout *Rujub* and the *Lodge*. Buchan's addition of the 'explorer and noted Big-game hunter' (vii) Sir Edward Considine to the assembled imperial glitterati in the *Lodge* pointedly argues the centrality of hunting to ideals of English manhood. Accordingly, we learn that Carey is safe from any disparagement of British orthodoxy because even the 'Tory member could not speak ill of one who was so noted a sportsman' (15). A similar judgement is extended, ultimately unwisely, in *Rujub* when the 'great shikari' Doctor Wade (48) is convinced by the insurgent rajah of Bithoor's offer of a day's shooting that he is, despite growing concerns, 'a first-rate fellow' (100).

Likewise in *Rujub*, to the subalterns Richards and Wilson, tiger hunting represents an opportunity to prove themselves the right kind of men and to stimulate their incipient careers. At first 'burning to distinguish themselves' in the sporting field (103), an early failure in the face of their quarry rouses even greater levels of determination and excitement until faced with the prospect of 'wip[ing] out the disgrace' they can talk 'of nothing else' (166). A part of hunting's value for imperial masculinities is plainly its relation to military service, a long-standing connection that is widely deployed in British imperial fiction and hunting narratives. As long ago as the fifth century BC, Xenophon remarked on one of the chase's evident uses as a preparation for warfare: 'when men used to hunting make difficult marches under arms, they will not give in, but will endure hardship, because it is with hardship that they are accustomed to take wild beasts'.[62] In addition to bodily training, pluck and marksmanship, a sound knowledge of terrain honed in the hunt could be of considerable value on the battlefield: to General E. A. Alderson in a 1900 training manual on *Hunting as a School for Soldiering*, the hunter 'is already a more than a half-made soldier'.[63] In Ballantyne's *The Gorilla Hunters*, the young hero Peterkin offers an earlier, more evocative (and decidedly uncomfortable) correlation between the pleasures of the chase and the military requirements of colonial expansion in a self-confident synopsis of his youthful adventures:

> I've been fighting with the Caffirs, and the Chinamen, and been punishing the rascally sepoys in India, and been hunting elephants in Ceylon and tiger shooting in the jungles, and harpooning whales in the polar seas, and shooting lions at the Cape.[64]

The neat division of Peterkin's escapades into two categories of violence adduces the hunt as the natural counterpart of martial violence. For Buchan as well in his 1900 novel of Russian sponsored Indian insurgence *The Half-Hearted*, the two clearly complement each other. Faced with imminent danger the hero Lewis Haystoun takes solace in the valuable preparation afforded him by his experience of the hunt, blessing 'his sense trained by years of sport to a keenness beyond the townsman's'.[65] Hunting, however, while offering practical preparation for the army also blurs into military discourse in a more subtle and problematic way.

As the uprising reaches its conclusion, Haystoun declares pointedly, 'we've got a day's sport before us'. Military operations appear in themselves as a kind of venery, constituting in the more direct terms of the civil servant and army volunteer Sir Edward Braddon in a comment on the 1855 Santral rebellion in India, a 'splendid substitute for tiger hunting'.[66] This apparent interchangeability of hunting and war emerges in yet more shocking terms in the work of the chief scout and war hero Robert Baden-Powell who, in his account of the 1896 Matabele Campaign against anti-colonial insurgents in present-day Zimbabwe, depicts a predatory vigilance careless of its object: 'your gun is ready and every sense is on the alert to see the game. Lion or leopard, boar or buck, nigger or nothing.'[67] The categorisation of Africans and other racial groups as 'game' is already implicit in Peterkin's formulation and is a key implication of Henty's reimagining of the political and military machinations of the beleaguered British Raj in the unfolding crisis. For Dr Wade, the novel's alpha male, his contribution to the war effort is consistently expressed as an extension of his prowess on the sporting field. Despite his official non-combatant status as a medical man, he reassures himself as the rebellion commences that 'if I can shoot a tiger on the spring I fancy I can hit a Sepoy' (174). With slightly different orientation, in the final chapters, as the bloody British reprisals are set to begin, he reflects that 'I have always been a hunter, and this time it is human "tigers" I am going in pursuit of' (379). Wade's rhetoric exemplifies the movement from hunting as practical preparation for war to the identification of war and hunting through the metaphorisation of Indian revolutionaries as tigers. Bathurst, accordingly, is warned as British rule appears on the brink of restoration in the novel's later stages that the hamstrung Rajah of Bithoor, a leading figure in the rebellion, is 'a tiger – and a wounded tiger is most dangerous' (330). An extended version of this metaphor is offered earlier by Wade:

> A tiger's cub, when tamed, is the prettiest of playthings, but when it once tastes blood it is as savage a beast as its mother was before it. Of course, I hope for the best but if the Sepoys once break loose I would not answer for anything they might do. (153)

Wade's exploration of the apostasy of the sepoys frets on the duality of apparent domestication under the Raj with an underlying, inherent wildness. The return of the sepoy tigers from their tamed state as empire's playthings to their genetically determined state of insurgence evidently adds a powerful biological logic to the suppression of the 'Mutiny'. Having rediscovered the 'taste of blood', the sepoys may now in Britain's 'work of retribution' (379), legitimately in Wade's thinking, be subjected to treatment that appropriate to the most savage of beasts.

In turn, the centrality of the tiger as a metaphor of insurrection in the British mythology of power lends further significance to the literal depredations of colonial sport in the subcontinent.[68] In the first days of the rebellion, the military exigency of the situation seems initially for Henty's imperial establishment to outweigh the more apparently trivial assignment of a planned tiger hunt. Conversely though, in such a dire situation it becomes still more vital that the day's sport go ahead. The commanding officer Major Hannay explains that:

> [I]f, after all the preparations were made, we were to put the tiger-hunt off altogether, it would set the natives talking, and the report would go through the country like wildfire that some great disaster had happened. We must go back at once. [The] doctor urges that he should go out and kill his tiger. [If] the tiger is killed, it does not matter whether two or sixty of us went out. (172)

Beyond the generalised value of maintaining the semblance of normality as a gesture of imperial confidence, the tiger hunt is invested with an urgent importance. Without the possibility of a display of might on the usual extravagant scale, the *coup-de-grâce*, however modestly accomplished, emerges for the doctor and the major as the most pressing concern, as if the tiger's dead body might anticipate and enact a wider British triumph, revealing to the sepoy the inevitable fate of treacherous human tigers that flout the rule of order. It is perhaps unsurprising, therefore, to turn to a different colonial context that the hunter Considine in *A Lodge in the Wilderness* should support the 'right' of British servicemen to kill 'a score or two of natives in the way of duty' (306) as the object of the hunter's violence alternates between animal and man, disclosing a transferable skill deployed for both for leisure and conquest.

The colonial politics of hunting thus connect forms of otherness and types of violence, illustrating the intimacy of categories of species and race in the maintenance of British rule. In addition to affording an aggressively cautionary image of retribution to the insurgent, these connections also emerge in apparently more peaceful guise in what Pandian expresses as the trope of 'predatory care'. By this, colonial hunters identified themselves as tender-hearted protectors in a move aimed at 'securing the bodies and hearts of resistant subjects through spectacles of responsible force'.[69] As Pandian argues, British control of man-eating tigers in rural districts formed a powerful sign of imperial benevolence that operated alongside the 'administrative territorialization' of India in the 1860s and 1870s as an important component of British exploitation of India's forest resources.[70] While Henty's tale is clearly set at a slightly earlier phase of Britain's colonial interests, the administration of rural space is a prominent aspect of his vision of British imperialism in India. Bathurst, the novel's unlikely hero, is introduced as the selfless arbiter in a local dispute over land rights, listening 'to the statements of the old people of the village, cross-questioning them closely, and sparing no efforts to sift the truth from their confused and often contradictory evidence' (10). Pointedly, Henty insists on the indefatigable

Bathurst's unqualified success: 'His perfect knowledge of their language, the pains he took to sift all matters brought before him to the bottom, had rendered the young officer very popular among the natives' (11).

The novel's critical moment, however, comes when, significantly in the midst of the performance of these duties, Bathurst chances upon a tiger 'standing with a foot upon a prostrate figure, while a man in front of it was gesticulating wildly' (12). Confronting the snarling beast, in the text's opening plate (Figure 1), with fist clenched and legs astride in a heroic stance of masculine determination, he chivalrously rescues Rabda, a young Indian girl, and consequently endears himself to her father, the juggler Rujub who had appeared utterly ineffectual in the developing emergency. The hapless Rujub, indeed, is himself at risk as the tiger hesitates 'whether to strike down the figure in front or to content itself with that already in its power' (12). The illustration of Bathurst's triumph over the man-eater develops a tradition of visual representation of tigers in the context of colonial strife perhaps most famous from a *Punch* cartoon of 1857 (see Figure 2). Here the British lion drives the Bengal tiger away from the body of a white woman, suggesting contemporary stories of brutal Indian violence against British women while depicting a counterattacking British fearlessness. In substituting an Indian for a white victim, *Rujub* carefully extends the range of Britain's predatory violence from protection of its own to a far wider remit, bringing Indian colonial subjects into the safety of British care. Indeed, in *Rujub* the white man is consistently cast as the protector of the helpless indigene. The news, later in the novel, that a man-eater had 'carried off herdsmen on two consecutive days' (122) is greeted by an immediate demonstration of imperial resolve so that Britain is proclaimed by an appreciative populace as the salvation from the rapacious embodiment of mayhem and peril. As Rujub asks in the wake of Bathurst's heroism: 'Would one of my countrymen have ventured his life to attack a tiger, armed only with a whip, for the sake of the life of a poor wayfarer' (14).

The most notable effect of this imperial benevolence in the face of animal aggression is to translate Rujub from a potential insurgent who has for years 'worked quietly against' the imperial establishment (278) to a willing servant of British rule who deploys his mysterious telepathic and clairvoyant powers against the rebellion. It is his warning of the impending hostilities that allows the British to save themselves from immediate catastrophe (186). When the British are besieged by sepoys it is his tireless labours that allow Bathurst to liberate his wife-to-be Isobel Hannay from her imprisonment by the lascivious Rajah. Speaking to Bathurst, Rujub describes the process of his conversion:

> The Feringhees have wrung nothing from the poor to be spent in pomp and display; they permit no tyranny or ill-doing; under them the poorest peasant tills his fields in peace.

Figure 1. 'Bathurst confronts the tiger'. G. A. Henty, *Rujub the Juggler* (New York: Mershon, 1901 [1893]), 12.

THE BRITISH LION'S VENGEANCE ON THE BENGAL TIGER.

Figure 2. 'The British Lion's Vengeance on the Bengal Tiger'. *Punch*, 22nd August 1857, 76–7.

> I have been obliged to see all this, and I feel now that their destruction would be a frightful misfortune. We should be ruled by our native lords; but as soon as the white man was gone the old quarrels would break out, and the country would be red with blood. I did not see this before, because I had only looked at it with the eyes of my own caste; now I see it with the eyes of one whose daughter has been saved from a tiger by a white man. (280)

Rujub's ventriloquial summation of the advantages of a British India hinges vitally on the intervention of the white man between the defenceless child and the tiger; while home rule for India means bloodshed, British dominion offers a security and justice that finds its epitome in Bathurst. Importantly, though, Bathurst embodies a different paradigm of manhood from the vigorous military adventurers that often appear in Henty, and one that indicates the oversimplification of Mawuena Kossi Logan's judgement in the sole recent monograph on Henty that his 'choice of hero […] is a never-changing one' and that his 'heroes are predictable' in the masculine stereotypes they portray.[71] Indeed, Bathurst's emergence in the early chapters of *Rujub the Juggler* as a nervous figure with a congenital terror of firearms creates a space in imperial discourse for an alternative, even effeminate, masculinity: not just the butcher or the fighter, but the diligent and sensitive public official who can yet act with courage and purpose when the need arises. Bathurst's effeminacy emerges most forcefully through comparison with Isobel. Reflecting on her and Bathurst's shared indisposition she remarks, 'I can understand that it is disagreeable for a man to feel nervous, simply, I suppose, because it is regarded as a feminine quality' (87). Even in the illustration of his defeat of the tiger, Bathurst contradicts the expected disposition of British manhood. As he is pictured above the tiger, the slenderness of his limbs and the unusual, protruding, almost breast-like, cut of his jacket offset the masculinity of his action with a feminised image that illustrates compassion as much as authority.

In depicting Bathurst's development from something of an oddity among his peers to a man lauded for his heroism, Henty offers what in the context of writing for boys is a conventional narrative of self-improvement that forms part of the form's educational agenda. As Henty's publishers were keen to point out in their introduction, Bathurst 'masters his fear, and gives a powerful lesson of what stern and unbending will-power can accomplish' (iv). Given his nervous character, Bathurst's engagement with savage Indian animals is of a different kind from the militaristic sport-hunting of his colleagues. He is 'not a shikari, but a hard-working official' (14–15) who 'takes no interest in sport of any kind' (92): as one colonial colleague exclaims with exasperation, 'he doesn't shoot, he doesn't ride – I mean he don't care for pig-sticking' (8). Bathurst, indeed, left the army in some disgrace following the discovery of his nervous temperament.[72] Henty's simultaneous celebration of Wade's macho predations and Bathurst's reluctant yet instinctive heroism allied to a meeker masculinity demonstrates an important tension in imperial reflections on wild beasts and one that is summarised by the former prime minister Lord Appin in Buchan's *Lodge*. Although he implies that a degree of force exercised for a 'beneficent purpose' is an unavoidable aspect of imperial governance, he also contends that 'the worship of brute force, of mere conscienceless power, is the most certain sign of degeneration' (77). While violence is used with powerful symbolic resonance to portray the development of colonial order through its contact with empire's animal and animalised human others, the danger of brutishness is one that must be guarded against. Bathurst's addition of a less overtly aggressive schema to colonial contact with wild animals fulfils this necessity, allowing colonial power to conceive of itself raised above the level of the brute, mighty but with a conscience, strong-armed but benevolent and socially responsible. Ultimately, this motif reinforces the otherness of the savage beasts of Henty's India and the ostensible dualism of human and non-human by moderating the more aggressive elements of empire's reform of the wilderness with a lighter touch more resolutely segregated from brutish belligerence.

This interplay of paradigms of masculinity is of central importance in reading imperial interactions with animals and is developed further beneath. A complementary aspect of the symbology of British imperial power in this context emerges in representations of the commodification of animal bodies. The development of colonial order and the flourishing of colonial manhood are expressed through the assimilation of animal others into the discourse of capitalist modernity, although, particularly in Buchan's *Lodge*, this process is somewhat ambivalent. For Buchan's characters, the deployment of animal remains relies for its value on the apparent failure of empire to entirely contain animal otherness in the processes of commodification, thus re-emphasising romance's investment in wilderness and imaging a masculine culture that, contrary to Bathurst, participates in as much as reforms animality.

Trophies and Trinkets

The use of animal bodies in empire's domestic and sartorial arrangements home and abroad was as symbolically significant as it was financially lucrative. Formed into a wide range of products, curios and mementoes, animals were contained and transfigured according to a prevalent, utilitarian view of nature as resource which supplemented the bald logic of economic gain with a pointed ideological investment in the processes of commodification. In terms of productivity, elephants were perhaps the most considerable of beasts, at least of those that dwelled on land. With the growing popularity of billiards in the nineteenth century and the piano's centrality in upper-middle-class entertainments, ivory and in particular the softer ivory of young East African elephants was very much in demand for the manufacture of balls and keys.[73] Simultaneously, the refinement of taxidermic technologies saw stuffed exotica become popular as household ornaments, while the fashion for decorative feathers in ladies' hats, often taken from African ostriches, but also more rarely from Asian birds of paradise, was another profitable enterprise among many.[74] The trade that facilitated such items was a prominent factor in the establishment and maintenance of colonial settlements and the plentiful, for a time at any rate, zoological raw materials constituted an enticing possibility for adventurous spirits.

Clearly, the increasingly widespread use of exotic animal bodies in Britain was part of a wider nineteenth-century growth in economic development and technical innovation. Thomas Richards contends that, 'between the Great Exhibition of 1851 and the First World War, the commodity became and has remained the centrepiece of everyday life, the focal point of all representation, the dead center of the modern world'.[75] Given the increasing prominence of colonial animal bodies in metropolitan capitalism, it is tempting to foist a pun on Richards' analysis: the 'dead center of the modern world' conveying not just the dominance of commerce but also, in the imperial context, the histories of predation behind many finished products. Capitalism's 'hold over England', as Richards opines, operated 'not only economically but semiotically', enabling what Nicole Shukin in a study of *Animal Capital* in contemporary culture describes as 'vacillations between economic and symbolic logics of power'.[76] The incorporation of animal otherness into a mercantile agenda powerfully emblematises the expansion of civilised order into the wilds, articulating the cultural centrality of violence against animals as animal objects are haunted with a significance deeper than profit.

The commodity, as Marx wrote in *Capital*, is 'an extremely obvious, trivial thing' as a functional object with clear 'use-value', yet also something that simultaneously abounds with 'metaphysical subtleties and theological niceties'.[77] Refining his argument with a famous example of striking relevance for environmentalists, Marx suggests that:

> The form of wood [...] is altered if a table is made out of it. Nevertheless the table continues to be wood, an ordinary, sensuous thing. But as soon as it emerges as a commodity, it changes into a thing that transcends sensuousness. It not only stands with its feet on the ground, but in relation to all other commodities, it stands on its head, and evolves out of its wooden brain grotesque ideas, far more wonderful if it were to begin dancing of its own free will.[78]

Marx's fantastic personification of the grotesque table illustrates the inscription of material objects within a semiotic system in which they become 'supra-sensible or social': items with connotations beyond their function and physical composition.[79] Specifically, the 'mysterious character of the commodity-form' consists in its reflection of the social relations informing the conditions of its production. To pursue this line with reference to an environmentalist agenda, the commodity might be seen to be comparably transfigured by ecological as much as social conditions. The commodity, therefore, is inhabited by the hunter's adventures in the wilderness, his situation in the wider matrix of colonial relations and even by the labour of the animals themselves in feeding and growing to constitute their own bodily selves. The object's 'metaphysical' value consists in the narrative of transformation that attaches to the finished physical form and evinces not only acquisitiveness and colonial power but also a keen fascination with animality that retains an investment in non-human otherness despite the politically evocative theme of order through appropriation and assimilation.

The commodity, importantly, is a closely related form of animal representation to the trophy. Although trophies were preserved principally as souvenirs, more often for personal gratification than as part of a larger entrepreneurial enterprise, mounted heads and skins of a hunter's prey evidently had economic value, as the number of commercial taxidermists in

Victorian Britain testifies.[80] The trophy's value, however, was more explicitly in its emblematic power. Its dual significance as both a hunter's prize and, as the OED expresses it, a 'memorial of a victory in war' reiterates the military, rather than commercial, associations of hunting. Appropriately, Henty dictated his novels to his secretary in a study lined with sporting trophies and military paraphernalia collected in his extensive campaigns abroad, providing him, lest he forget, with a forceful reminder of the ideological basis of his fiction.[81] Most frequently, trophies were prepared to bear as close a resemblance to the originary animal as possible while, conversely, the commercial use of animal bodies often involved a more radical transformation of the raw material, resulting in finished products that may only distantly evoke the animal source. Billiard balls, for example, might be a hundred per cent elephant without seeming to be elephant at all. Yet, despite their relative distancing from the animal's image, animal commodities both in large scale enterprises such as the ivory trade as well as the manufacture of less common trinkets and *objêts d'art*, provide a comparable symbolic charge to the more obvious appeal of the trophy.

The role of trophies in *Rujub the Juggler* neatly exemplifies their significance to the sportsman. Wilson, a young subaltern and enthusiastic hunter, imagines how he would utilise his prey to illustrate his mettle to his family and to the recently arrived object of his youthful affections, Isobel Hannay (later Mrs Bathurst) in a rather blunt gesture of masculine prowess. Examining the carcass of the tiger killed by Wade following his own missed shot he muses wistfully, 'If I had put a bullet into the brute, so that I could have said I helped to kill him, I should have liked the head to get it preserved and sent home to my people' (113). To Isobel, in similar vein, he laments: 'It was an awful sell missing him, Miss Hannay; I wanted to have had the claws mounted as a necklace; I thought you would have liked it' (114). The tiger's body appears for Wilson as a metonymic celebration of the hunter's qualities, potentially advertising his developing manhood and career prospects and allowing him, perhaps more importantly, to involve Miss Hannay in a pointedly Darwinian flirtation, his fitness as mate announced by the talons of his prey.[82] With only the tiger's claws apparent, the necklace constitutes a less noticeably bestial object than the head Wilson might have sent home to his family, but one that nonetheless derives its significance from the dominatory relation of man and animal that conditioned its production; the mute narrative of his valour in the field he would have liked to have been able to offer Isobel.

Henty's tiger-claw necklace is part of a flourishing nineteenth-century trend for the fashioning of zoological exotica into a remarkable array of odd, ingenious and sometimes very costly forms. Such objects' appeal lays in a rather whimsical charm, heartily approved in an 1896 article in *Strand*

Magazine by one William G. Fitzgerald who records a startling range of 'animal furniture' that had appeared in Britain's country houses, from giraffe chairs to crocodile dumb waiters to albatross-beak letter clips.[83] While they may lack the trophy's direct masculine suggestiveness, it is precisely the whimsy they embody that informs such articles' ideological significance: hyperbolically domesticated metropolitan accessories that testify to imperial power through their extraordinary, and at times comic, ingenuity.

In this vein, writing in *Hunting and Shooting in Ceylon*, Harry Storey gives a detailed account of the uses to which he has put his elephant conquests:

> Of trophies to be secured from our elephants the feet rank first – tusks you can leave out of the count – there are very few tuskers in Ceylon, besides which they are not allowed to be shot. These feet have to be most carefully cleared out, which is a wearisome job for your coolies, as they are a mass of bone and gristle, and then rubbed inside with burnt alum and saltpetre (Montagu Browne's mixture), filled with dry sand or straw, and put out in the sun to dry. Dull weather will soon cause them to 'sweat' and go rotten. They make fine footstools, liquor stands, or, if cut long in the leg, umbrella stands. I once designed and got made by Orr of Madras a very neat thing in the shape of bon-bon dishes made out of an elephant's toe nails. I selected the best nails, had them polished, lined with silver, and supported by two silver feet at the curved side. They came in handy as wedding presents. The ears can be split, part way down, lined with cloth or silk, and used as newspaper racks to hang on the wall. The tails are usually stuffed and hung up, but you can make bracelets out of the thick tail bristles.[84]

Storey clearly intends his readers to imagine him as quite the sophisticate, the world of bon-bon dishes and newspaper racks his elephant gestures towards indicating leisure and refinement; his appreciation of a 'very neat thing' hinting at the eye of a connoisseur. Elephant bodies, then, are invested with Storey's status in British society, but also, importantly, form an aspect of his narration of his colonial status. As he remarks on his coolies' 'wearisome work' in preparing the foot and later notes of the elephant's nails that he '*had* them polished', Storey takes his place as the overseer of a labour in which he personally plays no part, announcing the social and racial hierarchy in which he casts himself in colonial Ceylon. His role, rather, is in the acquisition of the raw material and he frames his account of the possibilities of pachyderm anatomy with gory details of his many elephant-hunting adventures. Blood pours out of wounds 'in torrents' and the ground is 'swimming in blood' before Storey turns to the more delicate matter of umbrella stands.[85] Accordingly, following his final tip that 'you can make bracelets out of the thick tail bristles', he leaves the reader with a final reminder that elephant shooting is 'exciting and

[...] possesses a fair amount of danger'.[86] Storey's reflections on animal bodies blend sophistication with raw masculine vigour, exemplifying a dichotomy in which elephants appear as both exchangeable commodities and embodiments of a savage nature, an interplay of the tamed and the wild that energises the animal's remains with intricate semiotic power.

Such elaborate transformations of animal bodies serve to convert potentially dreary and even commonplace trophies into articles more worthy of notice. Fitzgerald comments that:

> We have all seen hunting trophies – for the most part mournful looking heads – mounted in monotonous fashion and set up as ornaments in country houses; but he was really a 'dreffle smart man' who first thought of adapting these trophies to every-day use – turning them, in fact, into articles of furniture.[87]

As Fitzgerald depicts a society that relishes the peculiar he is also at pains, like Storey, to frame what might potentially seem kitsch with redeeming narratives of heroic encounters. He follows his initial celebration of the adaptation of trophies into furniture with a dramatic story of the provenance of a friend's hat stand: 'Fancy lounging into the entrance hall of a country mansion after a long ramble and throwing your hat on the horn of a rhinoceros, which identical horn was once half buried in the writhing body of your host.'[88] As much as inert domestic accessories, these objects are 'living' testimony to colonial power and male endeavour; the more extreme and unusual the modification of animal bodies, the more complete British authority over colonial nature appears to be, capable of shaping animals into whatever fanciful forms it conceives. Even more subtly, animal bodies that have lost practically all appearance of their animal origins can still silently narrate the overarching context of colonial domination. In *Rujub*, for example, Henty offers a hint of the semiotic force of billiards when Major Hannay reflects on the estimable Dr Wade: 'He is good all round; he is just as keen a shikari as he was when he joined the regiment, twenty years ago; he is a good billiard player' (21). For Hannay, Wade's skill at billiards sits fittingly next to his enthusiasm as a shikari as the mark of the right kind of chap, but it also forms a continuation of the mastery over animals he demonstrates in the field; the expert manipulation of the ivory balls around the table displaying a self-assured, casual control of the non-human, taming a dangerous beast into an imperial toy that integrates the elephant into the home.

The 'metaphysical subtleties' of the animal commodity, then, to return to Marx, reflect power dynamics that render the mute body eloquent with the imperial status quo. The literal process of *object*-ification of animals often carries with it, unsurprisingly, a sense of animals as already insentient things, existing only in relation to empire's belligerent and acquisitive intentions towards them. Fitzgerald records a Bond Street dealer who kept a 'stock of *live* parrots and cockatoos, so that aristocratic customers could select one for a swinging lamp' (original italics). 'After selection', he adds, 'the doomed bird was sent along to the taxidermist, killed immediately, and then mounted in the style chosen.'[89] While the lamp derives its charm from its animal source, the animals required are, conversely and curiously, always already marked out for their illuminatory purpose; if they define the unique value of the lamp, the lamp, on the other hand, defines them. Storey's elephants, however much he insists in his hunting tales on their intractable brutality, also seem destined from the start for their domestic end. The 'clearing out' of the elephant's foot that his coolies undertake is a telling locution that imagines the 'mass of bone and gristle' as an irritating obstruction to the proper constitution of this raw material in civilised society, as if these feet were always already umbrella stands.[90] But while in a familiarly utilitarian approach to non-human others the elephant's commodification seems destined from the start, the task of assimilation fails, in Storey's account, to entirely erase the product's animality. With the prepared foot still in danger of sweating in 'dull weather', the persistence of organic processes provides an ongoing narrative of Storey's conquest of the beast; the object's brute origins return to the fore to emphasise empire's success in subduing the recalcitrant creatures of these wild lands. This insistence, however, also conveys, and relishes, a continuing exteriority of the object to the colonial domestic, notwithstanding its evident assimilation, that emerges strongly in Buchan's *Lodge*.

Musuru's romantic appeal derives in significant part from its deployment of animality. Built on the proceeds of various forms of environmental exploitation, especially gold and copper mining, tobacco farming and teak forestry (11), Carey's house predictably contains many of the common animal furnishings of the imperial elite. The opportunity to acquire trophies is one of the numerous attractions of a stay at Musuru. Sir Edward yearns for 'a good eland head' (226) and when his desire is finally gratified Lady Flora admiringly reports that he 'thinks it a record, but he hasn't looked up Rowland Ward yet' (239). Rowland Ward, shorthand for the immensely successful and long-running *Rowland Ward's Records of Big Game with Their Distribution, Characteristics, Dimensions, Weights, and Horn & Tusk Measurements*, was the prime resource of trophy hunters and the centre-point of an obsessive quantification through which hunters could calculate their relative standing in the annals of sporting history.[91] In accordance with this predatory background, animal bodies blend with the opulent trappings of European cultural accomplishment in Carey's country house. Assembling in the 'Blue drawing-room' 'the most exquisite in its decorations' of all Musuru's rooms, the guests discover a space of awe-inspiring perfection:

> The books in the cabinets and on the tables were bound in vellum or blue morocco, and the few ornaments were of blue Sèvres ware or old ivory […] The lamps had shades of ivory silk, and in the soft light the pure colours swam in a delicate harmony as of a summer noon. The scene was so strange and perfect that most of the guests gave an involuntary gasp of admiration. (191–2)

In this sumptuous spectacle of interior design, ivory ornaments are arranged with calfskin vellum and sheepskin morocco leather to produce a display that is both refined and literally brutal. Such connoisseurship of commodified animal bodies consistently occupies Buchan in the brief digressions with which he sets the scene for his text's political discussions. The former prime minister Lord Appin is discovered admiring a 'beautiful cabinet, inlaid with agate and ivory' (197), while Hugh, entering the Green drawing-room, surprises 'Lady Flora Brune examining critically some Zanzibari ivories' (22). Like Storey's Ceylon, in Buchan's Africa the domestic realm is effortlessly infused with the animal presence, providing objects of appreciation that fit harmoniously into the household environment of a people carrying its ascendancy lightly.

An important note in this symphony of decor, however, is the strangeness that draws an 'involuntary gasp' from the Blue drawing-room's gathered company. As much as these arrangements indicate the potent authority of European civilisation they can also appear uncanny. Musuru's hall, in particular, produces an eerie and ambivalent atmosphere:

> Entering the house through the heavy brass-studded doors, you come first into a great panelled hall, floored with a mosaic of marble on which lie many skins and karosses, and lit by a huge silver chandelier. In a corner is a stone fireplace like a cavern, where day and night in winter burns a great fire of logs. Round it are a number of low chairs and little tables, but otherwise the place is empty of furniture, save for the forest of horns and the grinning heads of lion and leopard on the wall. (20–21)

While the 'silver chandelier' and 'mosaic of marble' compose an ambience of ease and social sophistication, the trophies intrude an elemental, almost archaic feel to the room, evoking next to the blazing fire and 'fireplace like a cavern' a sense of the outside enclosed within. The 'forest of horns' contained resolutely behind the 'heavy brass-studded doors' and accompanied by the oddly 'grinning heads of lion and leopards' captures the savage otherness of the untamed wilds, but significantly attains its affect through the trace of unassimilated animality these trophies still carry. Wealth is saved from decadence by the bodies' primal, organic presence that, as with Storey, witnesses the masculine prowess of the culture that produces such interiors. Accordingly, Buchan is also at pains to illustrate the processes that precede this representation of animals. One of the female guests describes her shock at intruding on an altogether gorier engagement with animal bodies than Lady Brune's critical examination of Zanzibari ivories: 'I found Colonel Alastair and Sir Edward in the stables skinning beasts, and they were so covered with blood and the place smelt so horribly that I could not stay' (43). Similarly, billiards, as in Henty's *Rujub*, appears a more brutal enterprise than might be expected as Lady Flora suggests, 'After tea let us go and find Colonel Alastair and Sir Edward and play games on the billiard-table. I think we both want a bear fight' (92). The choice of the soldier and the hunter as billiards opponents adds a masculine vigour to this quiet enjoyment reiterated by the curious metaphor of a 'bear fight' as they reprise their bloodier engagement with animal others in the cleaner environs of the house.

The interdependence of violence and luxury that emerges throughout the text is later summarised and conceptualised by Sir Edward when he argues that the adventurer is 'the electric force of civilisation' (136), facilitating the West's cultural achievements by his tireless, elemental endeavours in the wilds. Musuru, as a result, appears as a hybrid space. As Lady Flora comments, 'Savagery is on every side, and yet in half an hour's ride I can get back to my maid and a French *chef* and the latest English novel' (87). This pattern is both a familiar characteristic of hunting discourse and a favourite theme of Buchan's. As Donald writes, hunting is a 'strange amalgam of atavism and insistence on social caste, of primitivism and sophistication';[92] a blend of cultural accomplishment and a primal organic inheritance that complements what are perhaps Buchan's most famous lines, appearing in various forms in his work but most usually quoted from the anarchist Lumley's portentous judgement in the 1913 novella *The Power-House*: 'You think that a wall as solid as the earth separates civilisation and barbarism. I tell you the division is a thread, a sheet of glass.'[93] If this compromised binary opposition forms an ideal conceptual backdrop for the flourishing of romance by bringing these polarities into contact, it also clearly has relevance for theoretical questions of animality and in particular the Manichean division of man and beast.

MacKenzie's summary that 'big game hunting represented the striving and victory of civilised man over the darker primeval and untamed forces still at work in the world' is doubtless, as we have seen, broadly accurate, but it does not represent the full story.[94] While victory resonates through narratives of animal conquest and commodification, a vital aspect of the animal object's semiosis remains an ongoing otherness beyond assimilation that conveys the impossibility of entirely erasing an animal from its own body. Animal bodies retain an organic aura that fascinates and attracts colonial discourse; a savagery that remains intimate with civilisation so that the processes of commodification illustrate a complex psychic and political dynamic. On the one hand, the commodity, like Fitzgerald's cockatoos, appears to have always been a commodity, but, on the other hand, the animal never stops being an animal and infusing human culture with its brutal energy, imaging human incorporation into the non-human world. Reflecting on a residence decorated with 'skins and horns of beasts' in *The Prince of the Captivity* (1933), Buchan comments that the 'house [...] fitted its possessors as closely as a bearskin fits the bear'.[95] Interior design, as much as the mark of culture and sophistication, also in this form subtly clothes the inhabitants in a wider and wilder natural environment. In comparable terms, Donald explains the significance of trophies to the hunter *par excellence*, Roualeyn Cumming:

> Whereas trophies real or depicted, had traditionally been sporting mementoes of a largely decorative or symbolic nature, those that Cumming exhibited commercially in London in 1851 were intended to provide a voluptuous distillation of the character of wild Africa. They substantiated his racy narratives, but their deeper, metonymical purpose was to embody the *experience* of the hunt and the kill.[96]

Animal bodies, in this context, constitute a gesture of entry into and participation in the wilderness as abode of beasts; the embodiment of an experience that continues to haunt the commodified and re-presented remains and which illustrates the savage prowess not just of the individual sportsman, but of the colonial culture to which he belongs. The appeal of exotic trophies and trinkets is that they retain and relish animal otherness at the same moment as powerfully illustrating its reform.

This pattern offers a markedly different interaction of humans and animals through commodification from the paradigm of late twentieth and twenty-first century capitalism. As Cary Wolfe suggests in his reading of Carol Adams' seminal *The Sexual Politics of Meat*, 'the larger logic of commodity fetishism under modern capitalism [...] institutes a radical disassociation between the fetishized act of consumption and the conditions of production absented by it'.[97] The meat industry provides a disturbing and often cited illustration of this trend. The supermarket's vacuum-packed, mechanically recovered agglomerations of beige matter that constitute one of the urban West's principal modes of engagement with non-human beings clearly achieve their marketing triumph through their erasure of animal origins.[98] Evidently, as Michael Bilig writes in broader terms, 'the pleasures of consumerism would be routinely diminished by an awareness of the productive origins of consumer goods'.[99] The absoluteness of this objectification of non-human species comprises a forcible denial of 'an animal real' beyond human interests that operates in much less unqualified terms in the colonial theatres of Henty, Buchan and Storey. Despite the narratives of power with which empire's unruly beasts were upholstered, colonial romance trades on the remains of an animal presence in their representation: the 'glamour of the unknown' Carey's guests discover in Musuru's hybrid arrangements.

Such elision of the savage and the sophisticated exemplifies, to take a neat formulation from Shukin, 'the becoming-capital of animal life and the becoming-animal of capital'.[100] As central as this is to the naturalisation of colonial capitalism's dominatory rationale, it also indicates the instability behind the environmental and identity politics that serves big-game hunting. The imperative to appropriation is shot through with nostalgia for the wildness of animal presences; the domestic is permeated by, as much as segregated from, 'the animal' as Manichean categories of difference become subtly indistinct. Rather than being excluded from the human, animality is consistently included in the expression of a cultural accomplishment that aims to encapsulate what is most human. Consequently, what we might call the ecology of adventure fiction (the vision it encodes of human and non-human interrelatedness) is an uneasy mix of environmental desire and environmental violence that seeks to reassert the human as a part of the natural, but which routinely characterises this sense of belonging as a struggle to be separate from the natural. This ecological model is a central aspect of both the literary form of imperial romance, with its emphasis on wilderness and contest, and of the imperial ideology it seeks to unfold, with its determination to transform yet relish the wild.

Importantly, the technologies of animal representation that developed as part of Victorian commodity culture were also an integral aspect of another related strand of colonial discourse and another mode of signifying empire's non-human others. The commodity and the trophy blurred also into the specimen, the embodiment of zoological truth that articulates an intricately involved nexus of knowledge, power and violence. Natural history provided romancers with an alluring context for adventures in the earth's wilder reaches and one which raises key questions concerning racial, gender and species identity. In promulgating an ostensibly ideologically neutral objective order of creation, natural history often served to naturalise colonial structures of domination. The scientific animal body was invested with the self-confidence of a culture busily containing the world in a scientific order that constituted a crucial aspect of many colonial romances' didactic, patriotic agenda. As boys were introduced to the tasks of specimen collecting and preparation, however, numerous problems arise in the construction of masculine power, particularly involving the signification of violence. Just as the administrator Bathurst adjusts paradigms of masculinity, so representations of the naturalist illustrate the discovery of another form of colonial subjectivity in engagements with exotic animals. Classification emerges not just as a series of technologies and practices for signifying non-human others, but also, critically, as a means of signifying the self. If the processes of commodification unevenly banish animality from imperial order, narrations of natural history comparably evince an inconsistent distribution of categories of savagery and animality that problematises the strict segregation of the scientist from his specimens.

Chapter Two

SCIENTISTS AND SPECIMENS

Truth's Body

In a chapter titled 'The Animals: Territory and Metamorphoses' from *Simulacra and Simulation*, Jean Baudrillard considers a confession that he suggests science requires of animals, a confession that he writes 'in the final moment' is of 'rationality':

> Animals must be made to say that they are not animals, that bestiality, savagery – with what the terms imply of unintelligibility, radical strangeness to reason – do not exist, but on the contrary the most bestial behaviours, the most singular, the most *abnormal* are resolved in science, in physiological mechanisms, in cerebral connections etc. Bestiality and its principle of uncertainty must be killed in animals […] Everywhere bestiality must yield to reflex animality, exorcising an order of the indecipherable, of the savage, of which, precisely in their silence, animals have remained the incarnation for us.[1]

As Baudrillard argues later in the essay, 'In a world bent on doing nothing but making one speak, in a world assembled under the hegemony of signs and discourse, their [animals'] silence weighs more and more heavily on our organisation of meaning.'[2] Science's effect is to make wordless bodies eloquent with reflexes, mechanisms and behaviours, to produce a body of knowledge from the uncertainty of animal presences. While Baudrillard's work is centred on the late twentieth century's industrial-scientific regime, these processes are a continuation of the concerns of natural historians in the golden taxonomic age that went hand-in-hand with nineteenth-century imperial expansion. In tracing colonial natural history's deciphering of unfamiliar animals into Western patterns of meaning, this chapter proceeds from an analysis of its violent ideological structures and material procedures, to a consideration of the debates surrounding natural history's role in education and in boy's own fiction and to close readings of works that exemplify the complexity of male subject formation through this mode of engagement with empire's non-human others.

In 1923, the American sculptor, taxidermist and pioneer of the museum wildlife diorama Carl Akeley outlined his hopes for the planned African Hall at the American Museum of Natural History and described the arduous process of producing 'truth' from exotic animal bodies:

> It is ordained that the projected Roosevelt African Hall of the American Museum shall follow the ideals and customs of modern museum exhibition. Into it shall go nothing but the truth. Forty groups of African mammals and probably two and three times forty species will be represented in their natural environment, doing normal and natural things. And when we say that in this great hall only truths are to be represented, we are committing ourselves to an enormous task; for we mean by such a statement that every detail in relation to an animal must be carefully studied at first hand by the men who are to prepare and assemble these groups. A vast amount of toil is involved in physical preparation, but, before that work is undertaken, labor equally great and even more important will be necessary to correct inaccurate theories that have persisted about little-known African animals.[3]

Akeley's statement provides a significant summary of an ideologically loaded convention of animal representation that had been continually refined in the West throughout the nineteenth century in concert with developing commodity culture. His pioneering and dramatically large-scale work was a high point, even perhaps a culmination, of this tradition, poised in the 1920s on the brink of a terminal decline ushered in by the development of moving pictures. For Akeley 'truth' inheres in a mimesis of the 'natural environment', the representation of animals 'doing normal and natural things', so that the public might almost forget themselves in a museum as they embark upon an imaginative journey to another continent.

According to the 'ideals and customs of modern museum exhibition', animals are carefully arranged among imitation foliage in front of a skilfully painted backdrop. If 'truth' comes from nature it also comes from display. Akeley's task demands the replication of the natural environment but also necessitates the removal of the animal from it. The museum building itself appears in part to confer 'truth' on its exhibits. In Akeley's ideal paradigm of the animal exposition, it is difficult to ignore the presidential greatness of the surrounding hall. '[I]n this great hall only truths are to be represented'; the grandiose fabric of the museum both lends its seriousness to the 'enormous' undertaking it houses and also draws significance from it, its eminence justified by the bodies it contains. Akeley's portentous opening, 'it is ordained', conceals the author of this fantasy, preferring instead an ecclesiastical rhetoric, as if the hand of some unseen reverence is exercised in the museum, debarring error and preventing animal bodies, in Baudrillard's words, slipping 'behind the horizon of truth'.[4] An echo of the biblical flood adds to the theological resonance: the promise of 'forty groups' and 'forty species' of mammals to fill the hall recalls Genesis' epic rain and expresses the museum as a modern ark, where the earth's full complement of creatures will be preserved for perpetuity under the eye of God, with the twist in the tale that they will never disembark to repopulate the earth with their offspring. Indeed, preservation was a common synonym for taxidermy, as the manipulation of animal remains hints ironically at Noah's environmentalist task. Significantly, museum buildings across the Western world consistently drew on church architecture to invest their collections with an air of divine authority.[5] Akeley's pledge of the exhibition that 'into it shall go nothing but the truth' evokes a comparable legal testimony, a juridical atmosphere that encloses the hall, requiring an oath to guarantee and establish its contents' authenticity.[6] The modern museum is the home of 'truth', an animal's presence within its hallowed walls certifies that it has attained a certain status, no mere lifeless body or nameless beast but rather a specimen, the subject of learning, available to the visitors' casual gaze and the more scrupulous attention of scholars as a creature that is thoroughly 'known'.[7]

Behind this authorisation of animal remains, Akeley self-importantly reveals there lays a 'vast amount' of painstaking study and physical toil. Firstly, meticulous scientific observation identifies an animal's nature and then, the specimen safely secured, a gruesome craftsmanship diligently sets about reproducing this nature, to make it seem to live again. The desired aim of this labour is eventually to erase itself. Taxidermy's 'magical effects', as Donna Haraway explains, exist in the illusion that 'what is so painfully constructed appears effortlessly, spontaneously found, discovered, simply there if one will only look'. Taxidermy operates as 'the servant of the "real"', a tool for the 'construction, the discovery of form' that with its 'twin brother' biological science founds 'the civic order of nature'.[8] The installation of animals in a new municipal habitat consummates natural history's dream to pursue and capture the ontology of each living being, to assemble the multitudinous variety of the organic world into fixity and stasis, constituting, in Foucault's terms, a heterotopia 'that is itself outside of time and inaccessible to its ravages'.[9] Stephen Christopher Quinn's modern, official guide to the dioramas emphasises this temporality:

> Time has stopped. Birds soar in suspended animation. Animals gaze in perpetual fixed attention. Clouds hover motionless in azure blue skies. Behind the glass all of nature is locked in an instant of time for our close examination and study. All the details invite us closer. We are drawn to this place arrested in a moment,

where wild and illusive creatures are encountered up close. Wilderness envelopes us [...]

'Is it real?' is the most frequently heard question in response to the museum's dioramas [...] The effect is so convincing that one young diorama viewer was overheard saying, 'It's magic!'[10]

These simulacras' startlingly lifelike appearance offers a testimony to the technological wizardry of Western industrial culture and identifies the diorama as a combination of rationality and magic appropriate to the museum's situation as a secular cathedral. Importantly, animals exist in this domain not as individuals, but as the eternal representatives of species, the brass name plates on the display case uttering their vicarious taxonomic confession. The production of this calm and timeless 'truth' was a viscerally materialist process, not only a question of what an animal is, but of the practices its body is subjected to, the traffic and transfiguration of its remains that completes its migration from wild thing to exhibit.

While Akeley's museum project was involved with the trade of dead animals, the related venture of the zoological garden was engaged in the more problematic, and hardly less bloody, matter of transporting the living. During the late nineteenth century it was estimated that only around one in ten of animals caught would make it alive to their European or American enclosures and only about half were ever embarked.[11] Nonetheless, the export of exotic fauna from Africa and India was for some a lucrative business. The German entrepreneur and zoo pioneer Carl Hagenbeck successfully dispatched tens of thousands of animals and more than a hundred thousand birds to zoos in Europe between 1866 and 1886.[12] Shipping companies began to specialise in the zoo trade, learning the art of animal transport from circuses and by the twentieth century the fatality rate of animals destined for zoos had been reduced to a more manageable level.[13] To those occupied, like Akeley, in the quest for zoological 'truth', it would seem that such a resource would be invaluable in discovering details of animal anatomy and activity. Rather than relying on a reconstructed version of the animal to represent the 'truth', here was the 'truth' itself, breathing and feeding, if somewhat chastened in its confined new circumstances.

Yet in the nineteenth century and for some time thereafter, living zoo animals were of comparatively little interest to natural historians. Indeed, it was not until animals had died that they became of real scientific value. Waiting lists of anatomists grew for the remains of precious exotica. Ritvo records a request from a fellow of the Zoological Society (the organisation responsible for London's first zoo in 1828) for the 'testes of the Society's lion, in the event of the death of that animal', while the Irish surgeon general was similarly keen to acquire the head of their kangaroo.[14] Accordingly, the decease of an elephant in Regent's Park in 1847 provided when dismembered and dispersed ample material for numerous interested parties[15] and in France the distinguished zoologist Cuvier was always keen to profit from demises at the Paris gardens. Zoos, therefore, as Baratay and Hardouin-Fugier argue, more often than not functioned mainly as 'annexes, maintaining biological reserves waiting to be used'.[16] Although zoo proprietors were keen to distinguish their enterprise from commercial menageries, frequently emphasising their collections' supposed scientific importance and even in some cases restricting admissions to a knowledgeable elite, the zoological garden unavoidably developed into a space of public interest, at times, of sensation, in a way that the exhibition of stuffed animals was never quite to become.[17] In a pamphlet *On the Extent and Aims of a National Museum of Natural History* (1862), Richard Owen contended with a disdainful allusion to populist animal entertainments that the purpose of the natural history museum was 'of a wider and higher nature than to gratify the gaze or the love of the marvelous in the vacant traverser of its galleries'.[18] Indeed, economic pressures ultimately demanded that zoological gardens embrace their popular appeal as a spectacle so that the living zoo animal may be characterised as a resource more alluring for the holidaying public than for the working intellectual.[19] Again in the words of Baratay and Hardouin-Fugier, 'the nineteenth century confirmed the division that had emerged in the early modern period: to the layman the enjoyment of the living, to the scholar the use of the dead'.[20]

The march of 'truth', then, went hand-in-hand with death, illustrating natural history as an aspect of imperial violence and a deeply problematic enterprise from the point of view of animal ethics. While observations in the field were, as Akeley contends, of tremendous importance in the naturalist's craft, the availability of the animal carcass in the Western metropolis, whether it had arrived living or dead (but preferably dead), was the *sine qua non* of zoological progress. Hunting was inextricably linked to natural history right up until the 1920s when Akeley's African expeditions were among the last formal, and rather guilty, scientific hunts.[21] Indeed, the absence of moderation in the natural history hunt for most of the nineteenth century was expressed in a strikingly blithe attitude to the possibility of animal extinctions that reinforces the conception of the museum as a deathly ark, a bleak reconfiguration of Noah's conservationist mission that participates in empire's wider antagonism to the savage beasts beyond its regime of human order.[22] Over many years, therefore, the demands of natural history underpinned an industry of sizeable proportions that invites comparison with more strictly commercial enterprises. Before science could receive the evidence that would be installed in its records, animal bodies had to pass through many hands: the hunter or naturalist on the front line, his staff of 'natives' often charged with the disposal of innards when the specimen was prepared in situ, functionaries at ports and on board ship. More peripheral figures also played their part: guides and interpreters, suppliers of the arsenical soap used for preserving skins, in parts of Africa the tribal kings who allowed access to their lands. Men like Hagenbeck and institutions such as the Zoological Society were in effect substantial employers and central participants in the wider politics of the Western presence overseas.

At the height of the global taxonomic boom of the nineteenth and early twentieth centuries, then, the gathering and collation of natural history specimens from the new worlds of Africa, South America and the East involved considerable energy and financial outlay. Frequent expeditions departed in search of the strange and wonderful fauna of foreign lands, their discoveries reported in a growing number of scientific periodicals and in the proceedings of numerous natural history societies. As a result of increasing exploration of foreign lands, the number of 'known' mammals had risen according to Owen from two thousand to three and a half between 1855 and 1862.[23] Often the naturalist provided the first contact of the Western power with a new territory, returning not only with new specimens but with information about the terrain and peoples of these lands that would be of considerable value to any more systematic incursion. As Richard Drayton remarks of natural scientists, 'like merchants and missionaries, they often led, rather than followed the flag'.[24] If economic motives were an important part of imperial expansion, natural history was most definitely a worthwhile investment. Botanists in particular played a vital role in the development of European colonial interests. Farming was a key ingredient of the flourishing, or otherwise, of settler societies and much work that was carried out in this cause took place in the botanical gardens that came to function, in Donal McCracken's words, as 'economic depots to encourage and service plantation agriculture'.[25] Animal husbandry both in the colonies and at home similarly stood to benefit from the widening knowledge of animal physiology that zoology produced and new endeavours such as South African ostrich farming were particularly reliant on the input of naturalists although some other experiments in domestication were notably less successful. Writing in 1898, the zoologist W. H. Flower reflected sadly that 'British-grown armadillo has not yet appeared upon the menu-cards of our dinner-tables',[26] a disappointment reflecting the initial intention of the London Zoological Society at its formation in 1825 to collect 'such living subjects of the animal kingdom as may be introduced and domesticated with advantage in this country'.[27]

The relation of natural history and empire was not only apparent beyond Western shores, however. As the taxonomic enterprise gathered momentum, sites were evidently required from which to coordinate and administer this venture and in which to store its rapidly accumulating products. The foundation of the American Museum of Natural History in 1869 that was to contain Akeley's African Hall was one of many similar institutions that sprang up in the West. In Paris the Muséum National d'Histoire Naturelle received a new building in 1889 after having prospered as the most important centre of European natural history since the late eighteenth century. Berlin's Museum für Naturkunde was finished in the same year while many smaller cities also hosted significant collections.[28] In London, a dedicated Natural History Museum finally opened in 1881 after it had been realised in the 1850s that Britain's natural history stores were outgrowing their previous home in the British Museum. For Owen this moment had been anticipated keenly for many years as a powerful marker of Britain's global status:

> The greatest commercial and colonizing empire of the world can take her own befitting course for ennobling herself with that material symbol of advance in the march of civilization which a Public Museum of Natural History embodies, and for effecting which her resources and command of the world give her peculiar advantages and facilities.[29]

Natural history museums, and like them zoos, stood as emblems of state success and expanding influence: exemplars, to return to Pandian's analysis, of empire's 'symbology of power'. Like the proliferation of animal commodities, these sites provided a narrative of political domination and national prowess. Competition between rival colonial powers added urgency to this undertaking as the museum and zoo functioned as powerful metonyms of relative success in the scramble for territory.

Natural historical 'truth', then, was a potent political force. The quest for scientific exactitude and completeness that would leave no being unassimilated into its pages was a project that was embraced widely and with resolve. Akeley's intention to 'correct inaccurate theories that have persisted' evokes a project with a determined sense of impetus, a work of continual improvement in which each age was to build on and supplant the errors of the past until the final, all-inclusive, incontestable book of species might go to print and the world's museums display their full set of treasures. This endeavour is commonly said to have originated in the work of the eighteenth-century Swedish naturalist Carl von Linné, or Linnaeus. Linné believed, in terms that are clearly recalled in Akeley's later formulation, that 'in natural history, errors cannot be defended nor truths concealed'.[30] As he instigated his momentous task of ordering all natural forms into a single system of classification, he began the long journey towards an ultimate natural history.[31] Linné's order, first suggested in the 1735 *Systema Naturae*, and refined in many subsequent editions, was to be expressed through the introduction of a Latinate binomial system of identification that could be applied to all life-forms, expressing both genus and species and thereby also providing a sense of the relatedness of distinct animals. Linné's was not the only system to be designed during this period (the French naturalists Michel Adanson and the Comte du Buffon were to offer alternative visions later in the century) and by the beginning of the nineteenth century many British naturalists, as Ritvo suggests, considered his principles 'quaint and artificial'.[32] But his influence was nonetheless widespread: the Latinate binomial was adopted extensively and with enthusiasm and is still used today.[33]

But perhaps of more far-reaching significance, however, is Linné's situation of natural historical truth in relation to theology. Lisbet Koerner comments on Linné figuring himself as both Moses and Adam on frontispieces to his works and taking the line of 1 Kings 17:8 'and the word of the Lord came unto him' as a prophecy of his classificatory mission.[34] Natural history, and Linné himself, were represented, therefore, in the loftiest terms: to name the animals again was to be the second Adam, to fulfil divine will and to demonstrate the divine unity in animal creation, or as one Victorian sentimentalist was to express it, the 'God-written poetry of nature'.[35] Referring to himself grandly in the third person, Linné remarked, 'God has suffered him to peep into his secret cabinet. God had suffered him to see more of his created work than any mortal before him. God has endowed him with the greatest insight into all natural knowledge.'[36] While at times Linné conceded the artificiality of his system, he never doubted that he was ultimately moving towards the expression of a natural order underlying the artificial, nor that his task witnessed divine glory and would serve to reveal God's natural plan to wider human notice. Like Moses on Mount Sinai, Linné was no less than an emissary of God.

This conviction that the natural world contains an innate order that requires only the appropriate attention of the scientist to expose it has received influential analysis in Foucault's *The Order of Things*:

> Order is, at one and the same time, that which is given in things as their inner law, the hidden network that determines the way they confront one another, and also that which has no existence except in the grid created by a glance, an examination, a language; and it is only in the blank spaces of this grid that order manifests itself in depth as though already there, waiting in the silence for the moment of its expression.[37]

While order, for Foucault, resides only in the grid of knowledge that expresses it, it must also, like Akeley's divine order of species, be known to exist beyond this, to be 'already there'. In terms of natural history, unnamed animals constitute the 'blank space' on the grid; concealed from science in some deep jungle, they nonetheless already belong to a species and a genus, their identity already fixed. New species are said in natural history to be 'described', a practice that consists, exactly as Foucault articulates, of 'a glance, an examination, a language'. This pattern, as is clear in Linné's identification of his role, privileges the visual, aiming, as Foucault goes on to argue, 'to bring language as close as possible to the observing gaze, and the things observed as close as possible to words'.[38] Such access to the secrets of nature establishes the power of its practitioner and necessarily excludes those not able to obtain it. For Linné, classification confers a priestly authority; but in the decades that followed it was more prominently utilised in the temporal service of colonial power as a potent form of self-assertion that aimed to monopolise 'truth' for a global elite and to declare European pre-eminence.[39]

Indeed, the frequent naming of new varieties after renowned Europeans is a clear signal of the connection of Western power and natural history specimens. Whereas it was considered bad form for a naturalist to name an animal after himself, patrons and dignitaries were frequently remembered in the Latinate binomial. Sir Stamford Raffles, the influential Southeast Asian colonial administrator is commemorated, for example, in twenty three organisms, including the rather dubious honour of giving his name to *Rafflesia Arnoldii*, the world's largest flower, sometimes referred to as the 'stinking corpse lily'.[40] As David Spurr, substantially influenced by Foucault, writes, albeit over simplistically, 'all knowledge of nature, or of the Other, is but an elaboration of the process of inscribing one's own name onto the unknown'.[41] Classification meant, therefore, the enclosure of the world within Western cultural structures and the erasure of indigenous animal nomenclature; it provided a mark of ownership and an emblem of the subordination of other traditions to Europe.[42] The 'truth' of an animal could in these terms only ever arise in the West.

The assimilation of natural history specimens into a Eurocentric system of knowledge also operated, as many critics have argued, as a metonym of the wider imperatives of imperial order. John M. MacKenzie notes that the 'emergence of natural history specialisms [...] was itself both an impulse towards and a symptom of the developing yearning to order and classify human affairs through imperialism'.[43] Accordingly, Ritvo claims of Raffles that his 'activities as a naturalist echoed his concerns as a colonial administrator: he made discoveries, imposed order and carried off whatever seemed particularly valuable or interesting'.[44] The production of scientific 'truth' further buttressed the ideology of empire by resolving beings into a 'natural' hierarchy of higher and lower animals, those destined to exercise dominion over others and those that were unavoidably their prey. Ethnology included human varieties in this pyramidal structure of life on earth so that the European could contentedly look to science for a validation of racial superiority. The conclusions of Darwin while in many ways a problematic contribution to the ideology of natural history, added to this a sense of colonial success as automatically demonstrating its own justification: merely, in Herbert Spencer's famous phrase, the survival of the fittest. In Foucauldian terms this subsumption of the world into European modes of representation constitutes itself a form of violence. Foucault wrote that 'we should conceive of discourse as a violence we do to things' and Gayatri Spivak, following Foucault, describes Western imperial knowledge as an 'epistemic violence'.[45] In natural history, as in other arenas of imperial engagement, this subtle form of forceful control is inseparable from a corporeal brutality, from the animal bodies that litter its advance. Natural history, therefore, appears as an unholy alliance of domination and destruction: an order of death that despite its intended movement towards zoological truth, (towards animals as themselves) constitutes a Euro/anthropocentric regime through which colonial discourse expresses a sense of its own centrality.

Yet while this account of power and classification may be persuasive, it is important not to underestimate the polyvocality, indeed the confusion, of colonial natural history. Rather than a unitary and internally consistent undertaking, nineteenth- and early twentieth-century taxonomy is a story of contradiction, argument and fashion, of explosive controversies about creatures and their relation to one another that made and ruined reputations. Organisms, for example, not infrequently migrated between designations as disputes between naturalists were resolved and reopened. Classification often illustrated a notable unpredictability, perhaps most striking to a modern readership in the inclusion of bats as one of the four genera of primates in Linné's original *Systemae Natura*. The vexed question of relative difference and similarity between creatures also beset the natural historical establishment. Among the schisms of natural history in this period is the division of taxonomists into what Ritvo describes as 'lumpers' and 'splitters', those keen to gather creatures together under one classification and those who preferred to separate them into ever finer divisions.[46] Writing in 1857, for example, the distinguished natural historian and eccentric Yorkshire aristocrat Charles Waterton complained that the 'divisions, and subdivisions of species in the birds, perplex me beyond measure, and [...] make me as angry as the "fretful porcupine"'.[47] A single species, furthermore, could at any one time have several designations from different naturalists and be related in a variety of ways to a variety of seemingly irreconcilably different beings. As Ritvo explains, 'the conviction that species were somehow real – that in labeling a group of organisms with a Latinate binomial, taxonomists were identifying an identity that had existence independent of the naming process – flourished in spite of a striking absence of consensus about the nature of the entity in question'.[48] As T. H. Huxley wistfully remarked in his review of Darwin's *Origin of Species*:

> Even in the calm region of entomology where, if anywhere in this sinful world, passions and prejudice should fail to stir the mind, one learned coleopterist will fill ten attractive volumes with descriptions of beetles, nine-tenths of which are immediately declared by his brother beetle-mongers to be no species at all.[49]

The significance of this state of flux is that classification was not immune from a certain unease; the naming process as much as it appears to assert authority also witnesses provisionality and the failure of authority. Foucault, in the preface to *The Order of Things* narrates the supposed inability of aphasiacs to arrange differently coloured balls of wool into like groups in a passage that may be seen to have relevance to the negotiations of colonial taxonomy. At first, the aphasiacs are able to produce a pattern:

> But no sooner have they been adumbrated than all these groupings dissolve again, for the field of identity that sustains them, however limited it might be, is still too wide not to be unstable; and so the sick mind continues to infinity, creating groups and then dispersing them again, heaping up diverse similarities, destroying those that seem clearest, splitting up things that are identical, superimposing different criteria, frenziedly beginning all over again, becoming more and more disturbed, and teetering finally on the brink of anxiety.[50]

For the aphasiac, it is the lack of language, the absence of an ordering faculty that produces this confusion. For the colonial naturalist, the vast array of unassimilated organisms outside language (even if their place in language is waiting for them) mirrors this bewilderment: a proliferation that demands order, yet seems to defy it. The anxiety that the aphasiac edges towards, then, is also a component of natural history. If this nervousness is discernable at times in the heated arguments of anatomists, it is perhaps more prominent in the popular fictional representations of colonial natural history that emerged at the margins of this discourse, texts not constrained by scholarly propriety and able, even required, to embrace the more fraught aspects of the enterprise. In fact, romance, and in particular the boys' adventure, embodies a number of tensions that accumulated around natural history.

If the parallel development of the museum and the zoo as the metropolitan loci of colonial taxonomy testified to an uncomfortable involvement of serious-minded scholarship and tawdry spectacle, the imperial romance strikingly encompasses these poles. On the one hand providing their readership with instruction on the sober subject of natural history, these texts were also, on the other, seldom shy of titillating the audience with marvellous and monstrous beasts. Indeed, for many naturalists a less rigidly scientific speculation was an integral aspect of their work and the imperial romance offered a welcome, if at times problematic, counterpart to more sombre articles. Writing in 1861, the inventor of the aquarium and populariser of natural history P. H. Gosse claimed in the significantly titled *The Romance of Natural History* that alongside the approach of the theoretical anatomist and the field observer was an equally valid 'poet's way' in which the naturalist deals 'not with statistics, but with the emotions of the human mind – surprise, wonder, terror, revulsion, admiration, love, desire, and so forth – which are made energetic by the contemplation of the creatures around him'.[51] Animal bodies in this context are, therefore, not only the objects of a scientific gaze but of aesthetic appreciation or horrified recoil that consistently informs and adds to the instability of taxonomic division. Consequently, the hunting of exotic natural history specimens expresses not just the self-confidence and determination of science but also a more ambivalent mindset. The naturalist, despite his role as the ambassador and herald of imperial authority, is involved in a range of debates concerning the nature of his interaction with his specimens, particularly in terms of the acceptable limits of cruelty, the meanings of violence and the relation of these to questions of human identity. Ultimately, the identification and description of the natural historian, the narration of his characteristics and attitudes and his relation to other species of the imperial male, as well as to non-human species, is frequently just as complex and variable as the classification of his wonderful and alien subjects.

Boy's Own Science and the Meanings of Violence

The naturalist-adventurer's common deployment in the boys' literature of the second half of the nineteenth century reflected and encouraged the growing popularity of natural history pursuits among Britain's youth. Publications such as the *Boy's Own Paper*, or the *BOP* as it was popularly known, established by the Religious Tract Society in 1879, gave considerable space to natural history, offering practical tips on the collection and identification of specimens along with racier fictional depictions of the naturalist at work. Behind this policy was a belief among many Victorian educationalists in the moral value of natural history to the juvenile population. Science constituted, as Richard Noakes claims, 'an important part of the *BOP*'s strategy of producing an entertaining and wholesome serial that would please middle-class boys and their high-minded parents and teachers'.[52] The project's urgency arose in response to the extensive circulation of other, less salubrious texts: 'penny dreadfuls' which, with their focus on crime and violence, were widely seen to be exerting a harmful influence over the young. As a spokesman for the Religious Tract

Society explained in the year of the *BOP*'s first publication, '[t]hese illustrated papers [...] are eminently fitted to train up a race of reckless, daredevil, lying, cruel and generally contemptible characters'.[53]

The *raison d'être* of the *BOP* and of several other similar papers that were founded in this period was,[54] therefore, to produce responsible and morally continent young men; to instil moderation and discipline in place of excess and recklessness; to be, as an advertisement for the *BOP* in the *Publisher's Circular* expressed it, 'at once readable and healthful, entertaining and instructive'.[55] Generally, and particularly by those personally involved in the project, it was considered to have been a notable success. Reporting on the one hundredth anniversary of the Religious Tract Society in 1899, the *Times* reported that:

> The *Boy's Own Paper* which has [...] had a brilliant staff of contributors, was started with the special object of counteracting the pernicious influences of literature of the 'penny dreadful' type. It is now claimed that 'not only has the *Boy's Own Paper* supplanted most of the low-class literature and become a profitable publication, but it has also won the hearts of thousands of boys and helped them in the paths of wisdom and goodness.[56]

Importantly, the triumph of the *BOP* over 'low-class literature' in winning boys to virtue carries a double meaning. 'Penny dreadfuls' were both substandard publications beneath the 'higher' works of the socially concerned presses and also the texts most readily devoured by the 'lower' social classes. While Noakes is correct to point out that middle-class moral concern was central to the *BOP*'s inception, it was in the working-class communities purportedly most vulnerable to the perils of degeneracy that its mission was seen to be most pressing. In an 1888 survey of juvenile literature, Edward Salmon argued that the achievement of the *BOP* as 'the one real antidote to these poisonous sheets' was all the more significant in that it was the 'only first-class journal of its kind which has forced its way into the slums as well as into the best homes'.[57] Despite Salmon's judgement of the success of the *BOP* in this area, there remained, however, a marked tension in boys' literature concerning the divergent social classes of its intended readerships: was it really possible to direct one text to rich and poor boys alike? Issues of marketing and pricing arose alongside literary questions of style and content, and ultimately questions of literacy, as publishers reflected on how best to reach and, where necessary, reform their audiences. Ballantyne's attempt in the 1860s, for example, to produce a series of short fictional but morally instructive volumes for the urban poor under the title Ballantyne's Miscellany foundered on their prohibitive cost at a shilling each and the works were quickly repackaged in more lavish binding for wealthier readers.[58]

Nonetheless, natural history was seen to offer a beneficent influence across social classes. Writing in 1870, the year, significantly, of the introduction of universal schooling through the Elementary Education Act, T. H. Huxley expressed the profound and far-reaching 'Educational Value of Natural Historical Sciences':

> Leave out the Physiological Sciences from your curriculum, and you launch the student into the world, undisciplined in that science whose subject-matter would best develop his powers of observation; ignorant of facts of the deepest importance for his own and others' welfare; blind to the richest sources of beauty in God's creation; and unprovided with that belief in a living law and order manifesting itself in and through endless change and variety.[59]

If the 'penny dreadful' created deceit, daredevilry and cruelty, natural history was firmly implicated in the production of opposite qualities, providing a combination of practical and moral learning that gives emphasis to the divine 'law and order' circumscribing human endeavour. Accurate observation, particularly, was widely identified as a quality that would stimulate virtue and retard the growth of vice. In the words of the former prime minister Gladstone in 1879, natural history observation was 'the best and most efficient means of education of the senses' and promised to lead a boy away from 'grosser forms of enjoyment'.[60] In accordance with Foucault's interest in the classifying gaze, vision again emerges as a key aspect of natural history's operation: the prospect of blindness to the 'beauty of God's creation' conveying in Huxley's statement the importance of learning how to look.

Moreover, natural history's prominent incorporation into Baden-Powell's 1908 manifesto for the development of British boyhood, *Scouting for Boys*, testifies to its enduring significance as a source of education and improvement. *Scouting for Boys* offers many 'practices' by which the scout can engage in the interesting matter of studying and collecting his local wildlife; honours were awarded for 'drawing correctly the foot-tracks of twelve different animals or birds' or for naming 'twelve different kinds of fish and [...] the points by which they may be recognised'.[61] That the task should ask for twelve of each provides, perhaps, a numerological hint of the overarching Judaeo-Christian context; but more generally the assignment involves a quiet and attentive thoughtfulness that aims to assemble the facts of creatures without the need for violence. Indeed, although Baden-Powell concedes that big-game hunting is one 'of the best things in scouting', the natural historical opportunities of the chase are importantly seen to temper the urge to violence. Of the hunter's prey, or more appropriately the naturalist's specimen, Baden-Powell felt that, 'the more you see of them the more you see the wonderful work of God in them' and went on to stress that '[n]o scout should ever kill an animal unless there is some real reason for doing so, and in that case he should kill it quickly and effectively, so as to give it as little pain as possible'.[62]

Similarly, the Rev. J. G. Wood, an editor of the *BOP* and for many years the cornerstone of its natural history writing, announced in the preface to his 1881 *Boy's Own Natural History* that his aim was to induce his reader to 'look upon the great plan of Creation more as a whole than merely as an aggregation of separate parts' and to 'notice how wonderfully each creature is adapted for its peculiar station by Him who has appointed to each its proper position'.[63] The violence that accompanied this endeavour was to Wood, as to Baden-Powell, unfortunate but unavoidable. In an 1879 article in the *BOP* 'On Killing, Setting and Preserving Insects', he argued:

> We can not apply our minds on a higher subject than that which is afforded by the works of the Creator, and it is impossible to do so without destroying life.
>
> I have no scruple in killing any insect if I need it, but think it little short of a sin to destroy one without very good reason for doing so. I have no sympathy with 'sport' as exhibited by shooting creatures merely for the sake of killing them or displaying skill.[64]

Wood's insistence on the necessity of a judicious, justifiable violence clearly distinguishable from wanton brutality is a recurrent theme of the *BOP* and produced elsewhere a startling feat of reasoning. In *The Illustrated Natural History*, Wood wished that humans would 'bind themselves never to inflict one unnecessary pang upon any living creature'[65] before going on later to contend that 'by some merciful and most marvellous process, the mode of whose working is at present hidden, the sense of pain is driven out from the victim as soon as it is seized or struck by its destroyer'.[66] Natural history turns away from cruelty in favour of a more restrained model of masculinity that intends to moderate the aggressive pleasures of hunting. Although by Akeley's time such justifications were waning, science was an important factor in the continuing legitimacy of blood sports in the first years of the twentieth century. In an essay as late as 1921 on 'Sport and Literature', John Buchan contended of hunters, '[w]e have become naturalists, too, the best of us – naturalists first and sportsmen afterwards'. The 'naturalist-sportsman' was to Buchan 'the true lover of the wilds', providing a mark of civility that often in his novels identifies a thoroughly decent man: vigorous yet also decorous, thoughtful and self-possessed.[67]

The value of producing a generation of boys devoted to natural history and able to control their violent impulses is clearly connected to changing moral attitudes to animals in the nineteenth century. The visceral production of truth from animal bodies did not take place in an ethical vacuum, but involved a series of complex negotiations of animal welfare and ideals of manhood, and their relation to ideas of class and degeneration that are particularly prominent in the self-consciously moral format of boy's literature. By the time the *BOP* first went to press, a conception of animal rights was firmly, if inconsistently, established in both official and popular attitudes. The success of the Society for the Prevention of Cruelty to Animals since its establishment in 1824 led to Queen Victoria granting it royal approval in 1840 to produce the RSPCA. Acts of parliament were passed in 1822, 1849 and 1854 to provide for the punishment of brutality to domestic animals and an act forbidding cruelty to wild animals in captivity was passed in 1900. The Humanitarian League, founded by the Eton schoolmaster Henry Stephens Salt in 1891, continued to campaign for more humane treatment of animals and were able to achieve the notable victory of the abolition of the Royal Buckhounds, although as Salt pointed out there remained for many years no legislative protection for wild animals in their natural habitats. The anti-vivisection movement was another important strand of developing animal welfare initiatives, while in literary terms the 1878 publication of *Black Beauty* illustrates, as Heather Schell summarises, 'the Victorian era's increasing public sensitivity to animal pain'.[68] Neither was scientific hunting immune to criticism. An anonymous pamphlet of 1865 titled *Animal Cruelty* contended that 'of all the cruelties which are inflicted by the depravity of man on his guiltless fellow-animals, the most abominable are those committed by persons in the position of gentlemen, under the pretext of science'.[69] Animal rights is framed by the author, therefore, as an opposition of gentlemanliness and depravity that expects those in eminent social positions to be able to raise themselves above such base practices. For those involved in the formation of the SPCA, such a connection between social position and compassion towards animals was a ready assumption. At the society's founding meeting, the chairman expressed their aim as not just 'to prevent the exercise of cruelty towards animals, but to spread among the lower orders of the people [...] a degree of moral feeling which would compel them to think and act like those of a superior class'.[70] In many ways, therefore, the aspirations of the animal welfare lobby were not entirely dissimilar to those of the *BOP*. As Ritvo writes, '[i]f animal suffering was caused by people in need of moral uplift, then to work for the protection of brute creation was simultaneously to promote the salvation of human souls and the maintenance of social order'.[71]

Clearly, Baden-Powell's and Wood's justification of the destruction of animal life offers a response to this discourse that aims to protect the young naturalist from accusations of degenerate cruelty. It is also framed, however, by the relation of scientific violence in writing for boys to other agendas.

If animal bodies could be used to train boys to refrain from the unnecessary and potentially criminal violence that saturated penny dreadfuls, they could also be used, as we have seen, to train boys in the ostensibly noble and responsibly restrained violence of martial engagement. Ultimately, in an era of imperial expansion and consolidation boys needed to be inured to blood and taught to shoot. Although Baden-Powell is happy at times to dwell on the gentler instruction natural history affords, his ideal of scouting is essentially a form of paramilitary training that often emphasises the transferability of the naturalist's craft to more urgent situations. Learning to observe and stalk specimens would doubtless, like other forms of hunting, stand a boy in good stead in future military campaigns, as well as ensuring he would get plenty of fresh air and exercise. Indeed, the development of fit male bodies that the practices of the field naturalist would engender was clearly part of its appeal to a nation anxious about the potential consequences of urban growth and a connected physical debility for Britain's military and imperial future. Natural history, therefore, served a variety of moral and patriotic purposes that encouraged its establishment in the mainstream of school life, but which also relied on an uncomfortably fine distinction between different usages and levels of aggression. Often in the *BOP*, articles arguing the moral obligation of the young naturalist to refrain from unnecessary killing would appear in the same edition as stories celebrating the sporting feats of colonial soldiers or explorers. Violence, science and moral decency formed an uncomfortable and troublesome alliance; animal bodies were deployed variously and unevenly as markers of human moral progress or corruption, as the sign of a gentleman's learning and soldierly prowess or as the emblem of degeneracy.

Furthermore, involving natural history in a discourse of social improvement in fiction required a balance between entertainment and instruction that was often difficult to strike. Salmon, for example, concluded of the boy's adventure novelist Captain Mayne Reid that he 'was too fond of natural history and detail to be palatable to the youthful mind'.[72] His dogged insistence on using what another boy's own writer Gordon Stables described as 'break-jaw Latin' instead of vernacular natural history terminology was perhaps taking the didactic intentions of the genre too far, adding an unwanted hint of the schoolroom to the fun.[73] Other authors trod the tightrope more successfully. Salmon praises Ballantyne for accomplishing 'for science and natural history what neither Jules Verne nor Mayne Reid succeeded in doing. His style is so racy, his knack of silvering the pill so happy, that he plunges a boy into the depths of abstruse questions without giving the victim time to consider if he likes the dose or not.'[74] While the obligation of 'silvering the pill' confirms a sense among Victorian adults of the importance of evangelising science among youth, it also illustrates the necessity of compromise in the formation of the natural history adventure genre. Significantly, as Patrick Dunae writes, part of the success of the *BOP* was gained by 'co-opting some of the violence and non-conformity which had characterised the disreputable papers'.[75] Just as boy's own writing aimed to encompass both lower- and middle-class readerships, it was also connectedly caught between conflicting generic expectations, aiming to combine the educative virtues of a sermon with the more dubious satisfactions of a 'pernicious' popular literature. The fictional instruments of an improvement that hoped to lead boys away from lives of vice and dissipation remained ironically substantially indebted to the very texts that were identified as degenerate. As a genre, the boy's own adventure kept one foot in the pulpit and the other in the slums, aspiring to higher things but necessarily still attached to a disreputable literature that made the pious message palatable. While seeking to contain excessive brutality, therefore, these texts also paradoxically allowed space for the sheer thrill of violence, a contradiction that emerges powerfully in two of the most prominent, but now entirely critically neglected, fictional depictions of the naturalist in the boy's own genre.

Among the 'brilliant staff of contributors' to the *BOP*, Henty and his friend and biographer George Manville Fenn were among the most widely read and prolific. Fenn began his involvement in 1883 and Henty in 1895 after having worked for many years on the rival publication *Union Jack*.[76] Henty's novel of the Ashanti War *By Sheer Pluck* (1884) and Fenn's tale of Southeast Asian adventure *Nat the Naturalist* (1882) offer an important insight into the instabilities and complexities of the violent truth producing mechanisms of science in boy's fiction, into the inflection of hunting that natural history creates and into the ideological burden placed on exotic animal bodies. These texts, like most of their authors' works, were received warmly by reviewers as wholesomely appropriate reading for a juvenile male audience. The *Academy* described Fenn's book as 'a capital book for boys, especially for those who have a taste for collecting', while *The Christian Leader* enthused of Henty's work that 'morally the book has everything that could be desired, setting before the boy the bright and bracing ideal of the English gentleman'.[77] *By Sheer Pluck* is somewhat unusual in Henty's œuvre in taking a naturalist as its main character, although Henty himself, according to Fenn, was a keen amateur natural historian, particularly in his youth.[78] Fenn, on the other hand, embraced natural history consistently, publishing among his almost two hundred novels a sequel to *Nat the Naturalist*, *Through Forest and Stream* (1885) and several other adventures overseas that take the natural history expedition as their frame.

In harmony with a familiar Victorian pattern in boy's fiction, each novel provides a story of triumph over adversity that gives the readership a map of their own potential, if they only have the resolve to discover it, offering a structure of peril and psychic and physical testing recognisable as a key element of the romance mode. Frank Hargate, the hero of Henty's tale, is, despite a naturally gentlemanly bearing, orphaned, impoverished and eventually destitute, before he manages through hard work and determination to move towards his proper place in society.[79] Fenn's hero, Nat, another orphan, has at least the guardianship of his aunt and uncle to begin from, although his story is a comparable journey from disadvantage to responsible adulthood. From the start of each text, the educational and developmental value of natural history is made clearly apparent. When Nat is absented from school by his naturalist uncle Dick to help with the cataloguing of his specimens from a recent sojourn in South America, Dick defends the action by explaining to Nat's anxious aunt Sophia that 'he is learning the whole time he is with me', citing geography, Latin and handwriting as among the areas of his educational progress (49). In *By Sheer Pluck*, Frank learns from his father at an early age that 'a student of natural history must be more than a mere collector, and that like other sciences it must be methodically studied' (16). He later pursues his natural historical enthusiasm through school field clubs that offer boys the opportunity of 'long rambles in the country in search of insects and plants' (28) and which were central to the dissemination and development of Victorian natural history.[80] Perhaps more importantly, alongside the practical involvement of natural history with the educational establishment, each text also presents a firm sense of the particular sensibility of the young naturalist that addresses the relation of science and character.

Henty opens his novel with Frank, playing truant from a school cricket match, watching intently a chaffinch with its brood, its nest threatened by a 'small black snake', until the arrival of another boy 'running up like a carthorse' frightens away the objects of his interest (9). The second boy is quick to remind Frank where his obligations lay: 'I never saw such a fellow as you are Hargate. Here's the opening match of the season, and you, who are one of our best bats, poking about after birds and snakes' (10). Frank duly hurries to the cricket field and happily redeems himself in the eyes of the team captain by helping to save the town eleven from ignominious defeat at the hands of the 'home boarders', playing a 'a steady rather than a brilliant game' and gaining himself notice as a 'good sturdy sticker' (10). Without waiting to 'join in the general talk over the game', Frank then rushes home to his mother and young sister, explaining as he arrives fifteen minutes late for tea that it is 'not my beetles and butterflies this time. We have been playing a cricket match' (13). Frank appears as a quiet, diligent and solitary figure, committed to his duties to the school and his family, yet somewhat outside the main clique of boys. While he is 'ready to join in a game of football or cricket if wanted', he 'vastly preferred to go out for long walks with his […] net and his collecting boxes' (15), so that, more explicitly, his 'habits of solitary wandering and studious indoor work had hindered his becoming the chum of any of his school-fellows' (16). *Nat the Naturalist*, offers a similar paradigm of the relation of masculinity and natural history. Like Frank, Nat is rather removed from his contemporaries, confessing 'somehow I didn't get on well with the other boys, for I cared so little for their rough games'. Instead, on school holidays he prefers 'to look for lizards in the furze, or to catch the bright-coloured sticklebacks in the ponds, or else to lie down on the bank under one of the trees, and watch the efts coming up to the top' (8). Natural history fills the time allotted to a more rough-and-tumble boyishness, offering a quieter pastime exemplified in Frank's 'steady' and 'sturdy' cricketing technique and far removed from recklessness and daredevilry.

The attractions of domestic natural history for the boy heroes quickly pale, however, next to the more exhilarating enticements of colonial specimen hunting. The excitement of potential new scientific discoveries, the lure of mysterious foreign terrain and the chance to prove oneself against more testing opponents than the modest British fauna, haunt Nat and Frank's natural history rambles through the British town and countryside. In Henty's novel, Frank, ranging the Kent fields with a specimen net, encounters a mad dog with hair 'rough and bristling' and 'its head down and foam churning from its mouth', moving ominously towards a young girl (32). Instinctively acting to protect her (not unlike Bathurst in *Rujub the Juggler*), Frank at first shoots at the dog with his blow-gun before, as it rushes at him with 'a savage growl', forcing the net over its head to restrain the animal until help arrives and two farmhands dispatch the dog with pitchforks. The blow-gun, a gift from his dead father's travels, is of the type 'used by some of the hill tribes in India' (15) and adds a trace of the colonial exotic to the scene, subsuming the familiar surrounds into a more charged environment that waits in the future. The unlikely containment of Frank's vicious opponent in the flimsy net identifies a natural progression in his specimen hunting, from humble insects to the dangerous beasts that will one day fill their place and for which his youthful natural history enthusiasm prepares.

In similar terms, having bought himself a toy crossbow, Nat pictures himself far away from his suburban home in Streatham. His 'old-fashioned garden with its fruit-trees' changes suddenly in his imagination 'into a wild jungle'; his aunt's cat transforms into a tiger which, as he stalks it through the undergrowth, appears as a thrilling object of fantasy:

> Here its striped sides were plainly visible, and, going down on hands and knees, I crept along between two rows of terrible thorny trees that bore sweet juicy berries in the season, but which were of the wildest nature now, till I could get a

good aim at the monster's shoulder, and see its soft lithe tail twining and writhing like a snake.

I crept on, full of excitement, for a leafy plant that I refused to own as a cabbage no longer intercepted my view [...]

Play as it was, it was all intensely real to me; and in those moments I was as full of excitement as if I had been in some distant land and in peril of my life. (13–14)

Nat's 'intensely real' pursuit of the tiger and, shortly afterwards, his similar pursuit of a lion in the form of his aunt's dog illustrates the homeland, as for Frank, as a training ground for more momentous later adventures, a practice field for dangerous encounters in menacing environments evoked by the 'thorny trees' and the 'writhing snake' of the cat's tail. The animals' existence for Nat as simultaneously pet and game also addresses a tension between the differing levels of acceptable cruelty to domestic and exotic animals. As a cat or dog, Nat's prey is clearly beyond the legitimate range of his aggression: Nat's aunt is horrified at his potentially dangerous games and when Dick later kicks the dog Nat is quick to rebuke him sharply (37). Indeed, Nat takes considerable care to protect the animals throughout his game, covering the tips of the crossbow bolts with cotton wool lest they be genuinely injured (13). The opening of the animal to this playful and harmless violence, then, anticipates the colony as a moral frontier in which animal bodies will be detached from tender considerations and legislative protection and in which Nat's exultant cry 'the monster is slain! the monster is slain!' (14) will finally be able to sound in earnest.

Importantly, both Frank's confrontation with the dog and Nat's game with his aunt's pets illustrate a movement away from the natural history hunt and towards a more purely sporting form of venery. In these early exchanges both Nat and Frank are big-game hunters rather than naturalists, uninterested in the relation of the animal to questions of taxonomy, but concerned instead with other significations of violence against animals. For Frank, his attack on the dog is an example of 'predatory care', the use of his masculine prowess to protect the vulnerable from a wild menace; Nat's interests, on the other hand, are focused on the simple adrenalin-fuelled pleasure of setting himself against a savage opponent and victoriously administering the *coup-de-grâce*. When each of the boys is asked to join a natural history expedition overseas, therefore, for Frank to Africa and for Nat to Southeast Asia, the offer arrives as the consummation of a long-held dream and as an opportunity for which they have been long preparing; to cross the threshold of romance against which they have been pressing. Yet, their future interactions with animals will, it seems, not only be governed by an overarching discourse of natural historical moderation that is central to their early opposition to the rough world of boys' sports and games, but also by a sense of violence as political duty and even, simply, as pleasure that illustrates their interest in more deliberately belligerent models of hunting and undercuts the ideal of restraint.

In Search of Nature's Treasures

While Nat's adventures in his Streatham garden look forward to foreign lands as a space of uninhibited, heroic encounters, the movement towards this frontier initially emerges as a narrative of developing self-control that appears to dramatise Wood and Baden-Powell's paradigm of a reluctant, but justifiable violence. Under the tutelage of his Uncle Dick, Nat learns on their journey to manage his boyish gusto and to nurture the gentler qualities that earlier set him out from his peers as Fenn insists on the fundamental morality of natural history. Asked before they depart by Nat's guardian Joe if it is not cruel to shoot the 'lovely creatures' that appear among his specimens, Dick provides a statement of the relation of natural history to hunting that offers Nat both a legitimation of their impending mission and a warning as to its proper conduct:

> Well, yes, it has struck me in that light before now [...] but as I am working entirely with scientific views, and for the spread of the beautiful occupants of this world, I do not see the harm. Besides, I never wantonly destroy life. And then [...] if you come to think out these things you will find that almost invariably the bird or animal you kill has passed its life in killing other things upon which it lives [...]
>
> [A]nd as for you, young man, you may take this for a piece of good advice – never kill for the sake of killing. Let it be a work of necessity – for food, for a specimen, for your own protection, but never for sport. I don't like the word Nat; there is too much cruelty in what is called sport. (46–7)

The naturalist emerges, therefore, as a thoughtful figure who carefully considers the implications of his actions, adamant that there must always be a reason for killing more meaningful than pleasure. Specimen hunting is validated paradoxically here both by the higher aesthetic purpose of bringing natural beauty to a wider notice and by comparison with the natural behaviour of lower animals, a theme that will emerge in due course as a significant one in both Fenn's and Henty's texts. Later, as the two adventurers begin their task in the Indonesian forests, Fenn gives further emphasis to the justifications of the enterprise as Dick insists, 'Let's collect, Nat [...] and make a splendid set of cases of birds and insects; but let's have no wanton destruction. I hate to see birds shot except for a purpose' (121). The display of nature's treasures, with its implications of moral and educational improvement, raises their actions above an unrestrained aggression into which Nat in the early stages of their journey finds himself, by counterpoint, instinctively drawn.

Aboard ship en route east, a group of sailors catch a shark, which throws Nat across the deck with a sweep of its tail as he unwisely approaches. Flying into a rage he moves to attack the dying creature: 'I was so angry and mortified that I jumped up, opened up my great jack-knife, and was rushing at the shark, when my uncle laid his hand upon my arm' (94–5). Dick's advice to 'take your lesson like a man' (95) offers a moral of gracious defeat, but also seeks to marshal a youthful petulance and to hone the discipline the naturalist requires in the field. Ultimately, Nat learns his lesson well, reflecting later of a particularly abundant habitat for tropical birdlife in terms reminiscent of his uncle that '[w]e could have gone on shooting […] as long as we liked, but that would have been wanton work' (142). In a similar construction of aggression, Henty bemoans the sporting impulse and eulogises a more appropriate scientific mindset. As Frank and his naturalist companion Mr Goodenough are about to begin their work in the largely unexplored African jungle, Goodenough laments that, 'One or two explorers have made their way there, but these have done little towards examining the natural productions of the country, and have been led rather by the inducements of sport than by those of research' (113). Attentiveness and taxonomic subtlety take priority over the big-game hunter's bluster, just as Frank prefers his birds and beetles to his classmates' rougher pleasures. Yet despite the implicit privileging of the scientific expedition, when Frank arrives in the vicinity of the eagerly anticipated specimens, it is not the discovery of new species or the understated practices of classification that supply the narrative dynamic. Indeed, although on their first foray into the jungle the travellers secure several rare birds and five that are 'entirely new', (139) Henty quickly directs his readers to more thrilling matters.

Setting out into the jungle once again, Frank is pleased to observe a number of butterflies and kingfishers as he walks by a stream, but his brief speculations on natural history are interrupted by a cry from his Houssa companion:

> Looking round he saw, at the edge of the stream below him, a huge alligator […] Its mouth was open, and Frank, as if by instinct, fired the contents of both barrels into its throat. The animal rolled over on to its back in the water and then turned as if to struggle to regain the bank. The Houssa, however, had run up, and, placing the muzzle of the gun within a foot of its eye, fired, and the creature rolled over dead. (140)

Such an instinctive assault on the alligator clearly offers a different mode of interaction with animals than the attentive scrutiny of the natural historian: an immediate, primal response to an unexpected danger. Indeed, the absence of a scholarly dimension to the encounter is ironically emphasised by Henty's erroneous insertion of the restrictedly North American or East Asian alligator into the African domain of crocodiles. Frank's decisive action introduces two of the most consistent and arresting tropes of the sporting narrative, the lethal and intimate penetration of the animal body right down its throat and through its eye. While Frank may be excused from accusations of an improper or wanton violence by the implication of self-defence, Henty's imaging of the moment betrays a brutal aesthetic of violence incompatible with the reluctant belligerence of natural history, offering a display of vigour in which the African and the adventurer appear significantly as uneasily complicit partners. Shortly afterwards, a leopard provides a similarly gory depiction of victimhood as Frank and Goodenough set about obtaining this rare skin for science:

> He had been hit by two bullets. The first had struck his shoulder and exploded there, inflicting so terrible a wound that it was wonderful he had been able to move afterwards. The other had struck him on the back, near the tail, and had burst inside him. (146)

The animal's death is a spectacular, even sensational moment that gladly embraces cruelty. As the narrative zooms in on the bullet, exploding and then bursting inside the leopard's body, Henty invites his readers to a victorious imagining of animal suffering that relishes rather than resists violence and causes Goodenough's objection to the casual destructiveness of sport to ring hollow.

These incidents are pivotal to the novel's progression in a number of ways. Henty's interest in the interior of these animals in a sense reproduces a scientific insistence on the importance of an examination of internal forms and processes to the natural historian. The professor of natural sciences F. W. Rudler remarked in 1876 that as 'long as we look merely on the outside, our acquaintance with the animal kingdom must needs be superficial and unsound'.[81] As Henty allows the reader's imagination to infiltrate the animal's body, he plunges into the core of natural history, but rather than construing the moment through a gaze that pays attention to structural detail, he hints instead at the animals' tactile experience: at the wounds that decimate this structure. In this instant, *By Sheer Pluck* announces its abandonment of natural history and its movement towards an alternative signification of animal bodies. The earlier death of the maddened dog in the Kent fields appears in terms that protect the reader's gaze from its corpse as the bloody job is accomplished quietly and even with a touch of pity: 'the men [...] speedily dispatched the unfortunate animal' (33). There is, on the contrary, nothing 'unfortunate' about the alligator or leopard. Crocodiles, indeed, if this is what Frank's prey is, operated as a common symbol of radical otherness, inhabiting, in the words of Leighton and Surridge in a recent essay on the nineteenth-century racialised crocodile, 'the underbelly of empire, the slime at the bottom of the river'.[82] More generally, exotic animals exist beyond sentiment, as if their bodies were unfeeling, except that it is their capacity to experience the bullets' deadly impact inside them that provides Frank's hunting with its macabre frisson. While the animal rights movement often mobilised descriptions of animal suffering in newspaper and periodical articles to generate sympathy for abused creatures, there is nothing of compassion in Henty's visceral report.[83] Rather, his lurid prose announces a moral difference of domestic and exotic species that allows the gunshot without a hint of transgression and reproduces a broader colonial differentiation between Britain and its others.[84] These savage African brutes, like the Raj's recalcitrant tigers, may, it seems, be subjected to anything without qualms: a form of animal racism that excludes them from the moral agenda attached to natural history, although as exotic species they are paradoxically among the specimens most desired.

Compared to Fenn's narrative of developing restraint, *By Sheer Pluck* produces an opposite movement away from a carefully circumscribed aggression and towards an instinctive state beyond a tender-hearted interest in animal welfare. Frank's confrontation with the alligator is a moment of transformation for him, from the quiet and studious boy we meet in the opening chapters to a vigorous young man, always prepared for any violent occasion. There is, therefore, a familiar ideological purpose to this gruesome introduction to Africa beyond the instinctual pleasure of destruction. Natural history for Frank is a stepping stone to service as a soldier that continues the preparations for manhood and patriotic responsibility that began at home with the cricket match and his confrontation with the mad dog. Frank, indeed, is following in his father's footsteps in combining colonial soldiery and science as natural history finds its value to a significant extent, as Baden-Powell would agree, in the preparation it offers for armed service. The moral of Frank's encounter with the alligator is, Mr Goodenough advises, 'the necessity of always keeping his eyes on the watch' (140). Natural history has put Frank in the right place at the right time and allowed him his first experience of violent action in the colonial setting. Accordingly, in the chapters following the deaths of the alligator and leopard, scientific interests fade into the background of the novel as Henty embarks on the characteristically detailed retelling of the Ashanti campaign with Frank recast as military hero, using his new found prowess along with his innate 'pluck' to help subdue insurgent Africans. For Henty, killing animals leads to killing natives in a movement that recalls the intimacy of speciesism and racism. Clearly, the ideal of restraint remains an important element in military discourse, expressing British intervention as responsible and beneficent rather than haphazardly aggressive. Violence when controlled and sanctioned by the state is ostensibly the laudable expression of a virile masculinity that encompasses notions of justice, fair play and, when appropriate, moderation. As long as the pleasure of killing is bridled to the national good there need be no fears for a boy's moral well-being.[85]

But vitally, Henty's slippage between categories of violence raises profound difficulties concerning the role of natural history in a boy's education and also, connectedly, questions of the nature of the boy. It also clearly implicitly addresses questions of literary form and the problem, as Joseph Bristow summarises, of taking violence 'away from the recently named hooligan and restyl[ing] [it] for the respectable boy'.[86] The natural history adventure rather than lifting a boy away from a degenerate, 'dreadful' violence appears in Henty's work only to subtly incorporate it in the 'legitimate' brutality of imperial expansion, producing a boundary between forms of violence that may be hard to police. The evident pleasure of killing, while ostensibly for Henty marshalled by the state, casts a shadow over the formation of the decent, upstanding boy in the pursuit of natural historical truth as the purity of the endeavour comes under scrutiny. Indeed, although Fenn does not supply his readers with such grisly 'specimens' as Henty, there is nonetheless also a marked tension in *Nat the Naturalist* surrounding the strict discipline with which the adventurers approach their task as they set about assembling their collection of nature's treasures. In fact, Fenn's ideal of masculine self-possession participates in a complex negotiation of beauty and death that leaves the reader with an unstable and inconsistent notion of natural history's moral framework.

In a key moment, investigating the interior of an Indonesian island, Nat appears innocently to revel in the marvellous beauty of animal creation as he considers a tree covered with flowers:

> All about this beautiful little birds were flitting, and as we watched them for some time I could see their feathers flash and glitter in the sunshine, as if some wore tiny helmets of burnished gold and breastplates of purple glittering scales. No colours could paint the beauty of these lovely little creatures. (193)

In contrast to *By Sheer Pluck*'s fascination for the prey's interior, Fenn's interest is captured by the specimen's surface. As the birds appear to Nat's gaze their beauty clothes them protectively in miniature armour, as if their glittering colours, seeming like tiny helmets and breastplates, might help to direct Nat's predatory intentions to loftier matters, to the sheen of an exterior lovely beyond the reach of art. The birds are clothed momentarily in an illusion of invulnerability that distances the text from the worst excesses of cruelty and emphasises the pleasure that is gained in the birds as specimens, as the truth of themselves, rather than in the thrill of their suffering. Nat and Dick watch the birds intently, as Nat expresses it, 'so interested in what we saw that neither of us thought of firing' (193). As they are called away to breakfast by their companion Ebo, Dick wistfully remarks that '[n]o stuffed specimens of ours will ever reproduce a hundredth part of their beauty' (193). The hunter-taxidermist's craft appears self-defeating, the birds fleeting splendour may never be transported to the homeland and contained in a glass case: ultimately, perhaps, the traveller may as well lay down his gun and devote himself to the ephemeral pleasure of observing these creatures in their natural habitats. Such an intention tinges imperial science with an environmentalist sensibility that complicates readings of colonial natural history as straightforwardly dominatory.

Indeed, in the early stages of Nat's natural history adventures in Asia, the entrancement of natural beauty overwhelms the seductions of cruelty. Watching a group of 'beautiful scarlet lories', Nat again becomes involved in an aesthetic experience that supplants aggressive intentions:

> I was so utterly taken up by the beauty of the sight that I forgot all about my gun, but knelt there watching the lovely little long-tailed birds, climbing by the help of their beaks, in and out amongst the branches [...]
>
> I had seen stuffed specimens before, but they seemed so poor and common-looking beside the velvety softness and brilliant colouring of these smooth-feathered, lively, rounded birds, and I kept on enjoying the sight to so great an extent that I am sure the flock would have escaped had not my black companion shook my arm violently, and pointed to my gun, when, recalling the object of my journey, I raised it, took careful aim, and fired. (119–20)

The intervention of the racially stereotyped 'black companion' Ebo to remind Nat of his purpose suggests a duality that haunts the act of specimen hunting. While he is only looking, Nat is the connoisseur, minutely appreciating the birds' lustrous plumage; as soon as he raises his gun he becomes, for a moment, the savage, led by the instincts of his primitive guide, just as Frank in *By Sheer Pluck* finds himself acting in concert with his African servant. Nat's intellectual and emotional elevation comes to a rude conclusion with the slow deliberation of the denouement as he remembers his rifle: 'I raised it, took careful aim and fired.' The gunshot is both a duty but also itself a form of pleasure, something to be relished and lingered over as much as the magnificence of the natural world, containing its own aesthetic and artistry as Nat's developing skills with a rifle see him gather a substantial bag of these rare treasures.[87] This accomplishment in the technologies of violence compromises Nat's development as the civilised paragon of British restraint as the visual pleasures of the natural historical specimen and the more visceral gratifications of the violence required to secure them are entwined in the travellers' pursuit of their ostensibly lofty aim.

Despite his education in self-control, collecting for Nat is a source of exhilaration that produces a bodily excitement related problematically to the aesthetic enjoyment of bird life. As the adventurers start inland for their 'first shooting expedition', Nat experiences anticipation as a physical response to the excitements that lay ahead, evoking a mixture of enlightened and base interests. With his 'pulses throbbing, and every nerve in a state of tension', Nat looks forward eagerly to his 'first gloriously feathered trophy' (115). Notably, his expectation of acquiring a 'trophy' rather than a specimen repeats the text's earlier blurring of the distinction between the big game and the scientific hunt. His adrenaline flows in response both to the gloriousness of the creature and to its inexorable movement into his collection. Later, on hearing of the birds of paradise they are shortly to encounter, Nat again is hardly able to control himself: '"Oh Uncle!" I cried as my eyes glistened, and I felt my cheeks flush at the anticipation of seeing one of these noble birds before the muzzle of my gun' (169). For Nat, the wider and gentler natural historical processes of observation, classification and exhibition are telescoped into the 'muzzle of [his] gun' and into the action which inevitably causes the birds' beauty to fade and decay. The gunshot, then, is an instant shaded with ambivalence, a concession to a lower self that acknowledges its relative failure in terms of an aesthetic justification for natural history, but which nonetheless constitutes an imperative that can not be gainsaid. Specimens must be collected, science must advance; but ironically this procedure for Fenn can not consistently correspond to the moral advance of the naturalist.

Particularly, Dick on an interval in their specimen gathering raises the question of the adventurers' distinction from the 'savages' that Nat is in fear of meeting:

> 'And do you feel sure, uncle, that there are no savages here?'
> 'None but ourselves, Nat,' said my uncle laughing.
> 'Well, but we are not savages, uncle,' I said.
> 'That is a matter of opinion, my boy. I'm afraid the birds here if they can think about such things, would be very much disposed to look upon us as savages for intruding on their beautiful domain to shoot one here and one there for our selfish purposes.' (177)

Fenn here explicitly develops the moral questioning of natural history that inheres in Ebo's timely interruptions of the travellers' reveries. As he reminds the reader that they only shoot 'one here and one there', Dick continues to insist on the restraint that governs their endeavour and emphasises sensitivity to issues raised by animal welfare lobbyists; yet he also evokes a fundamental contradiction that the text fails to resolve. Dick goes on to provide a disquisition on animal consciousness that argues the capacity of birds for feeling, even tenderness. His reflection is halted, however, by the realisation that as he speaks 'we are [...] losing chances to get lovely specimens of foreign birds' (180). Again this moment highlights the relation of animal welfare to colonial geography, but also involves Nat and Dick in a pursuit that is unsure of its justification and of its effect on those who practice it. Indeed, as Dick's lecture comes to a close Nat hears a 'shrill wild call' and wonders if, after all, 'savages were near' (180) as the resumption of their collection re-installs them into uncivilised surrounds with savagery perhaps much more closely connected with them than they would like to think. The scientific expedition, then, is unexpectedly akin to 'natural', savage patterns of predation and victimhood.

In this context, Nat's imagining of the glittering martial surface of the exotic birds operates not so much as a deflection of violence but as a teasing invitation to it. The birds, it seems, are dressed for war, prepared for the gunshot in their tiny armour as their beauty is necessarily connected to the warlike impulse that intends to rob them of it. For Nat, natural history is a game of simultaneously standing admiringly apart from the specimen and grasping tenaciously towards it, of watching and devouring, fixating on the glorious surface only to fantasise intruding on the matter beneath. Eulogising on the last bird he shoots in New Guinea with its 'lovely bluish tint' and 'magnificent plumes of rich blue and green', he concludes as he examines the carcass, 'It was a feast to gaze upon so lovely an object of creation, and I felt more proud of having secured that specimen than of any bird I had shot before' (241). The bird's movement into its allotted position in the natural history collection and its fulfilment of Dick's aim to 'spread [...] the beautiful occupants of the world' appears as the consumption of a feast laid out for the hungry naturalist that imagines both scholarly distance and bestial intimacy and gives powerful emphasis to the contradictory impulses gathered in the natural history hunt.

Both *Nat the Naturalist* and *By Sheer Pluck*, therefore, provide models of developing manhood that reveal the moral and ideological complexity of killing animals for science. On the one hand the duality between violence and restraint, between savagery and learning expresses the generic situation of the boy's own natural history adventure between the lower attractions of the 'penny dreadful' and the higher aims of socially concerned publishers. It also may be read not simply as a contradiction, but as an embodiment of the ideal full attainment of a gentlemanliness that, like the conventional figuring of British colonial rule, is both forceful and benevolent, able to adapt itself to any circumstance: the kind of cultivated vigour articulated by Buchan's Musuru. These are young men capable of aggression if the need arises, but also able to govern themselves resolutely and happy to retire back into a quieter scientific reflectiveness. As Ballantyne had phrased it in *The Gorilla Hunters*, the 'boys who are most loved in this world are those who are lambs […] in the drawing room, but lions in the field' (73). Henty, in particular, seems keen to demonstrate that a boy can be a naturalist and a hero and seems to find no problematic in the extension of natural history into war, in the same way that he recruits the administrator Bathurst to military service when the need arises. Fenn's text contrastingly takes a more anxious and introspective view of the relation of science and violence, fretting at the hint of savagery that it seems to supply and to an extent questioning the naturalist's mission. This divergence exemplifies the distinct focus of the two authors, the contrasting interests of the war correspondent and the natural history enthusiast. The distinct settings may also play a part in the emergence of diverging agendas: while Africa is stereotypically a land of barbarism, the East may more easily be associated with the kind of opulent beauty and the refined sensibility, and sensitivity, the birds of paradise evoke.

Perhaps most significant, however, is the descent towards animality that boy's own scientific violence implies. Just as Lord Appin in Buchan's *Lodge* signalled the danger of an overinvestment in '*brute* force', the trajectory of Fenn's text in particular construes violence as a form of degeneration that sees the Briton become the brutish savage, tellingly intermediate between human and animal in imperialist evolutionary hierarchies. This need not necessarily be a bad thing for imperial romancers, as the enthusiasm for the commodity's bestial trace indicates. The facilitation of a human animal nature that the scientific hunt reluctantly and inconsistently supplies, indulges romance's atavistic inclination and proto-environmentalist critique of industrialisation. This interplay of violent and restrained aspects of the self is fitting both artistically and politically, promoting a versatile masculinity appropriate to both imperial conquest and administration and to the generic requirements of romance. Yet the natural historian remains, on the other hand, a problematic figure.

If Henty and Fenn are clearly situated slightly differently in relation to the duality of the scientific hunt, they nonetheless have in common a firm sense, notwithstanding the apparently mainstream concerns of science for boys, of the naturalist as outsider, as a marginal and at times dysfunctional figure despite his well-remarked implication in imperial politics. Indeed, natural history often appears, perhaps rather surprisingly, not so much as an aspect of an ideal colonial subjectivity, but rather as a kind of infection. *Nat the Naturalist* begins with Nat's aunt characterising his early scientific researches as 'whims and fads' (5), while *By Sheer Pluck* concludes with Frank's friend the soldier Dick Ruthven playfully remarking as Frank settles down into a related scientific career as a physician that he is 'a good soldier spoiled' (352). For Henty, while a boy may be both a naturalist and a hero, it is perhaps hard for him to be both at the same time and the antipathy between natural history and a wider duty, embodied initially in the cricket match, is never quite resolved in the text. Ultimately, Frank is able to play his patriotic part only because he moves away from the restrained ideals of natural history and into the military fray. The relation of natural history to the Empire is perhaps, therefore, more complex than many critics are prepared to allow, not only in its ambivalent relation to violence, restraint and the moral agenda of boys' adventure but also, connectedly, in its production of men who appear to defy the normative expectations of masculine virtue. If natural history is instituted as the pathway to colonial power in terms of the violence it necessitates, the colonial presence it ushers in and the hierarchies it supposes, it also discloses a narrative of marginality, magic and inadequacy that problematises its violent, dominatory structures and the privileged status of the white male coloniser.

Animal Magic

The natural historian's power in the colonial outpost is constructed not just by material and epistemic violence, but also, relatedly, by the superior social position he automatically assumes through the lofty nature of his scientific engagements with animals. In an 1869 account of his travels and researches in the East Indies, *The Malay Archipelago*, the celebrated naturalist A. R. Wallace describes his involuntary elevation among Aru Island society when he is called on by a group of islanders to explain 'what all the animals and birds and insects and shells were preserved so carefully for':

> They had often asked me this before, and I had tried to explain to them that they would be stuffed, and made to look as if alive, and people in my country would go to look at them. But this was not satisfying; in my country there must be many better things to look at, and they could not believe that I would take so much trouble with their birds and beasts just for people to look at. They did not want to look at them; and we who made calico and glass and knives, and all sorts of wonderful things, could not want things from Aru to look at. They had evidently been thinking about it, and had at length got what seemed a very satisfactory theory; for [an] old man said to me in a low mysterious voice, 'What

becomes of them when you go on to the sea?' 'Why they are all packed up in boxes' said I. 'What did you think became of them?' 'They all come to life again, don't they?'[88]

The old man's conclusion seems intended as a comic illustration of the indigene's ignorance next to the European adventurer's knowing sophistication. Nonetheless, his supposition of the magical properties of Wallace's carefully organised collections forms a significant element of the naturalist's own sense of his endeavour in these distant regions and one that forms an important part of Henty and, to a lesser extent, Fenn's depictions of natural history. For a Western readership, the juxtaposition of Wallace's intention to make the specimens 'look as if alive' and the Islander's presumption of a magical reanimation is the difference of reason and superstition; a distinction that causes Wallace to concede shortly afterwards, with some embarrassment, 'And so I was set down as a conjurer and was unable to repel the charge.'[89] The 'calico and glass and knives' that to him are the product of commonplace manufacturing practices become invested in this setting, to these people, with a mystical energy that is readily transferred to Wallace's boxes of skins. The mere display of taxidermic artefacts to a curious and distant populace appears to the old man, by contrast, bafflingly insufficient and ultimately, necessarily, a cover story. As the islanders mistrust the naturalist's description of his task, Wallace is able to remind his readers of the racial hierarchies that frame his expedition, but also, as he does so, he is led to imagine the West through the islanders' gaze. The play of magic and technology that unfolds in the priestly guise he finds himself inhabiting and the determined rationality his project is inscribed within affirms the naturalist's higher purpose through a complex interweaving of viewpoints. It is not just Wallace's own serious-minded commitment to natural history that ascribes its value, but his appreciation of the hint of the miraculous it carries for the uninitiated. Through this specular process he is able to represent himself as both an amused rationalist and an esoteric practitioner: as a holder of humdrum mysteries, the ambassador of a materialism that invents itself anew in the marvel of the islanders.

Taxidermy's 'magical effect', to return to Haraway's phrase, is clearly, to some degree, transferred to the West to be reprised in the museum-goers' sense of wonder at the uncanny *trompe-l'œil* of the exhibits, an experience for Quinn still current in the twenty-first century. Wallace's islanders offer a hyperbolic version of this experience that expresses natural history's strategic role in the developing power relations of the colonial encounter, depicting both the supposed intellectual backwardness of other peoples and allowing for the mystification of the West. Science is here elevated to ritual. The violent masculinities that shade Henty's and Fenn's portrayal of the natural historical enterprise seem, particularly through Foucault's and Spivak's analysis of discursive violence, a logical counterpart of this subtler self-empowerment. Indeed, *By Sheer Pluck* and *Nat the Naturalist*, in common with numerous other boys' adventures, display the might of the adventurers not only through their derring-do and ballistic expertise but in their proficiency in scientific processes alien to the initially bemused but latterly awed populations they meet. Goodenough in Henty's tale, for example, is quick to point out on their arrival in Africa that their intentions will be sure to produce perplexity among West African peoples:

> The people perfectly understand that white men come here to trade; but if we said our object was to shoot birds and beasts, and to catch butterflies and insects, they would not believe us in the slightest degree, but would suspect us of all sorts of hidden designs. (122)

As with the Aru Islanders, the antipathy of Henty's Africans to science induces them, Goodenough speculates, to suspect some occult, or at least clandestine, alternative agenda. A narrow interest in trade is the limit of their comprehension of the travellers' ambitions and within this context, as Goodenough later contends, the naturalist's activities are peculiar and pointless: his treasures 'absolutely valueless in the eyes of the native' (202). This apparently inevitable alienation of other peoples from science was a theme that also informed Ballantyne's imaginings of colonial natural history in this period. In the 1885 tale of Krakatoa, *Blown to Bits*, for example, a characteristically stereotypical rendering of the speech of the African servant Moses outlines his stupefaction at his Dutch employer's passion for natural history:

> 'Das de most 'straord'nary craze I eber know'd men inflicted wid!' said Moses that night, as he sat smoking his pipe beside the Dyak boy. 'It passes my compr'ension what fun dey find runnin' like child'n arter butterflies, an' beetles, an' sitch like varmint. My massa am de wisest man on eart', yet *he* go a little wild dat way too – sometimes!'[90]

Moses' disparagement of the extraordinary craze of specimen collecting aims for Ballantyne to confirm the African's place below the European naturalist in a racial hierarchy, revealing the black man's own childlike nature in the identification of white men running 'like child'n arter butterflies' as they labour, on the contrary, to advance the cause of science. The 1910 handbook to the British Museum's ethnographic collections illustrates the supposed differences in mental structure that inform this contrast. Primitive man, it avers, 'does not distinguish between similarity and identity, between names and things, between the events that occur in dreams and real events'.[91] Science is thus itself assurance of the justification of the European's placement of himself at the top of nature's hierarchy.

In Fenn's and Henty's texts, this opposition of natural history and indigenous peoples is illustrated by a significant inability of the naturalists' servants to satisfactorily fulfil their duties with respect to their masters' collecting missions. Goodenough complains as he sets a group of Fans to the task of gathering butterflies that the specimens were 'often spoilt irreparably by their rough handling' (167). Similarly, Uncle Dick in *Nat the Naturalist* grumbles that 'natives […] are very rough preservers of birds' and produce specimens that are 'little better than rubbish', a theme he later returns to when associating the poor quality of the 'plumage worn in ladies' bonnets' with the manner in which the preserved skins of birds of paradise were 'roughly dried by the natives' (215).[92] The incompatibility of Africans and Indonesians with these tasks emphasises the skill and sensitivity that ostensibly inheres in the white hands of the coloniser and necessitates a division of labour in the field through which the remains of the lifeless animal are separated into those parts appropriate to the naturalist and those upon which it befalls his servants to work. Nat describes the partitioning of the day's bag of treasures: 'we secured the birds we had shot, and going back my uncle and I set to and skinned them, handing over the bodies to Ebo to cook, while we carefully preserved the skins, admiring them all the while' (153). As Nat and Dick feast their eyes on the birds, Ebo set himself to the more visceral task of preparing to feast the body. Likewise, as Frank and Goodenough search Africa for animal skins, they do not forget to supply their party with the more immediately useful portions of the local fauna, shooting two hippopotami to the 'joy of the Fans' who attend to the preparation of the remains as the adventurers begin their quest for the inedible yet more significant products of the forest (139).

The dismemberment, preparation, storage and consumption of animal remains, therefore, participates in the categorisation not just of natural history specimens but also of the humans involved in these various procedures. Although the patterns of Western engagements with exotic animals, as we have seen, are unstable, the essential structure is that to the appetitive other the innards are assigned, while the lustrous surface is reserved for the naturalist whose enlightened gaze can appreciate this finer aspect. Whenever these exterior parts of the animals are used by Africans in Henty's novel, they appear as a kind of primitive display that suffers by comparison with the signification of such items in the Western agenda. As Henty describes traditional African dress on his heroes' first arrival in the 'Dark Continent', he insists on the usages of animals as a clear marker of evolutionary development:

> They wore coronets on their heads adorned with the red tail-feathers of the common gray parrot […] Some wore only a strip of goatskin hanging from the waist, or the skin of a tiger-cat, while others had short petticoats made of cloth woven from the inner bark of a tree. (132)

Despite the regal suggestiveness of the coronets, it is merely the 'common gray parrot' that adorns these natives as they appear ignorant of natural historical value. With these animal products hanging unscientifically on the African body as utilitarian coverings or mere ornamentations, Henty depicts an ostensibly unenlightened sensibility against which the Western technological manipulation of the animal body he turns to immediately afterwards appears astounding.[93] Again it is through the eyes of the 'native' that the Westerner is able to realise the full import of his own miraculous appearance:

> The idea of the people of Central Africa of the whites is that they [...] live at the bottom of the sea and are possessed of great wealth [...] They believe the strange skins they wear are manufactured from the skins of sea-beasts. When night fell Mr. Goodenough fastened a sheet against the outside of the chief's hut, and then placed a magic lantern in position ten paces from it. The Fans were then invited to gather round and take their seats upon the ground. A cry of astonishment greeted the appearance of a bright disc. This was followed by a wilder yell when this was darkened, and an elephant bearing some men sitting on his back was seen to cross the house. The men leaped to their feet and seized their spears. (133–4)

Goodenough's astonishing depiction of an elephant with his magic lantern aims to construct a disjunction between the material animal of African culture and the symbolic or represented animal of the industrialised West. While to Africans animals are confined to their corporeal substance, to Henty's adventurers they appear through image and illusion as a sign of the coloniser's dominance over the natural world. As the Fans leap to their feet to protect themselves from Goodenough's play of light and shadow, the adventurer appears as a shamanic figure, the mediator of nature to the African, installing himself in a position of unassailable power, invincible in the technologised culture the Fans read as magic. The white man's clothing, in confirmation, can only be seen by Africans as the 'skins of sea-beasts' rather than the result of the intensive processing of organic materials that characterised nineteenth-century textile manufacture.

The shock of the white man's appearance in central Africa is then literally realised when Goodenough uses a battery to channel an electric charge through a group of the Fans before he then shows them 'several simple but astonishing chemical experiments, which stupefied them with wonder; and concluded with three or four conjuring tricks, which completed their amazement' (135–6). Throughout the expedition Goodenough relies on the same strategy to establish himself in a position of magical power over the tribes he encounters; Henty later reprises, 'In crossing the country [...]

the white men were the objects of lively curiosity, and the exhibition of the magic lantern, the chemical experiments, and conjuring tricks created an effect equal to that which they had produced among the Fans' (201). Famously, Rider Haggard in *King Solomon's Mines* exalts his African adventurers through a similar combination of magic and scientific knowledge, most notably through the prediction of an eclipse that astounds their hosts and wins them a reprieve from an unpleasant fate.[94] In *Nat the Naturalist*, a comparable pattern emerges, albeit in less spectacular style, Ebo watching, for example, 'the boiling of the kettle [...] with the greatest of curiosity' (131). The zoological, taxidermic project that Fenn and Henty describe is situated, therefore, within a context of Western technological mastery that ultimately guarantees the naturalist ascendancy over the inhabitants of these wild regions. As Chrisman, writing on Haggard, remarks: 'the operations of science and magic fuse within the romance to produce an authoritarian style of imperial legitimation'.[95] Natural history is but one element of a culture of machines, procedures and images against which colonised peoples seemingly have no defence.

As science establishes animals in its Western system of signification and representation, it effects a transubstantiation of animal remains, like that undergone by the commodity, through which their materiality magically embodies the imperialist tenets of order, power and violence; a conjuring trick that revels in the identification of taxidermist and magician. Empire's racial project thrives through a hierarchy of engagements with animals, but not without irony. Buchan's interest in Musuru's bestial furnishings performs a similar kind of relish of animals as ornaments that Henty appears to disapprove among the Fans; while Fenn and Henty's complex negotiations of savagery and violence create further problems in the production of clearly demarcated ethnic boundaries in interactions with wild beasts. But despite these ambivalences, Henty's text is notable for an extraordinarily virulent racism that partly hinges, in terms of marked relevance for readings of colonial natural history, on conceptions of hygiene. Frank and Goodenough's experiences of West African towns and villages offer an insalubrious image of squalor that constitutes a commonly articulated point of difference between colonisers and Africans. In Sierra Leone, the 'houses were constructed entirely of black mud, and the streets were narrow and filthy beyond description' (122). In Accra, later in the novel, the British presence seems to some extent to have moderated this native disregard for sanitation as '[s]ome effort had been made to keep the [principal street] free of the filth and rubbish which everywhere else abounded' (298). In familiar terms, this trope is transferred to the inhabitants of these regions: as one African chief confesses, 'I jus' dirty little naked nigger like de rest' (171). By comparison, Goodenough despite his death of dysentery appears untainted to the last, his inner cleanliness ultimately encapsulated by his grave placed hygienically 'on a rising spot of ground beyond the marsh' (246).

Contrastingly, however, in *Nat the Naturalist* natural history opposes rather than disseminates ideals of hygiene and plays an important role in constructing science as much as a rather questionable practice as a mystical tool of Western power and colonial expansion. As the colonial naturalist is assured of his magical potency in the eyes of the indigenous populations, he is contrarily troubled in the homeland by a domestic gaze that seems to undercut the possibility of fulfilling a moral and political ideal through science. If Henty's naturalists ultimately aspire to the creation of an empire of cleanliness among the swamps and jungles of central Africa, in Fenn's novel Nat's tyrannical, asepsomaniac Aunt Sophy aims to instil a comparable sanitary regime within her suburban home. At the outset of the tale, Sophy begins the lament that consistently frames Nat's developing interest in natural history: 'I haven't a bit of peace of my life with the dirt and dust. The water-cart never comes round here as it does in the other roads, and the house gets filthy' (6–7). Faced with such an endeavour she employs herself with 'a cloth and feather brush from morning to night' (7) and greets with dismay Nat's and his Uncle Joe's early experiments in taxidermy: 'And a nice mess you'll both make, I dare say', she cries, only to be slightly mollified by her husband's promise 'but not indoors, my dear. We shall be very careful' (25–6). Likewise, Dick reports a similar reproach from Sophy to his early scientific researches: 'She used to tell me that I should come to no good […] when I began to make a mess at home', he remembers (38).

Nat's interest in natural history, then, necessitates a removal from the home and into a convenient outhouse that Sophy characteristically dismisses as a 'nasty untidy place' (47). This local segregation from a feminised domestic world prepares for Nat's adventures overseas in a similar way to his early games with his Aunt's pets, while allowing the male readership to share a joke at the interfering, shrewish female presence Nat will leave behind him in the homosocial exile of colonial natural history. Notions of hygiene in this context seem petty and unworthy of Nat's higher intentions, as if Aunts, like Africans, are incapable of apprehending the purposes of science. Yet while Fenn evokes natural history as a movement away from feminised space and as an exile from hygiene, Henty on the other hand intriguingly figures Frank's nascent career as a natural historian as a literal movement into a female environment. Finding employment before his departure overseas in the East London shop of Mr Horton, an aging and broken-spirited naturalist, Frank, much to his satisfaction, is provided with accommodation in the former room of Horton's deceased daughter:

> Frank […] like[d] it greatly. It was the front room on the second floor. The old man's daughter had evidently been a woman of taste and refinement. The room

was prettily papered, a quiet carpet covered the floor, and the furniture was neat and in good keeping. Two pairs of spotless white muslin curtains hung across the windows. (94)

In the light of Henty's later fascination with the minutiae of animal suffering, such attention to the delicate arrangements of feminised interior décor strikes a curious note. Taxidermy remains separate from the domestic sphere, confined to Horton's back room and allowing for the 'spotless' hygiene of Frank's new home; but the happy installation of the hero in this space, however, raises questions concerning the wider cultural location of natural history and taxidermy in the domestic metropolis.

Importantly, Frank does not just inhabit a different gender arena, but he also arrives in a peripheral socioeconomic domain. When his gentlemanly boyhood companion Ruthven tries to discover his old friend in his new London position, he finds himself moving away from the familiar sites of privilege and into a region that perhaps more than any other would have evoked to a contemporary readership failures in urban sanitation: 'I tried the places in Bond Street, and Piccadilly, and Wigmore Street [...] to begin with. Then I began to work east' (100). This movement into the darker reaches of London clearly forms part of Henty's rags-to-riches social agenda, but also suggests Fenn's playful association of natural history and filth. Natural history, it seems, inevitably proceeds through a series of exiles, to back rooms, sheds, slums and finally colonies; at first banished for its infringement of ideals of hygiene, but latterly exported to disseminate them. At the same time the naturalist moves towards and away from images of defilement, his relation to ideas of gender and sexuality also undergoes a restless process of renegotiation. Frank's adoption of the daughter's furnishings clearly expresses the aspect of himself that sets him apart from his sportier peers and which marks his innate outsidership from the novel's outset. His early eagerness to explain to his mother as he is late for his evening meal that he has been delayed by cricket and not by his 'birds and beetles' (13) suggests perhaps the naturalist's own sense of his hobby as a disappointment to a normative agenda. In the eyes of his mother, Frank frets, natural history is neither magic nor power, but shame. Furthermore, his taxidermic prowess serves not the higher aims of the Empire, but functions largely as a form of kitsch that insists on Frank's involvement in the feminine domestic setting. His first commission, to stuff the pets of a sailor's wife, is a notable success: Horton remarks of Frank's arrangement of a cat and macaw 'Wonderful! I should have thought them alive' (91). But this magic, destined only for the mantelpiece, expresses only Frank's continuing marginality in terms of Henty's preferred masculinities, a world away from the gloriously masculinised trophies of Buchan's Musuru.

Connectedly, Frank's apparent settlement at the end of the novel for the life of a bachelor doctor (compared to the soldier Ruthven's marriage to Frank's sister) reflects a sense in both Henty's and Fenn's tales that natural history is somehow fundamentally incompatible with heterosexual normalcy. Goodenough lives largely untouched by feminine influence. Unmarried, he prefers instead the wild life of the colonial outdoors and the companionship of fellow naturalists. Having no close living relatives, he leaves his substantial legacy to Frank, allowing, on the one hand, the tradition of male natural history to continue, but also expressing a kind of dysfunction that inheres in his name: a man who while good enough could perhaps in some ways be better; a man characterised ultimately by lack. While *By Sheer Pluck* offers Henty an opportunity, as in *Rujub the Juggler*, to illustrate the possibility of marshalling and utilising an errant masculinity for the state, natural history in itself, despite Frank's military accomplishments, remains suspect and peripheral, even deviant. As W. H. Flower confessed, natural history often involves 'a curious condition of mind or "idiosyncracy"' (62) and more specifically, as Mary Louise Pratt summarises: 'the naturalist figure often has a certain androgyny about it'.[96]

If Henty imagines natural history as a form of effeminacy, Fenn, on the other hand, frames it more combatively as an attack on the feminine domestic realm, an ongoing battle with the restrictive hygienic energy represented by Sophy. While Frank's taxidermised macaw seems destined to please its female audience, Nat's first ineffectual attempt at taxidermy on his Aunt's parrot brings him only her disapproval, making him 'less a favourite than ever' (34). His magic is reserved for the more telling colonial arena. Nonetheless, there are elements in which Fenn's gendering of the naturalist evinces a similar pattern to Henty's. Uncle Dick, like Goodenough, seems all at sea in the domestic setting and hankers for the undomesticated environment his expeditions provide. Nat, meanwhile, is finally reconciled with his Aunt following his return from his scientific adventures in the Eastern seas as success in natural history seems at last to grant him access to the suburban hearth: Sophy is now, he notes, 'very kind and different to what she had been of old' (255).

If Foucault's aphasiacs' confused arrangements of wool, therefore, evoke in some measure the complexities of gathering the organic world into a coherent system of classification, they may also depict the uncertainty that gathers around the representation of the naturalist. The naturalist is a figure that defies categorisation: both liminal and politically central, violent and restrained, the matter of rollicking adventure and the author of sober truths, determinedly male and prone to effeminacy, simultaneously an agent of imperial hygiene and the perpetrator of mucks and messes. As much as he seeks to dominate the animal kingdom, both discursively and materially, the naturalist is also compromised by his involvement with it. The production of zoological 'truth', on the one hand, is a violently hierarchical enterprise that forcefully segregates human from animal. As such, despite the nineteenth-century origins of the concept of ecology, boy's own natural history to an extent runs counter to what we would think of today as an ecological mode of being, characterised by attention to the interrelationships between organisms and nourished by a respect for life. On the other hand, however, the natural historian is called upon to question his own situation in the order he constitutes and to lament the violent practices through which it proceeds in a way that works against this dominatory trajectory. While MacKenzie writes that the 'curiosity, classificatory power and destructive capacity of the hunter in the service of […] scientific knowledge […] epitomised Western man's command of a global natural world', the relation of the naturalist to the animals he practices on is evidently more complex than this model allows.[97]

These ambivalences in the imagining of the naturalist were strikingly encapsulated in the 1860s in what was perhaps the most sensational event of Victorian natural history. The cultural construction of the gorilla comprised an intriguing narrative of race, hygiene and degeneration that raised profound questions concerning the relation of representation and the material animal and led unavoidably to the examination of the human self as a specimen reflected in the eyes of the animal other.

Chapter Three

THE ANIMAL WITHIN

Gorilla War

Sharing 97.7 per cent of their genes with *Homo sapiens*, gorillas are among the most intimate of humanity's animal relations and have often stimulated uneasy and ideologically charged reflections on human origins and identity. Discourses of race, gender and class, in particular, have long accumulated in relation to the gorilla body. As Donna Haraway writes more broadly in *Primate Visions*, 'The primate body itself is an intriguing kind of political discourse.'[1] Consequently, what became known in the 1940s as primatology may, as Erica Fudge comments, tell 'us as much (if not more) about ourselves as […] about our animal others', providing the basis for what Haraway terms simian orientalism: the 'construction of the self from the raw material of the other'.[2] If Fenn's and Henty's narrations of natural history indicate the complexities of human subject formation in encounters with exotic animals and demonstrate the instability of the romance as a vehicle for ideals of masculinity, gorillas provide a hyperbolic embodiment of these anxieties. Their entry into natural history in the second half of the nineteenth century comprises a remarkable and understudied narrative of the cultural production of earth's largest primates in which a number of boundaries appear under stress. With their uncanny likeness to *Homo sapiens*, gorillas unsettle the generic distinctions between natural history and fiction as much as the evolutionary borders between human and animal. Representations of encounters with these extraordinary creatures provide some of the most sensational and evocative moments of nineteenth-century natural history writing, which in turn offered an unmissable opportunity to authors of boy's adventures. What emerges most forcefully in this context is the ambivalence of the category human and the uncertainty of evolutionary hierarchies even in texts strongly associated with an imperialist agenda.

In the months and years following the 1859 publication of Darwin's *Origin of Species*, the question of human exceptionalism was prominent in academic debate and the public imagination. As Freud would later comment in trenchant terms, Darwin's work 'tore down the barrier that had been arrogantly set up between man and beast',[3] reducing the primacy of humankind to a sordidly selective business of fighting and breeding rather than an elective consequence of divine preference. Evidently, the psychological and theological effects of this concept were deeply felt. Samuel Wilberforce, the bishop of Oxford, in his review of the *Origin* in the *Quarterly*, expressed his certainty of the ultimate incompatibility of evolution with his Christian tenets:

> Man's derived authority over the earth; man's power of articulate speech; man's gift of reason; man's free will and responsibility; man's fall and man's redemption; the incarnation of the Eternal Son; the indwelling of the Eternal Spirit, – all are equally and utterly irreconcilable with the degrading notion of the brute origin of him who was created in the image of God and redeemed by the Eternal Son assuming to himself his nature.[4]

While the creation of man in the image of God revealed his paramount position on earth, Darwinian logic advanced an altogether more disturbing, and for Wilberforce 'degrading' possibility. To Disraeli, speaking in 1864, the question was simply, 'is man an ape or an angel?'[5] The response of evolutionists was clear. As Darwin later expressed it in *The Descent of Man* (1871), 'Man still bears in his bodily form the indelible stamp of his lowly origin.'[6]

Famously, this troubling evolutionary ancestry formed the matter for a heated exchange between Wilberforce and Huxley, an influential pro-Darwinian, at the thirteenth annual conference of the British Association for the Advancement of Science in Oxford in 1860. Spurred on by boisterous support, the bishop taunted Huxley with his simian antecedence, reportedly asking whether he was 'related by his grandfather's or grandmother's side to an ape'.[7] Wilberforce's sarcasm trades on the well-established signification of apes as symbols of a degradation that exiled man from grace and decency. Richard Owen, for example, ended one of his several treatises on primates with a lengthy quotation from Henry More's *Conjectura Cabbalistica* (1662) that reminds his readership of the ethical contexts of his subject:

> And of a truth, vile epicurism and sensuality will make the soul of man so degenerate and blind, that he will not only be content to slide into brutish immorality, but please himself in this very opinion that he is a real brute already, an ape, satyre or baboon.[8]

The opposition of man and primate, then, is historically structured as doubleness; the 'ape, satyre or baboon' providing an emblem of moral, especially carnal, danger, that threatens descent down the ladder of creation.[9] As Haraway summarises, 'Traditionally associated with lewd meanings, sexual lust and the unrestrained body, monkeys and apes mirror humans in a complex play of distortions.'[10] One of the immediate repercussions of Darwin's work was to make these disturbing connections both more intimate and more real, not just a metaphor for man's failings, but an integral, and potentially scientifically demonstrable, part of his being: a narrative of brutishness deciphered in the human form.

Debates around man's 'brute origin', then, could hardly have had higher stakes. As post-Darwinian arguments gathered momentum and became increasingly impassioned, non-human primates were instituted as the focus of investigations of renewed intensity. Apes became a hermeneutic problem. In them was concealed, it was supposed, the secrets of evolution (or of creation); their bodies witnesses to God's plan or even, prospectively to more avant-garde interpreters, to his absence. If man's image was haunted by the body of the ape, apes, conversely, were inseparable from what they might say about the human as the commonalities and distinctions of monkey and man were held to disclose a narrative of the most far-reaching significance. Although close attention was paid to simian hands and feet, it was particularly monkey brains that emerged in the late 1850s as the prime site for excavation in the quest for conclusive evidence of the precise relation of man to his fellow primates. More particularly still, arguments honed in on the *Hippocampus minor*, now more commonly termed the *calcar avis*, a protrusion at the back of the brain that was considered by Owen to be unique to the human cerebellum, and verification of *Homo sapiens*' exceptional status among mammals.[11] For Owen, this was ample proof that '[m]an is the sole species of his genus, the sole representative of his order and subclass'. Consequently, he was led to conclude an essay 'On the Classification and Geographical Distribution of the Mammalia' (1859) with the most self-assured pronouncement: 'Thus I hope has been furnished the confutation of the notion of the transformation of ape into man.'[12] But while Owen distanced himself from the most radical and controversial implications of Darwinism, Huxley on the other hand was a determined supporter of an evolutionary connection between man and ape and offered a directly oppositional reading of the primate cerebellum, asserting that the '*Hippocampus minor* is neither peculiar to, nor characteristic of man', but rather could be found in 'certain of the higher Quadrumana', specifically 'any of the true Simiae'.[13] Accordingly, to Huxley, mankind must be understood as ultimately a part of and not apart from the rest of the mammalian order:

> No absolute structural line of demarcation wider than that between the animals which immediately succeed us in the scale can be drawn between the animal world and ourselves; and I may add the expression of my belief that the attempt

to draw a psychical distinction is equally futile, and that even the highest faculties of feeling and of intellect begin to germinate in the lower forms of life.[14]

At times Huxley was careful to temper his conviction in the organic unity of species with a reminder of the evolutionary development of man beyond other organisms. '[N]o one', he argued, 'is more strongly convinced than I am of the vastness of the gulf between civilized man and the brutes; or is more certain that whether *from* them or not, he is assuredly not *of* them' (original italics).[15] But nonetheless, the scientific identification of man's bestial heritage was unavoidably a serious challenge to the Victorian self and to conceptualisations of humanity's place on earth.[16]

The '*Hippocampus* controversy', as it came to be known, was to run on for many years, not only as a scientific debate but also as a contest between two men whose scholarly antagonism was fostered both by deep personal dislike and by the desire to be recognised as the pre-eminent British naturalist of the day. Unlike the gentleman amateurs of Fenn's and Henty's novels, these were very much scientific professionals whose vested interests have often been voiced by commentators on the scientific ructions of this period. Owen's biographer Nicolaas Rupke contends that his subject's 'emphasis on man's elevated position in nature was inseparable from his effort to secure the support of the Anglican establishment for the realisation of his museum plans'.[17] The younger Huxley, meanwhile, who in 1869 was to coin the term 'agnostic', had no such religious investments to protect but a fierce careerist ambition that he felt Owen was only too keen to obstruct. In 1861, however, the question of the hippocampus was overshadowed by a related, though altogether more evocative controversy that added spectacular new material to researches on human origins, while also revealing the profound ideological commitments of nineteenth-century primatology beyond, though still connected to personal feuding. The 'Great Gorilla Controversy' as it was termed by the *Times*, or in the punning words of the *Athenaeum* the 'Gorilla War', is the story, among much else, of the sudden rise and collapse of one man's reputation that caused a commotion in the scientific establishment and a frenzy of interest in popular literature and the press.[18]

When Paul du Chaillu disembarked in London in 1861 with a cargo of stuffed gorillas and a stock of thrilling anecdotes, he was immediately hailed both as a bold adventurer and a distinguished contributor to the pages of science. Speaking not long after his arrival to the Royal Geographical Society at whose invitation he had set sail for England, he received the warmest praise and fullest support from an audience that included several of the most illustrious figures of British natural history. Introduced, in the words of the *Times* correspondent Geographicus, by the 'warmest encomiums from Professor Owen', du Chaillu was 'enthusiastically cheered by the crowded assembly' who were not to be disappointed by what followed. Geographicus writes:

> [A]s one of the oldest Fellows of the Royal Geographical Society [...] I never attended any meeting of that body at which a deeper interest was excited than on that occasion, when the great hall at Burlington-house was crowded to excess and when the chairman (Sir R. Murchison) expressed himself as being most anxious that the great merits of Mr Du Chaillu should be fully and widely recognized.[19]

Another observer unstinting in his praise was the future prime minister William Gladstone who

> thought it no presumption to say that they had heard that night one of the most modest, talented and enterprising of modern travellers; and the rich and rare discoveries which he had communicated had been developed and applied to many of the highest and most important points of knowledge by a man of the most brilliant genius.[20]

Gladstone's 'brilliant genius' was Owen who had first heard from du Chaillu in December 1860 when he received a letter from New York in which the explorer offered to 'place my specimens of the Gorilla and the African apes at your service for such studies as you may wish to make of them'.[21] Owen's early analysis of these bodies immediately conferred academic legitimacy on du Chaillu's discoveries and the two men began a long friendship that was to endure even the later vicissitudes of du Chaillu's fortunes. In 1861, however, there seemed little doubt concerning du Chaillu's future place in the annals of natural history. He was dubbed the 'lion of the season' by the press and even Huxley was initially and unusually in agreement with Owen, as he too celebrated du Chaillu's 'magnificent collection'.[22] Its implications for studies of human origins were also not lost in these early exchanges with Owen remarking, 'when we came so near to ourselves as we did in the comparison of this tailless ape the interest became truly exciting'.[23]

Du Chaillu, then, at this time appeared to offer an enticing combination of scholarly rigour and a pure excitement that unfolded both in his dramatic storytelling and in the extraordinary and almost completely unfamiliar taxidermised specimens that provided the backdrop to the series of lectures that followed his notable debut. The *Times* was keen to emphasise in a report on the Royal Geographical Society meeting that his rather theatrical performances should in no way be held to compromise his more serious purpose:

> Strikingly attractive and wonderful as were his descriptions, they all carry in themselves an impress of substantial truthfulness. Of this no one who has formed

the acquaintance of M. Du Chaillu, and looked into his bright and piercing eye, can for a moment doubt.[24]

The *Field* took a similar, if slightly more visceral position on du Chaillu's credentials, its natural history correspondent F. T. Buckland reporting enthusiastically that '[h]e had killed no less than 21 gorillas. He was telling no stories – no romances: he had brought with him 21 skeletons.'[25] If the *Field* was pleased to convey du Chaillu's reliability to its readership, it was also not shy of utilising the sensation value of the gorilla to boost its own profile with one of du Chaillu's gorillas being gratefully borrowed to adorn the front window of its office in the Strand.[26] Truth inhered, then, both in the person of du Chaillu himself and in the undeniable presence of his exhibits. His personal history also seemed to announce his impeccable qualifications for an adventurous vocation. The son of a French trader in what is now Gabon, he spent three years in Africa as a teen, where he was to learn several African languages, before moving to America on his father's death in 1851. Becoming a naturalised American citizen, he secured a license from the prestigious Boston and Philadelphia natural history societies to collect zoological specimens and returned to West Africa in 1855 to spend a further four years in its remote and largely uncharted jungles.

Of all the African fauna that was known or speculated about in this period, the gorilla was evidently, and increasingly in the light of debates in Europe, by far the most substantial lure to the ambitious collector. *Troglodytes Gorilla* had first been described in the *Boston Journal of Natural History* only in 1847 by two American scholars, Thomas Savage, a missionary and amateur naturalist for many years resident on the West African coast and Jeffries Wyman, the Harvard professor of anatomy. Savage having been detained at a mission house on the Gaboon River as he waited to return to America was shown a skull, 'represented by the natives to be that of a monkey-like animal, remarkable for its size, ferocity and habits'. Concluding it to be a 'new species of Orang', he obtained before his departure 'several crania of the two sexes', along with a few other bones which he passed on to Wyman for a more detailed zoological analysis.[27] Rumours of enormous, hirsute man-monkeys in the far African interior had circulated for many centuries, the fifth-century BC Carthaginian sailor Hanno being generally supposed to have made the earliest reference to this mysterious and disquieting brute.[28] These 'wild men of the woods' occupied a space between natural history and the fantastic that is neatly encapsulated in the full title of a 1699 treatise on chimpanzees by one Edward Tyson: *Orang-Outang, sive Homo Sylvestris: or, the Anatomy of a Pygmie Compared with that of a Monkey, an Ape and a Man. To which is added, a Philological Essay Concerning the Pygmies, the Cynocephali, the Satyrs, and Sphinges of the Ancients. Wherein it Will Appear that They are all Either Apes or Monkeys, and not Men, as Formerly Pretended.*[29] Tyson's identification of his topic flickers between science and myth and, although Wombwell's travelling menagerie had exhibited a chimpanzee called Jenny in 1855, gorillas were still the stuff of legend. Savage and Wyman's article could claim to be a significant and long-awaited contribution to a blind spot in knowledge of the natural world, but their carefully argued, learned essay was unable to separate gorillas from their mythic heritage. Their evidence was perhaps too sparse to adequately contest so long-standing a tradition and or perhaps the West was simply unwilling to concede absolutely and irrevocably the materiality of this fabulous beast.

Charles Waterton's 1857 'New History of the Monkey Family', for example, presented by its author as the definitive account of the subject, made no mention of gorillas and began with a scathing and pointed dismissal of supposedly fantastic elements in primate studies:

> In the course of this treatise, I will do my best to remove from my old grandmother's nursery, accounts of the monkey family which deserve a better place; allowing at the same time a multitude of absurdities to remain there, as mental food for little children.[30]

In his task of separating 'accounts of the monkey family' into their proper genres, the gorilla was firmly consigned to the category of 'zoological romance'[31] and even du Chaillu's impressive shipment failed to shake him in this conviction, as he dismissed these specimens as differing 'little or nothing, except in colour, from the red Ourang-Outang'.[32] On the other hand, Owen had benefited from the opportunity to study one of Savage and Wyman's skulls and then from the later gift in 1858 of an entire pickled gorilla, to be exhibited the following year at the Crystal Palace and subsequently in the British Museum.[33]

Owen was able to publish two works that took gorillas as their central focus. The first in 1848 reflected on Savage and Wyman and agreed with their conclusion that the skulls did indeed constitute a previously unknown species. Then in 1859 in a substantial appendix 'On the Orang, Chimpanzee, and Gorilla', he mixed typically dry osteological investigations with some surprisingly populist conjectures on gorilla behaviour that illustrates this problematic beast still flourishing in its mythic terrain. By the time du Chaillu burst onto the London social and intellectual scene, therefore, the gorilla was still largely up for grabs as a scientific entity, a creature concerning which, as Buckland in the *Field* recapped in 1861, 'the facts were so few and the evidence so scanty'.[34]

Du Chaillu in his *Explorations and Adventures in Equatorial Africa* released in the summer of 1861 by John Murray, the same publisher Darwin had used for the *Origin*, wasted no time in announcing the natural historical significance of his recent journey. Simply in terms of the volume of his collection, his undertaking seemed remarkable. 'I shot, stuffed and brought home', he claimed, 'over 2000 birds of which more than 60 are new species, and killed upward of 1000 quadrupeds, of which 200 were stuffed and brought home, with more than 80 skeletons' (viii). There were also twenty new mammals including two new apes, *Troglodytes Calvus* and *Troglodytes Koolo-kamba*, and, most importantly, evidence too of an animal 'of which hitherto naturalists and the civilized world knew so little that the name even was not found in most natural histories' (1). In fact he boasted to be, 'the first white man who has systematically hunted this beast, and who has at all penetrated to its haunts' (341). Du Chaillu's characterisation here of the gorilla's territory as a 'haunt' tellingly evokes a double meaning from which his text extracts considerable mileage. As much spectres as specimens, du Chaillu's gorillas despite their unquestionable value as objects of science consistently emerge from the dark African woods as apparitions on the very edge of reality.

Indeed, the gloomy light from which they materialise frequently appears as an aspect of their eidetic character, as if such specimens could never truly exist in the clear light of day. This trope was among many that excited comment from du Chaillu's detractors. James Lamont, a correspondent of the *Morning Advertiser* wondered 'who ever saw a forest so dark in daylight?' and reflected on the likelihood of the huntsman securing his prey in such murky surrounds.[35] Du Chaillu's prose, however, is insistent on the point: 'Often', he emphasised, 'they choose for their peculiar haunt a wood so dark that, even at midday, one can scarce see ten yards' (297). The explorer's first gorilla encounter in 'the most dense and impenetrable part of the forest' accordingly represents the moment in terms that make the most of this ghostly ambience:

> Presently before us stood an immense male gorilla. He had gone through the jungle on all fours; but when he saw our party he erected himself and looked us boldly in the face. He stood about a dozen yards from us and was a sight I think I shall never forget. Nearly six feet high […] with immense body, huge chest, and great muscular arms with fiercely glowing large deep grey eyes, and a hellish expression of face, which seemed to me like some nightmare vision: thus stood before us the king of the African forest […]
>
> His eyes began to flash fiercer fire as we stood motionless on the defensive, and the crest of short hair which stands on his forehead began to twitch rapidly up and down, while his powerful fangs were shown as he again sent forth a thunderous roar. And now truly he reminded me of nothing but some hellish

dream creature – a being of that hideous order, half-man half-beast, which we find pictured by old artists in some representations of the infernal regions. He advanced a few steps-then stopped to utter that hideous roar again […] and here, beating his breast in rage, we fired and killed him.

With a groan that had something terribly human in it and yet was full of brutishness, he fell forward on his face. (70–71)

Du Chaillu's allusion to previous artistic 'representations of the infernal regions' both alludes to the longstanding tradition of ungovernable, sinful primate nature and also exiles the animal from the natural world into the supernatural. As a 'nightmare vision' and 'hellish dream creature', the gorilla is open to a range of speculations and rhetorical flourishes that need not be confined to the sober, wakeful demesne of natural history, although evidently the concerns of contemporary science still provide a vital element of the moment's frisson. Half-man half-beast, the monstrously hybrid gorilla bestrides taxonomic boundaries and dramatically embodies immediately post-Darwinian anxieties, over which du Chaillu appears, in some senses, to triumph.

Despite its 'immense body' and 'great muscular arms', the 'king of the African forest' ends the scene by falling forward rather pathetically on its face as the animal makes its obeisance to the new imperial (and evolutionary) monarch, exultant in his mastery. And ultimately, notwithstanding a pang of pity for the terrible familiarity of his quarry, the resemblance of hunter and prey is a vital aspect of the thrill of gorilla hunting: it is, du Chaillu insists, 'this lurking reminiscence of humanity, indeed that makes one of the chief ingredients of the hunter's excitement' (352). The *coup-de-grâce* symbolises both domination and catharsis (a term that will come into closer consideration in the final section of this chapter). In triumphing over the gorilla of the dark forests, du Chaillu is also conquering the gorilla within, illustrating, as Owen had asserted, that man is the 'sole species of his genus', or as du Chaillu himself expressed it, that there lies a 'vast chasm […] between even the lowest forms of the human race and the highest of the apes' (376).

Yet despite his victory, the reimagining of the eyes of the gorilla in this vital moment offers a challenge to the explorer that is not easily dismissed. As the gorilla looks the hunters 'boldly in the face', du Chaillu's prose is drawn to the 'fiercely glowing large deep grey eyes', the chain of adjectives evincing a fascination that reappears when the eyes ominously begin 'to flash fiercer fire'. Du Chaillu's proto-colonial dominance stumbles on the boldness of the animal's gaze and its unshaking direction towards him. In the jungle's half-light, the gorilla, perhaps paradoxically, is associated with a hyperbolic visuality that raises profound problems for the ideological assumptions of African exploration, particularly in the frequently reproduced illustration that accompanies the scene (see Figure 3). Du Chaillu, his African gun-bearer and the gorilla provide a stereotypical evolutionary triad that toys with notions of likeness and difference and appears to offer, as Janet Browne suggests, a series of oppositions: 'Mankind versus nature; [...] civilisation versus the wild; humanity confronting the beast within.'[36] The posture of the three, each with legs parted and an elbow crooked, structures the scene around a commonality that is offset by the clear dissimilarities between them. Du Chaillu himself features neatly dressed in his white safari suit, steady on his feet with his gun aimed decisively at his prey. Behind him, the gun-bearer in only shorts and a necklace, with his weapon pointing ineffectually skywards appears to lose his footing faced by the naked and deliberately anthropomorphised gorilla that completes the scene. Befittingly, the animal appears in rather theatrical mode: its tragic, even Shakespearian, stance staged by the proscenium arch of the overhanging branch. In this play du Chaillu, then, as becomes the new king of the forest, takes his place at the top of a hierarchy, in civilised costume and smaller than the others, yet secure in his mastery of his weapon; vastly more powerful if somewhat remote in the background of the composition.

The direction of the gorilla's huge bulging eyes towards du Chaillu, however, reiterates that the encounter is as much specular as spectacular. As the reader looks on the monstrous beast in its final moments, the beast stares back and the sure-footed explorer is situated inescapably in its gaze. Indeed, the only eyes available to the viewer are the gorilla's with du Chaillu's face concealed by his hat and the tilt of his head. The emphasis is unavoidably not on seeing

Figure 3. 'My First Gorilla'. Paul du Chaillu, *Explorations and Adventures in Equatorial Africa* (London: John Murray, 1861), 71.

but on being seen. A slight air of startlement wrinkles the gorilla's features and underlines the troublesome experience of being experienced through animal alterity, as the adventurer is called upon to witness himself from the most radically other of perspectives, a scopic positioning that may be elucidated by Homi Bhabha's postcolonial theorisations of the gaze:

> In the objectification of the scopic drive there is always the threatened return of the look; in the identification of the Imaginary relation there is always the alienating other (or mirror) which crucially returns its image to the subject; and in that form of substitution and fixation that is fetishism there is always the trace of loss, absence.[37]

The scopic drive of natural history, the Foucauldian glance is deeply troubled by this exchange. While the scene's composition aims to illustrate the empowerment of the colonial presence (the imposition of the self on the other), the 'return of the [gorilla's] look' destabilises the animal's objectification in the coloniser's power-hungry gaze; confronting du Chaillu with his own otherness in the gorilla's apprehension. To Jacques Derrida in his essay 'The Animal That Therefore I Am (More to Follow)', this experience of being experienced by an animal, evoked for him by being caught 'naked, in silence by the gaze' of his cat,[38] informs a complex interplay of subjectification and alienation. The animal's gaze appears, on the one hand, as 'vacant to the extent of being bottomless […] uninterpretable, unreadable, undecidable, abyssal and secret'; but it also functions as the means for human self-definition, signalling the 'bordercrossing from which vantage man dares announce himself to himself'.[39] As with Browne's reading of the du Chaillu illustration, the self is thus constituted through a process of opposition, differentiation and exclusion; a declaration of oneself to oneself at the border with the other: marked by the animal's abyssal gaze. Derrida's figuring of this visual encounter as abyss, however, offers not just a reflection in which the human discovers itself through excluding what it resembles, but also absorption, configuring an emptiness into which the human disappears. As Simmons and Armstrong summarise, the 'gaze of Derrida's cat serves to undermine the ontological security of the human animal that so confidently distinguishes itself from it'.[40] Despite the ideological layers drawn into du Chaillu's 'first gorilla', this seminal confrontation pivots, ultimately, on its failure to erase this animal's challenge to human subjectivity. In contrast to A. R. Wallace's discovery of his own privileged colonial position through the eyes of the Aru Islanders, the gorilla's gaze threatens the naturalist's priority, arresting du Chaillu in his moment of triumph, shading the determinations of the scene with the gorilla's failure to recognise and validate his mastery. Significantly, as the gorilla war

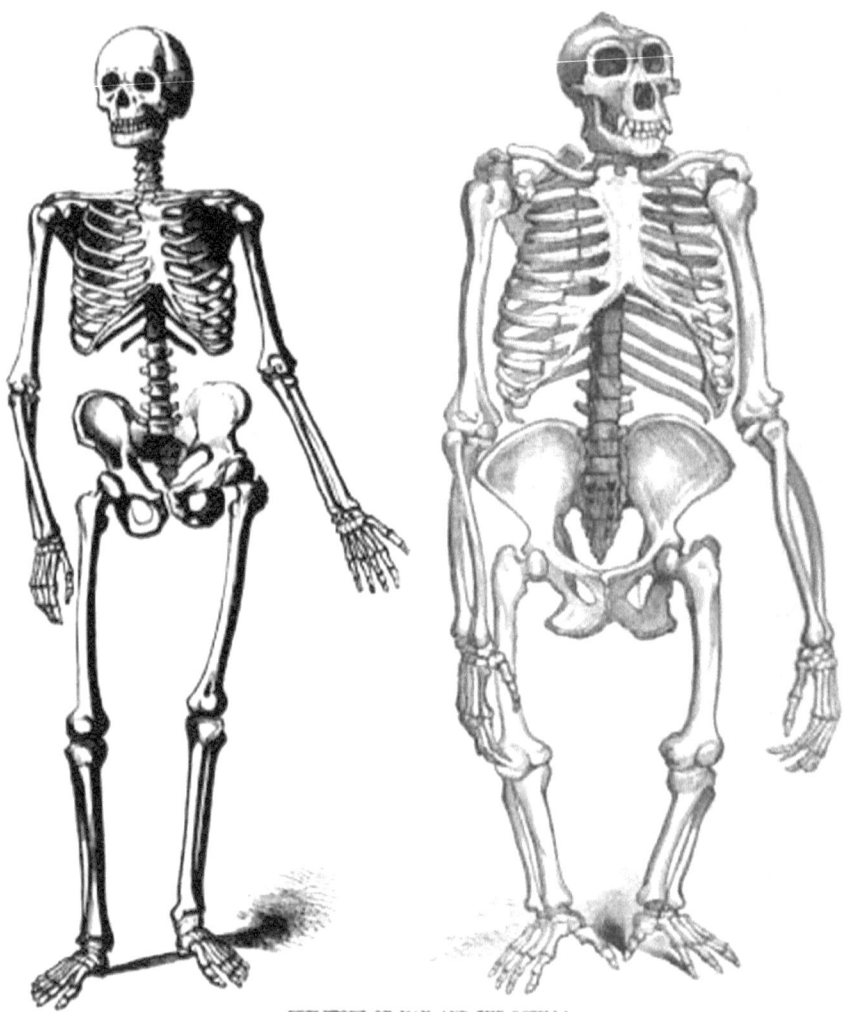

SKELETONS OF MAN AND THE GORILLA.

Figure 4. 'Skeletons of Man and the Gorilla, the latter drawn from a skeleton in my collection'. Paul du Chaillu, *Explorations and Adventures in Equatorial Africa* (London: John Murray, 1861), 370.

progressed, these complex negotiations of du Chaillu's position were to find a parallel in a series of more tangible questions that arose around the form and texture of the *Explorations* and the qualities of the man himself.

Errors and Accusations

Despite du Chaillu's overtly sensationalised account of his 'first gorilla', there was also plainly much in the *Explorations* that obeyed the more stringent, formal requirements of scientific discourse and reaffirmed the overarching gravity of the author's intentions. As McCook comments, du Chaillu was clearly in many sections of the work at least 'behaving as if he were a scientist'.[41] Throughout the text he offered reflections, at times lengthy, on geographical and anthropological points of interest, while appendices detailing every species, new and already recognised, he encountered on his expedition and describing the 'languages of Equatorial Africa' provided a final reminder that above all this text was conceived as a contribution to knowledge, notwithstanding the unscholarly overenthusiasm of the hunting scenes. A chapter 'On the Bony Structure of the Gorilla and the Other African Apes', furthermore, presented an academic overview of the debates and conclusions of nineteenth-century primate studies, complete with drawings and diagrams picturing the differences in osteological form and cranial capacity between the great apes. A depiction of human and gorilla skeletons side-by-side (see Figure 4) reinforced du Chaillu's emphasis on the uncanny relation between them, but in a mode evidently far removed from the earlier drama. Stripped down to the barest elements of form, du Chaillu's skeletons provide a static and methodical illustration of species identity that gives only the faintest hint of the theatrical in the left arm of the human figure, outstretched as if in introduction of his evolutionary cousin. The specimens' faces are even turned slightly away from each other in a coy gesture of separation that compensates for the thrilling similarities discovered in the gloomy African forest.

Du Chaillu's text, then, appears as an amalgamation of the zoological and the mythic, encompassed by the dual title *Explorations and Adventures*: an awkward balancing of two categories of representation that was perhaps more than anything responsible for the series of vigorous objections that before long overshadowed his initially widespread approval. Just as gorillas were neither one thing nor the other but liminal creatures on the cusp of the human/animal divide, so du Chaillu's text was comparably beset by confusions of literary taxonomy. John Edward Gray, keeper of zoology at the British Museum and a leading opponent of du Chaillu revealed his antipathy to this generic overlapping in a letter to the *Times*:

> If Mr. Du Chaillu had published his work as the 'Adventures of a Gorilla Slayer' I should have taken no notice of it, for the readers of such works like them seasoned to their palate. It is only as a work of a professedly scientific traveller and naturalist that I ventured any observations on it.[42]

It was du Chaillu's avowed scientific ambitions, then, clearly apparent in his adoption of the textual forms of natural history that brought the *Explorations* to Gray's notice and invited censure of its tendency to exaggeration. Gray's suggestion of an alternative title introduces a theme that occupied many of the work's critics. The *Athenaeum* asserted that for 'a solid book of serious travel, the style is rather airy', while the *Field*, perhaps unsurprisingly one of the publications most supportive of du Chaillu, conceded that the 'stories of his contests with the gorilla have had more particular attraction for the popular mind'.[43] Du Chaillu's fall from grace hinged at first on questions of tone and style: the seasoning, to follow Gray's metaphor, with which he flavoured his travels to the public rather than the academic palate. In opposing this inclination, Gray found himself following the same agenda as Waterton had in advertising his *New History of the Monkey Family* as the antidote to nursery storytelling. The danger, Gray argued, was that 'natural history may be converted into a romance rather than a science by traveller's tales if they are not exposed at the time'.[44] Du Chaillu's necessary exposure became in some quarters a battle for the dignity and integrity of science itself, an insistence on a textual purity contaminated by the *Explorations*' hybrid form.

In this context, unsympathetic commentators, including Gray, returned to the rather scant evidence of gorillas in European museums as a reference point from which to challenge du Chaillu's speculations and to reassert a scrupulous rationalism seemingly imperilled by such uninhibited expression. An anonymous reviewer of the *Explorations* in the *Morning Advertiser*, a popular and at times sensationalist publication, second only in circulation to the *Times* and at the forefront of the unfolding of the controversy, described 'feeling a degree of distrust' on first reading the work and in particular seeing the illustrations:

> A little examination shows the reader that they are not sketches from life made by the author, but elaborate pictures got up in England or in America of scenes which the draughtsman never witnessed […] To get at the actual truth, the first step would be to tear out all these wonderful pictures, and throw them away, and take our ideas of the animal from the reality in the British Museum.
>
> But having done this the next thing would be to blot out some of M. CHAILLU's astonishing stories.[45]

The rather drastic course of action the *Advertiser* suggests to the reader determined to get to the reality of the gorilla divides visual forms of representation into a clear hierarchy that hinges, appropriately, on the proximity of the illustration to the material animal. 'Elaborate pictures got up in England' situate the artist many thousands of miles from his subject while 'sketches from life' at least place it in his view. The 'reality in the British Museum', however, dispenses with the artist altogether and makes claim to an absolute purity and neutrality of representation: the animal as it unavoidably *is*. London's single entire preserved pre–du Chaillu gorilla provided, then, a salutary image of an originary being that might prevent, or at least rebuke, the over-imagination of zoological charlatans. Ironically, despite this insistence on the ultimate, extra-textual value of the specimen, the *Advertiser* could not resist an exaggeration of its own in the final lines of the article. Quoting Gray but with his own overenthusiastic flourish, the author claimed that 'stuffed gorillas have been pouring into Europe "for the last fifteen years"'.[46] The trickle of gorilla bones and bodies that had been trafficked from Africa (and more into France than Britain)[47] becomes, under the necessity of alienating du Chaillu from science, a far more substantial collection that serves to undermine the explorer's apparently original research, but at the same time problematises evidence as a disinterested declaration of truth. These few animal remains, the suddenly monumental 'evidence', are inserted into a narrative that runs deliberately contrary to du Chaillu's, wilfully constructing the Frenchman's untrustworthiness in his alienation from the scientific gorilla.

As much as du Chaillu was blamed for the illustrations in his work, he was also accused of not himself being their artist. In a letter to the *Times*, Gray identifies three previously published images of the gorilla that appeared in the *Explorations* without acknowledgement, two by Geoffrey Saint Hilaire at the Paris museum and a third, the gorilla skeleton reproduced from a photograph taken by a Mr Fenton 'for the trustees of the British Museum'.[48] Writing in the preface to the second edition of June 1861, du Chaillu offered a partial confession, conceding that four 'out of the 74 plates [...] have been copied' and adding that he regretted his failure to identify the original sources. On the subject of the Fenton photograph, however, he remained adamant, claiming defiantly that the gorilla skeleton 'is from a drawing of my own large specimen, and differs essentially from the other, as any comparative anatomist or careful observer may detect' (x). Du Chaillu's publisher John Murray was unequivocal in his support, writing in the *Athenaeum* that Gray was 'utterly mistaken' in his suggestion of plagiarism from Fenton.[49] Beyond this combination of admission and defence, an examination of the signatures that appear on many of the most dramatic illustrations reveals that the *Advertiser*'s suggestion of the employment of professional draughtsmen in England or America is probably accurate. The 'first gorilla' (Figure 3), for example, bears the name 'E. Whitney del' at the base of the image beneath the hunter's feet, while the plate titled 'Grand Reception by the Cannibals' carries the name 'Kanick' (75). The phenomenally popular, maverick preacher Rev. C. H. Spurgeon, who often drew congregations of several thousand, gave his opinion on the attribution of the illustrations in a lecture in support of and attended by du Chaillu:

> The fact is, this brave man can shoot gorillas but he cannot sketch; he may try his hand, but he is not at home in it. Very likely he has found somebody else to do it, and has been done the wrong way upwards.[50]

Du Chaillu's exact relation with the illustrations that appeared in his book is thus difficult to determine, while Spurgeon's curious locution 'the wrong way upwards' introduces a theme of inversion explored in the final section of this chapter. The visual texture of the *Explorations* emerges problematically as an interplay of field sketches by a diligent naturalist and works of imagination by hired draughtsmen, acting under only the vaguest zoological instruction and perhaps even in some cases, if the implications of Spurgeon's comments are to be believed, contrary to the author's intentions.

Doubts concerning the authorship of the text quickly followed the condemnation of the illustrations. A 'Fellow of the Zoological Society' corresponding with the *Advertiser* claimed that Huxley had identified du Chaillu as 'an 'illiterate, uneducated man, who could hardly speak or write English; [and] indeed his own language (French) very little better'.[51] Although du Chaillu's letters to Owen and Murray reveal a man with a sound, even elegant, grasp of his second language, the image of the ignorant foreigner fitted well with the growing atmosphere of implausibility that surrounded the adventurer. In the light of this, it was suggested that the *Explorations* American publishers Harpers' had employed one Dr Kneeland, a Boston naturalist, as a ghost writer to produce the 'astonishing stories' of which du Chaillu was presumably incapable, despite his protestation in the preface to the first edition that his book was the result of his own 'long and tedious labour' (ix).[52] The logical corollary of these allegations was speculation whether du Chaillu had in fact ever conducted any explorations in Africa at all. Drawing on his own contacts in West Africa, Gray in the *Advertiser* was among the first to cast such aspersions on the book's provenance:

> In the three or four letters which I have received from the Gaboon, during the last six or seven years, I do not find the slightest notice of Monsieur du Chaillu having been making any explorations, which, when we consider the small size of the European community there, one would expect to have been an object of interest.[53]

Similarly, the American naturalist George Ord in a letter to his close friend Waterton admitted that 'it is true that he has forwarded to the Academy some skins of African animals' but inserted the caveat that 'it is believed that these were not the produce of his own research, but were procured from traders who had visited the interior of the country'.[54] Waterton himself added a rather scathing development of this theme when he identified du Chaillu as 'no more than a trader […] possibly engaged in kidnapping negroes',[55] while a Mr Walker, himself a merchant in the region who had known du Chaillu 'for some years personally', according to Gray considered the *Explorations* 'neither more nor less than an amusing fiction' and doubted in 'common with most persons […] if M. du Chaillu ever killed or assisted to kill a gorilla'.[56]

Alongside these generalised protestations of authorial deception, more specific textual difficulties emerged. The chronology of du Chaillu's expedition implied, in the words of an anonymous correspondent of the *Athenaeum*, that '1856, 1857 and 1858 had between them four Julys!'[57] In similar vein a 'Puzzled Geographer' was lead to ask in the *Advertiser* 'what is the meaning of all this jumble? Is it consistent in a truthful traveller?'[58] The *Explorations* were further undermined by close examination of the specimens that the British Museum at Owen's suggestion had purchased from du Chaillu for what Waterton describes as the 'enormous sum of £500'.[59] Gray suggested that '[n]one of the skins of the gorilla exhibited by Mr du Chaillu offered any evidence of having been shot in the fore part of the chest, as invariably stated in his Narrative' and went on to cite in support of his argument the 'unanimous conclusion of numerous sportsmen and men of science, who have since examined both skins and skeletons'.[60] Owen, on the other hand, having remained a vocal supporter of his protégé, responded contrarily that 'the hole or rent is conspicuous; and that a gentleman who combines an acuteness of observation which has placed him high in science, with a well-known reputation as a skilful marksman and deer-stalker – Sir Philip Gray Egerton – concurs with me'.[61] Problems concerning the preparation of the specimens in the field also added to the discussion of du Chaillu's standing as Gray concluded that they 'could not have been prepared very far inland' and that du Chaillu was 'not a good preserver of skins'.[62] The gorillas that in du Chaillu's account had turned their startled eyes on the hunter in their final moments were now subject of a forensic scrutiny that saw very little of the animals themselves but much of the naturalist who had removed them (or not as the case may be) from their native forests. In this exchange the 'actual truth' required by the *Advertiser* shifted, significantly, from the zoological truth of the gorilla to the plausibility of their hunter.

These and related arguments were to rumble on throughout and beyond 1861. Academic quibbles were again enacted within wider personal and professional disputes: Waterton expressed his intention to 'absolutely hang this African ape in order to save from utter discredit what I have written on the monkey family', whereas the exchanges between Gray and Owen were intimately connected with political struggles at the British Museum.[63] The result was that, despite the continuing support of Owen, Murchison and the *Field*, du Chaillu was largely discredited as a serious natural historian. To the *Morning Advertiser*, he was a 'mere uneducated showman and dealer in skins'; more the menagerie impresario than the serious zoologist. To the *Athenaeum*, alluding to an earlier work of spoof African travels, he was a 'full-grown Munchausen'.[64] The expected value of du

Chaillu's specimens to science took second place to considerations of the man and his work. Darwin had little to say on the controversy, adding in a letter to his friend and fellow naturalist W. B. Tegetmeier that he had 'not read Du Chaillu [...] but I fear from all that I hear & read he deserves severity'.[65] In *Man's Place in Nature* (1863), Huxley's reflections on primates were similarly scathing of the significance of the *Explorations*' contribution to the field. Two years after du Chaillu had disembarked his spectacular cargo, information on the great apes was still, Huxley contended, at best sketchy: 'our knowledge of the chimpanzee and the gorilla', he wrote, 'stands much in need of support and enlargement by additional testimony from instructed European eye-witnesses.'[66] In a later passage Huxley enlarges on the absence of instructed eye-witnesses as he more specifically addresses du Chaillu's place in nineteenth-century zoology:

> If I have abstained from quoting M. Du Chaillu's work, then, it is not because I discern any inherent improbability in his assertions respecting the man-like Apes [...] but because in my opinion, so long as the narrative remains in its present state of unexplained and apparently inexplicable confusion, it has no claim to original authority respecting any subject whatsoever.
> It may be truth but it is not evidence.[67]

Huxley's dichotomy of truth and evidence clearly echoes earlier criticism of failures of the *Explorations* and reinforces the exile of du Chaillu from the scientific establishment. It also, however, concedes some significant ground denied him by many severer opponents. Notwithstanding his denigration of du Chaillu's narrative, Huxley allows the possibility that it may, almost by accident, still contain some genuine elements or at least the absence of 'inherent improbability'. The gap between this casual, even bumbling, truthfulness and a weightier scientifically admissible veracity or evidence restates the rigorous expectations of Victorian natural history that were at the heart of the gorilla war. But, as McCook writes, 'this controversy [...] illustrates the fragility of the process of legitimation of scientific knowledge in natural history during the Victorian era. Field observations in natural history depended very heavily on the perceived credibility of the person who made them.'[68] The facts did not simply speak for themselves; rather, they were inseparable from the personality behind the observing gaze and the perceived qualities or failings it brought to the task. Science, rather than an ideologically neutral empirical process, appears deeply invested. Accordingly, attention soon became fixed not just on questions of textuality and authorship in the *Explorations* but on an altogether more personal investigation of du Chaillu's origins and attributes.

That du Chaillu was by birth a Frenchman provided his critics with both a degree of comfort and a store of ammunition. A correspondent of the

Advertiser wrote with relief as the controversy began to take shape that it 'is a pleasure to think that the author is not an Englishman or otherwise the *prestige* of truthfulness that is affected to English travellers might be endangered'.[69] Such questions of national pride and racial virtue set against the suggestion of foreign defilement recur consistently throughout the first months of the debate. Waterton grumbled of the *Explorations* that 'such accounts [...] are no credit to the fascinating science of genuine zoology; on the contrary they mar and pollute it'.[70] In the *Gardener's Chronicle* he suggested a more intimate peril: 'our closet naturalists may gulp such foreign food as this, and praise its flavour, but I remove it disdainfully from my lips, as it ill befits them'.[71] Intriguingly, such gustatory images are common in the disapprobation of du Chaillu and his work. Gray's initial objections to a sensation hungry readership that liked things 'seasoned to their palates' were to progress along the digestive tract as the year progressed. Months later he was to write in the *Athenaeum* of 'the shallowness of M. Du Chaillu's pretensions as a naturalist, and the innumerable self-contradictions of a work which credulity itself cannot swallow entire'.[72] The *Advertiser* too lamented the 'taste of the vulgar reader' that afforded such speculations their evident success.[73] While du Chaillu's representations of the gorilla pivot on a visual peril, the complex moment of imagining oneself in the other's gaze, criticism of his work often prefers an oral frame of reference: contamination as flavour, the taste of foreign food; a text that seemed to promise dyspepsia. Du Chaillu was even to turn this trope against his attackers, commenting in the *Athenaeum* in a bitterly ironic reversal of some of the most extreme criticism that was to be levelled against him that Gray 'reminds me of the ape that grins a malicious snarl at the hand that has just given it a dainty'.[74]

This movement from the eyes to the mouth was to receive a startlingly literal enactment in an incident that took place at a July meeting of the Ethnological Society in London. With the Frenchman in attendance, a Mr Malone repeated the by now familiar accusation that du Chaillu was not the author of his work with on this occasion unusually dramatic consequences. The *Advertiser* reported the event with what it perhaps calculated as typically English reserve:

> Immediately after the chairman left the chair M. du Chaillu made his way through the crowd to Mr Malone, and after the exchange of a few words, terminated the discourse by spitting in his face [...] This very unusual termination to a scientific meeting caused great confusion, the English public being unused to so peculiar a method of answering the accusation of an opponent.[75]

While critics were worrying about the flavour of du Chaillu's prose, the problems of digesting it and even the threat of literary food poisoning, this scandalously ungentlemanly act explodes such delicate insistence on oral containment and gastric hygiene, propelling defilement not just towards the unfortunate Mr Malone, but to the 'scientific meeting' and the 'English public' he metonymically represents. Saliva, indeed, appears elsewhere in literary reflections on race and species as a powerful agent of contamination with approaches to it suggesting an index of evolutionary standing. Rider Haggard's 1915 gorilla novel *The Holy Flower* displays the Englishman Stephen Somers vomiting violently and instantaneously after drinking from a cup that has been licked by an African. Contrarily, Franz Kafka in his ironic 'A Report to an Academy' describes an ape happily licking its own face clean of human spittle.[76] The apparent restraint of the *Advertiser*'s reportage gives emphasis to du Chaillu's evident alienation from civilised, human surrounds: a British self-command that accentuates such foreign excess. Reflections on the melee in one of Ord's letters to Waterton signpost even more clearly du Chaillu's estrangement from decent society:

> It seems that a member having severely criticised the work, the author, who was present, became so incensed, that at the conclusion of the meeting, he had the audacity to spit in the critic's face, to call him a coward, and to threaten to shoot him! Is it possible that such an outrage should take place in a Society composed of English gentlemen, in the capital of the British Empire, and no one present to kick the blackguard out of the room?[77]

Ord's outraged concluding sentence offers a subtextual hint at one of the most telling and disturbing ingredients of the gorilla controversy. The evocation of the 'Society composed of English gentleman' reiterates a connection of nationality and temperament, suggesting not just the composition of the meeting but their innate English composure. Moving next to the 'British Empire', Ord places the society in its global context so that the final damning evocation of the 'blackguard' conveys not just a general depravity but a specifically racialised turpitude that threatens this island of composure from beyond its shores.[78] More evocatively still, *Punch* commented on du Chaillu's unusual strategy that 'such a way of arguing may be tolerated possibly at a meeting of Gorillas, but, happily, among Englishmen it has not yet been sanctioned'.[79] Du Chaillu's momentary loss of self-control, then, sees him rapidly descend the Victorian chain of being: from European adventurer, to African, to ape.

Indeed, the question of du Chaillu's ethnicity was a vexed one and a theme that particularly fascinated Ord and Waterton in their 1861 correspondence. Ord, especially, was keen to suggest that the first white man to kill a gorilla was in fact no white man at all:

> Some members of our Academy, who saw Du Chaillu, when he was here, say that the conformation of his head, give evidence of a spurious origin, the offspring of an African and a European; and a photograph of him which I have seen should seem to confirm this opinion. If it be a fact that he is a mongrel or a mustee, as the mixed race are termed in the West Indies, then we may account for his wondrous narrative; for I have observed that it is a characteristic of the negro race, and their admixtures, to be affected to habits of romance. When writing thus far, I received a visit from an old friend, who was introduced to Du Chaillu at the hall of our Academy; and he asserted that the aspect of the adventurer was not only forbidding, but that his manners were indicative of presumption and vulgarity. I applaud you for having inhibited so equivocal a character, in his attempts to enter the sanctuary of Walton.[80]

Just as his gorilla bodies were seen to testify against him, so du Chaillu's own form under the natural historian's trained gaze gave evidence against the authenticity of his text. Although he was cagey about discussions of his ethnic roots, it seems likely that despite his various claims to have been born in New York, Paris or New Orleans, du Chaillu was in fact born illegitimately on Réunion Island, a French colony off the coast of Africa, to a French father and a mother of mixed race.[81] He was thus a clear target for stereotyping assertions of racial inclination. His supposedly inherent tendency towards 'habits of romance' and a similarly characteristic 'presumption and vulgarity', consign him to a literary and social periphery against which Walton, Waterton's country estate, emerges as a 'sanctuary': a bastion of respectability that witnesses the danger without.[82] Here Waterton is protected not just from the undesirable company of a man so distant from the ideal of the English gentleman, but, more significantly, from the equivocation he embodies; an inbetweenness or doubleness that ultimately touched not just on ideas of race and genre but also on questions of species.

In his *Memories* (1926) the anthropologist and naturalist Edward Clodd, an intimate of du Chaillu's, reproduced the racial trope that served during the controversy to destabilise his friend's position still further: 'Paul's diminutive stature, his negroid face, and his swarthy complexion [...] made him look something akin to our simian relatives.'[83] In this period the connection of Africans and other non-white ethnic groups to primates was well-rehearsed both in scientific discourse and popular culture. A. R. Wallace for instance in an essay on 'Monkeys' in the *Contemporary Review* reflected that it 'is a very curious circumstance that, whereas the gorilla and chimpanzee are both black, like the negroes of the same country, the orang-utan is red or reddish brown, closely resembling the colour of the Malays'.[84] Indeed, du Chaillu himself repeated this supposition when reporting of a captive gorilla that the 'negroes would not have him as a companion for he was too much like one of themselves' (286). From the man with the 'bright and piercing eye' favoured

Figure 5. 'The Lion of the Season'. *Punch*, 25th May 1861, 213.

by the *Times* for his inherent truthfulness, du Chaillu's body now disclosed a different message as he degenerated in the course of the year from naturalist to specimen. He was in the rather ironic situation of being (through his dubious illustrations and questionable narrative) both too distant from the gorillas that formed the subject of his book, and (through the parentage speculated by his opponents) also too close to them.

In this context, the similarities that structured the excitement of the hunting scenes can be seen to return to haunt du Chaillu, even, eventually, to hunt him out of the scientific establishment. Despite the trim white safari suit and steady pose, du Chaillu's relationship with his prey ultimately appeared uncomfortably and comically intimate. An illustration that appeared in *Punch* earlier in the year may be read as a pointed commentary on the attitudes that du Chaillu was beginning to evoke. In the 'lion of the season' (Figure 5) du Chaillu appears in the guise of his discoveries approaching a terrified Englishman, captioned as an 'alarmed flunkey', whose paleness of dress and face emphasises the blackness of his companion. Here, a pun on exotic animals provides the nub of the cartoon. If du Chaillu was initially lionised by a too readily impressed London society, he was also from a very early stage gorillarised by an audience unsympathetic to this presumptuous outsider. The exaggerated man-monkeys he constructed ostensibly constituted a mirror in which his own ape-like nature was revealed. These animals were the romantic figures that expressed his own 'spurious' race and antipathy to the more thoughtful productions of serious natural history. Under this pressure, the cathartic violence of gorilla hunting takes on an extra edge: the need to purge oneself of the simian taint gains urgency by the proximity to oneself of the contaminating presence.

As du Chaillu's evolutionary intimacy to his prey retrospectively added spice to his aggression in the African forests, wider questions of race and violence were in due course to emerge at the margins of the controversy, most strikingly in Winwood Reade's 1863 *Savage Africa*. Reade, a wealthy socialite and amateur natural historian best known for his 1872 *The Martyrdom of Man*, set out for the territory of the *Explorations* in 1862 to test the truth of du Chaillu's findings and also he nonchalantly claimed to '*flaner* in the virgin forest; to flirt with pretty savages; and to smoke his cigar among cannibals'.[85] His conclusion that 'M. Du Chaillu has written much of the gorilla which is true, but which is not new; and a little which is new but is very far from being true' was evidently in line with the general consensus, but it is his comments on race that are this text's most unsettling contribution to the gorilla war.[86] Unsurprisingly, the supposed resemblance of Africans to the lower primates was a recurrent theme of his travelogue. While hunting gorillas he described the movements of his servant as 'like an ape crawling through the wood and feeding on his way'.[87] Further on, he offered a more general statement: 'Negroes are like monkeys which will caress you as long as you confront them; but shrink from them in fear and they will bite.'[88] It is Reade's concluding paragraphs, however, that reveal the most shocking ramifications of this ethnological structure.

Anticipating Africa's 'redemption' through the draining of its morasses, the watering of its deserts and the clearing of its forests, Reade offers a bleak conclusion for African peoples:

> In this amiable task they may possibly become exterminated. We must learn to look on this result with composure. It illustrates the beneficent law of nature, that the weak must be devoured by the strong.
>
> But a grateful posterity will cherish their memories. When the cockneys of Timbuctoo have their tea-gardens in the Oases of the Sahara; when hotels and guidebooks are established at the sources of the Nile; when it becomes fashionable to go yachting on the lakes of the Great Plateau; when noblemen, building seats in Central Africa, will have their elephant parks and their hippopotami waters; young ladies on camp-stools under palm-trees will read with tears '*The Last of the Negroes*'; and the Niger will become as romantic a river as the Rhine.[89]

While Reade presents his vision of a final solution at first in the passive tense ('become exterminated'), the brutality of this eugenic agenda quickly overlays the veneer of innocence, again, tellingly, through the operation of a metaphorical mouth. Reade returns his earlier anxiety at the bite of the ape-like negro with an all-consuming oral gesture, the 'devouring' of the weak by the strong that offers in its evocation of a 'law of nature' a Darwinian reading of colonial development. This agenda clearly follows the same basic structure as du Chaillu's gorilla hunting scenes: the stronger race or species affirms its position through its triumph over those below it in the hierarchy of organisms. But there are also for Reade ramifications of this trajectory for questions of genre. The romance of the Dark Continent is consigned at last to its proper place: the holiday reading of lachrymose girls on camp-stools and not the unworthy matter of scholarly attention. Literary form is thus subjected to a form of segregation that perhaps aims to resolve the confusions of the previous years, to fix texts into stable classifications just as natural history was endeavouring to settle the gorilla into a taxonomic home. The will towards this clear delineation of narrative species, however, stumbles at a number of obstacles. As works on the gorilla proliferated, fiction and fact continued to intertwine uncomfortably; the animal's abyssal gaze met with persistent games of otherness and resemblance that undermine the determinations of scientific and colonial order.

Further Confusion

In 1863 in a last ditch attempt to salvage his reputation as a natural historian and geographer, du Chaillu was to set off once again for Africa, this time armed with an array of scientific instruments, including a camera, that he hoped would allow him to produce the incontestable evidence lacking from his first expedition. The resulting 1867 volume *Journey to Ashongoland* began accordingly with a protestation of the genuine value of the *Explorations* to which he added a trenchant but generous-spirited condemnation of those for whom the 'novelty of his subject' had proved 'too striking':[90]

> Although hurt to the quick by these unfair and ungenerous criticisms, I cherished no malice towards my detractors, for I knew the time would come when the truth of all that was essential in the statements which had been disputed would be made clear.[91]

This renewed and self-confident pursuit for 'truth' was marked, in terms that anticipate Fenn's and Henty's paradigm of scientific self-restraint, with a determination to avoid wherever possible the violence that had formed such an integral part of the most stirring and problematic passages of the initial volume. His aim was not to 'slaughter unnecessarily these animals' but rather to engage in 'further study' of their habits.[92] Unfortunately for du Chaillu, the peaceful, scholarly intentions of this expedition were to meet with disaster. A live gorilla shipped for London died en route and a precipitate flight from a hostile tribe ended with his African bearers casting aside their precious load of 'photographs, instruments, stuffed animals, note-books, bottles of choice specimens in spirits and other valuables'.[93] Unsurprisingly, with little to add in terms of new findings or support for the old, this second narrative stimulated nothing like the interest of the first, either among the academic community or the sensation-hungry public. But while *Journey to Ashongoland* constituted du Chaillu's last, ill-fated attempt to play the part of the African explorer, it was by no means his final book on the subject as he set about an intriguing and probably financially shrewd change of literary direction.

In the late 1860s and into the 1870s and again at the beginning of the twentieth century, du Chaillu published a series of books that repackaged his African travels for young readers and embraced, in doing so, the kind of narrative texture a reader might expect from the *Adventures of a Gorilla Slayer* mooted by Gray as the more appropriate title for the *Explorations*. The first of these, *Stories of the Gorilla Country* (1868) opened with a rather bland explanation of his new project that belies the profound implications of the venture in the light of previous debates: 'I like children,' he wrote, 'and in

Figure 6. 'Death of a Male Gorilla'. Paul du Chaillu, *Wild Life Under the Equator* (London: Sampson Low, 1869), 195.

this book have written especially for them.'[94] In a parallel to the itinerary of his earlier celebrity he once again embarked on a lecture tour, this time in America and with a far different audience, but again with considerable success. Unavoidably, this change of generic allegiance casts a shadow over du Chaillu's continuing avowal of credibility: a confession that all along his work had been no more than nursery storytelling, or illustrative perhaps of the 'habits of romance' to which his racial origins affected him. Indeed, the second of the sequence, *Wild Life Under the Equator* (1869) reproduced almost verbatim the 'nightmare vision' of the first gorilla, complete with its 'hellish expression of face' and eyes flashing 'fierce fire' as the requirements of fiction demanded little alteration of the original scene.[95] As some elements of du Chaillu's gorillas remained constant in both textual forms, others, however, were revised in the shift. The years following 1861 saw illustrations of the gorilla evolve into new fantastically imagined forms which, in inverse relation to the progressive aims of zoology, appeared to remain gladly distant from the material animal as it continued to emerge in the pages of science. *Wild Life*

Figure 7. 'Gambo's Friend Killed by a Gorilla'. Paul du Chaillu, *Lost in the Jungle* (London: Sampson Low, 1870), 131.

Under the Equator revealed a far bulkier and more sinister gorilla (see Figure 6) than the *Explorations*' theatrical ape, emerging crouched from the dark recesses of the African jungle with a menacing line of teeth just visible in the gloom. *Lost in the Jungle* (1870), the last of this first trilogy, meanwhile, demonstrated that consistency was not of undue importance and figured the gorilla once more in upright posture, a shaggy and rather portly brute with features refined into a prominent, almost aquiline snout (see Figure 7) in a reworking of one of the most dramatic scenes of the *Explorations* in which a gorilla snatches and destroys a hunter's rifle. As if to reiterate the situation of the gorilla in lowbrow entertainment, the beast appears here somewhat akin to a circus strongman, the weapon bent beyond the stretch of physical possibility to emphasise the awesome powers of an animal now unbound by realism. Questions of strict accuracy no longer applied: the gorilla was safely cast in its exaggeratedly monstrous role.

Following the conventions of popular fiction, no diagrams or appendices were added to these later texts and no skeletons were posed to add a scholarly veneer to this spectacular matter. The liberation that these texts afforded from natural historical expectations also gave du Chaillu space for some sardonic allusions to the events of 1861. *Stories of the Gorilla Country* opened with a reference to the problems of chronology that had emerged among the earliest objections to the *Explorations*. 'In this book', he began defiantly, 'I have kept no chronological order.'[96] There may also, more pointedly, be significance in the descriptions of camouflage he introduced in these texts. Again in *Stories of the Gorilla Country*, he describes the effect of a disguise he adopts as he gathers with his African companions before embarking on the main business of the day: 'as extra preparation for the gorilla hunt [...] I had blackened my face and hands with powdered charcoal and oil; and my blue drilling shirt and trousers and black shoes made me look as dark as any of them'.[97] In the same circumstances, in *Wild Life Under the Equator* he notes 'blacken[ing] my face and hands with charcoal mixed with oil so that I might look like them'.[98] 'Blacking up' for the hunt allows du Chaillu to emphasise his underlying difference from the generalised 'them' that accompany him, but also might constitute a playful reference to the racial slurs he endured. In a sense du Chaillu is doing to himself what his most determined opponents had done to him and perhaps finally conceding his inevitable alienation from the scientific establishment: he was always destined to be an 'other' to British natural history just as his science was always destined to be romance.

For many years to come du Chaillu continued to be at the butt of natural historians' disapprobation. Carl Akeley, for example, in his *In Brightest Africa* (1924) returned to the notorious description of the first gorilla, determining to sort the passage into its factual and fictional components. He gave himself the task of putting into brackets what 'du Chaillu felt' and 'leaving outside what the gorilla did', and reached the conclusion that the gorilla 'did nothing that a domestic dog might not have done under the same circumstances'.[99] Akeley in this and other texts was influential in supplanting the persistently belligerent and hypersexualised gorilla of legend with the image of the generally peaceable, gregarious animal familiar to the late twentieth century and was clearly right to bring his scientific level-headedness to du Chaillu's flights of imagination, although the ongoing success of *King Kong* demonstrates the continuing mythic frisson evoked by the largest primate. Yet, ironically, some of what looked to nineteenth-century science like the most preposterous of du Chaillu's suggestions have subsequently found their way into mainstream scientific discourse. In the light of more recent researches some of Waterton's vituperations in the *Gardener's Chronicle* appear, in particular, comically misplaced:

> Satisfied in my own mind (after having paid attention to the monkey family for upwards of half a century) that apes pass their lives in trees, I am astonished to learn that the veritable ape which Mr Du Chaillu fell in with during his travels should always have been roaming at large over the ground. I come to the conclusion that he must have been labouring under some ocular delusion, and that he saw phantoms.[100]

Waterton's astonishment at the phantastic ground-dwelling gorilla reiterates the sketchiness of Victorian primatology and also demonstrates that du Chaillu was nowhere near the thoroughgoing charlatan he was painted; many of his delusions, indeed, in time would solidify into fact. An anonymous reviewer of du Chaillu's work also contended in a later edition of the *Chronicle* that the now iconic image of the male gorilla beating its breast, figured for the first time in the *Explorations*, should be regarded as 'a figurative expression thrown in for the sake of effect'.[101] With comparable self-confidence, Reade also informed his readers that the gorilla 'does not beat its breast like a drum'.[102] In writing about gorillas in this period, then, science and fantasy are inextricably intertwined: the material animal and its mythic twin inseparably joined despite the determined intention of the most qualified minds to keep them resolutely apart. More than just a question of style, genre or authorship this dilemma hinges on the gorilla itself, as if it was in a sense always already fictional, its dimensions and behaviours simply too much for a world unready for it: an animal 'too striking' as du Chaillu himself claimed.

Extraordinarily, some of the most intriguing evidence of the complex involvement of fiction and natural history in the Victorian gorilla appears not to have excited any comment in the 1861 controversy. While du Chaillu's critics were busy dismantling his reputation in whatever way they were able, there was one key source that seems to have escaped their notice. The appendix 'On the Orang, Chimpanzee, and Gorilla' attached to Owen's 1859 *On the Classification and Geographical Distribution of the Mammalia* included a passage apparently based on the evidence of a 'Bristol trader' that addresses the appearance and habits of the gorilla in terms which must have sounded very familiar to attentive readers of the *Explorations*:

> The hideous aspect of the animal with his green eyes flashing with rage, is heightened by the skin over the prominent roof of the orbits being drawn rapidly backward and forward, the hair erected and causing a horrible and fiendish scowl.[103]

Owen's gorilla, then, is represented in almost the exact language that so dismayed du Chaillu's detractors, terms which were then to reappear again shortly afterwards in the *London Illustrated News*' report of an animal with eyes 'flaring with a baleful emerald light when the fierce passions [...] are roused'.[104] The same 'hideous aspect', flashing eyes and fiendish demeanour haunt the text of a man who despite his numerous professional rivalries and disputes was universally acknowledged to be a scientist of gravity and standing. Owen also refers to a report of a 'gun-barrel bent and partly flattened by the bite of a wounded gorilla, in its death-struggle' that may well have inspired du Chaillu's depiction of such an incident.[105] A letter from du Chaillu quoted in Owen's son's biography of his father confirms, furthermore, that the adventurer was no stranger to this work. On the 22nd March 1861, the Frenchman wrote to the eminent naturalist:

> I think it is quite time that you should put your foot on the skin of an animal the anatomical character of which you have so thoroughly described in several of the memoirs you have published, and the reading of which has delighted me so much.[106]

This intertextual relation adds a further ingredient to Owen's steadfast and potentially personally injurious support of his friend and another layer to disputes over du Chaillu's authorship. At one level it reveals du Chaillu bolstering his own accounts of the gorilla with the most reputable of sources and emphasises the degree to which his personal characteristics as much as the substance of his narrative contributed to his downfall. More broadly, it also further problematises the myth of natural historical narrative purity in this era and shows the border between science and romance as permeable and fluctuating, a process of continuing exchange and contamination in which hybridity is the prevalent condition.

To take another example, A. R. Wallace's *The Malay Archipelago* (1869), another seminal work of scholarship dedicated solemnly to the genius and works of Charles Darwin, opens on a striking frontispiece captioned 'Orang-Utan attacked by Dyaks' (see Figure 8) that is far removed from the more restrained texture of the other illustrations in the work and probably from the pen of a different illustrator. Once again, the primate's near humanity is expressed both through an adjustment of its anatomical structure and in the dramatic composition of the piece. The Dyak and orang-utan come together in an intimate, if hostile, embrace that subordinates scientific discourse to the experience of the primate body, the imagined contact of its foot, arm and mouth on the native's naked skin perhaps surprising the scientific reader with an instant of narrative excitement and a vicarious thrill of danger more at home in the pages of a boy's own adventure. But despite the underlying menace of the scene, the orang's bite appears somewhat lacking in aggression, a brush with the flesh rather than a penetration of it that suggests an earlier, rather odd moment in Waterton's writing. Contesting du Chaillu's excessively violent depictions of primates in 1861, he offered his readers some curious evidence of their passivity. 'Apes are mild and harmless', he explained, 'I entered the cage of the huge red ape from Borneo, without any fear, and put my hand into its mouth whilst I examined its teeth. We kissed each other affectionately.'[107] While providing further confirmation of the oral fixation of Victorian primate studies, Waterton's fond discovery of the animal's gentleness displays a naturalist keen to experiment beyond the limits of his academic remit and to engage in an imaginary and sensory experience of the animal that sits awkwardly next to his often asserted commitment to an appropriate scholarly detachment.

The uncomfortable relation of science and sensation and between the scientist and his specimen that inheres in representations of gorillas in this period also forms an important context for some colonial fictions, most notably the work of R. M. Ballantyne. At the encouragement of his publisher and doubtless motivated by a family history beset by debt and bankruptcy, Ballantyne seized on the gorilla controversy to produce two novels in 1861, *Red Eric* and then *The Gorilla Hunters*, in which non-human primates take a significant role. A third novel, *Blown to Bits* (1889) draws on Wallace's *The Malay Archipelago* as well as the recent tragic excitement of the Krakatoa eruption in an adventure of the eastern seas in which encounters with the orang-utan continue his interest in the great apes and develop his exploitation of natural history exploration as a fitting stimulus for romping boy's romances.

The Gorilla Hunters forms the sequel to Ballantyne's breakthrough and best remembered novel *The Coral Island* (1857) and features his three adolescent heroes Ralph, Jack and Peterkin, now young men, in Central Africa in a quest for the 'great ape – the enormous puggy – the huge baboon – the man monkey' (19). While Ballantyne's text clearly had no zoological pretensions, it was nonetheless, rather remarkably, considered in some quarters to be 'true'.

Figure 8. 'Orang-Utan Attacked by Dyaks'. A. R. Wallace, *The Malay Archipelago* (London: Macmillan, 1877 [1869]), frontispiece.

The *Morning Advertiser* in its review of the novel shortly before Christmas was especially, and ironically, keen to celebrate Ballantyne's achievement:

> The author of this book for young readers has obtained considerable celebrity as a writer in a branch of literature demanding higher attributes than are generally accorded to it. Exaggerations must be avoided, in order that false impressions may not be made on the youthful mind; truth must be rigidly adhered to, for the least infusion of falsehood is fatal. Yet a stale or flat narrative will not do. Our author seems to be aware of these facts; his style, too, is every way suited to his readers; simple good Saxon, the best after all, for everybody. He has chosen a capital subject for his Christmas book, perhaps at present we could not have a more popular one than the Gorilla.[108]

The Gorilla Hunters, then, appears to satisfy the twin boy's own requirements of education and amusement: an entertaining narrative that leaves young minds unblemished by 'false impressions'. To the author of the review, this triumph is exemplified by the book's racial characteristics which carry with them distant hints of nutrition. Ballantyne's 'simple, good Saxon, the best after all for everybody' is devoured by the reader as a textual meat and potatoes, far removed from du Chaillu's emetic flavours and evidence of the rather surprising 'higher attributes' the reviewer discovers in this 'branch of literature'.[109] The elevation of the Scotsman over his dubious foreign predecessor is rife with contradictions. Ultimately, Ballantyne is simply doing what du Chaillu was blackballed for supposedly having done in the *Explorations*, constructing an elaborate fiction around the most uncertain of natural historical entities. Indeed, *The Gorilla Hunters* demonstrates a clear debt to du Chaillu in a way which significantly destabilises the *Advertiser*'s enthusiastic verdict on the text's veracity. In contrast to his later practice, this connection with an external source was unacknowledged by Ballantyne, but would surely have been recognised by his readers.

In accordance with the state of Victorian knowledge and clearly also as a device to heighten narrative tension, Ballantyne begins by identifying the existence of gorillas as a doubtful proposition. Peterkin, the most experienced hunter of the three, recently released from a naval commission, expresses his intention to 'shoot a gorilla, or prove him to be a myth' (19), while their initially fruitless attempts to track the animal down leads him to conclude with disappointment, 'I don't believe there's such a beast as a gorilla at all!' (181). Just as Ballantyne reproduces the natural historical context of du Chaillu's researches, he also recreates the dingy atmosphere of his forests. Walking through the 'dense, almost impenetrable underwood', the narrator Ralph concludes that it 'was altogether a gloomy, savage-looking country, and seemed to me well suited to be the home of so dreadful an animal' (212). Beyond the trio's specific experience of the jungle, Africa appears in general to partake of the uncertain, dreamlike setting du Chaillu discovered in his encounters with the gorilla. As they begin their enterprise, Peterkin remarks to his companions in terms that announce Ballantyne's coherence with one of the central tropes of his narrative form, 'But I say, boys, isn't it jolly to be out here living like savages. I declare it seems to me like a dream, or a romance' (35). The experience of being in Africa, then, in a figure that anticipates Reade's programme of de-romanticisation for the continent, remains inherently fictional until the determined hand of colonial improvement should gather it into nonfiction. As the adventures develop, 'the gorilla', typically, appears in Ballantyne, as in du Chaillu, as further demonstration of the oneiric ambience that surrounds the hunters. Once again the first contact with the terrifying beast emphasises the nightmarish and the devilish as Owen's imagining of the ape continues its intertextual journey. Ralph expresses the familiar combination of excitement and horror:

> Of all the hideous creatures I had ever seen or heard of, none came up in the least degree to this. Apart altogether from its gigantic size, this monster was calculated to strike terror into the hearts of beholders simply by the expression of its visage, which was quite satanic. I could scarcely persuade myself that I was awake! It seemed as if I were gazing on one of those hideous creatures one beholds when oppressed with night-mare! (217–18)

As if keen to miss nothing out, Ballantyne goes on to fill in other aspects of du Chaillu's representation of the gorilla's appearance as the story progresses. Approaching a later gorilla Ralph comments: 'His eyes glared horribly. The tuft of hair on the top of his head rose and fell with the working of his low wrinkled forehead in a manner that peculiarly enhanced the ferocity of his expression' (248). 'Roar upon roar' (248) resounds conventionally through the forest and the adventurers' emotions surface as readers would by now expect. Ralph admits following their first kill that:

> Pity at first predominated in my heart, then I felt like an accomplice to a murder, and then an exulting sensation of joy at having obtained a specimen of one of the rarest animals in the world overwhelmed every other feeling. (218–19)

Alongside the dichotomy of shame and satisfaction a hint of proto-colonial power politics is again apparent as hunting success sees the boys crowned masters of their new environment. In another echo of du Chaillu, Jack sends a bullet into the gorilla's chest whereupon 'the king of the African woods fell dead at our feet' (218). Although they feel at first 'like savages' in the jungle, the separation the hunters demonstrate from the peoples around them is a vital component of the ideological freight of Ballantyne's work. *The Gorilla Hunters* is among Ballantyne's most belligerently racist novels with African peoples depicted regularly and aggressively as 'niggers' with the white European installed seemingly without question on a higher rung of the evolutionary ladder. Equally significant is their distinction from non-human others they encounter. Despite Ralph's pang of sentiment towards his primate prey, as Peterkin reminds his colleagues with post-Darwinian impact, 'men are not beasts' (165).

But while Ballantyne's novel is structured around the theme of difference, it also derives much of its narrative interest from games of disguise and resemblance. An exchange of blackness and whiteness between the boys and their host King Jambai offers a similar scenario to the one imagined in du Chaillu's adventure tales. Appearing in ceremonial attire for the trial of one of his subjects, the king provides the travellers with an odd and slightly disturbing sight: 'His face was painted white, which had the effect of imparting to him an infinitely more hideous and ghastly aspect than is produced in the white man when he is painted black' (123). As the counterpart to this, the boys, as they plan the rescue of the defendant from an ordeal by poison, transform themselves too as Jack proposes that 'we undress ourselves, rub ourselves entirely over with charcoal and grease, so that they shall not recognise us and carry the girl off' (128). The relative success of these parallel disguises has its own racial message: it is far easier to climb down the ladder than to move up and, indeed, the descent of Ballantyne's heroes back into their evolutionary past goes further still in a series of doublings with non-humans that end in far more ambivalent resolutions than the familiar return to the inevitability of European dominance.

Particularly, it is Jack, the largest and strongest of the three, who at the novel's opening in an English village evokes images of the prey awaiting the hunters in the distant African jungle. Having not seen him for many years, Peterkin and Ralph fail at first to recognise the burly figure who alights from a coach. As Ralph offers to escort the stranger to a hotel, Peterkin comments with disbelief, 'you don't mean me to take this great ugly gorilla in tow?' (25). Jack's supposed resemblance to the animal is accentuated by a pun. Tow, a flax fibre commonly employed in taxidermy, adds a hint of the gorilla's fate to Jack's bestial appearance as Ballantyne's language evokes a specimen shaped by the naturalist's skilled attention. The power relation this process implies unfolds uncertainly, however, as the scene develops. Ralph, alerted by a sudden sound, turns to discover 'Peterkin struggling in the arms of the gorilla!' (26). In one of the text's numerous blurrings of friendship and violence, it is soon discovered that what appears to be aggression is in fact merely an affectionate, if vigorous, embrace, not unlike the Dyak's ambiguous hug of an orang-utan in *The Malay Archipelago*. The confusion between these poles, the reunion of friends and the hunter grappling with his quarry, is emphasised by the state into which Ralph slips as the realisation dawns that Peterkin's antagonist is, after all, only his old companion, Jack. 'I stood petrified', he admits. 'I believed that I was in a dream' (26). The rehearsal of the hallucinatory confrontation with a gorilla in this comparatively tame encounter reinforces the intrusion of intimacy into the dominatory mission they are set upon. Conquering primate others stumbles on this conflation of the other with the self and of hostility with tenderness as Ballantyne configures a violence unsure of its aims and its object.

Throughout the novel, Jack retains this alternate self in playful, running badinage between the companions. His simian dimensions even provide Peterkin with the rudiments of a plan as he suggests using Jack as a 'stalking-horse' to attract gorillas 'sure to mistake [him] for a relative' (28). Alongside the gorillarizing of Jack, Peterkin and Ralph also assume significant parallel identities. Reflecting on the time since their adventures in the Pacific Islands, Jack and Peterkin exchange thoughts on the effect of the years: '"There is no change in us except, indeed, that Jack has become a gorilla." "Ay and you a monkey," retorted Jack. "True and Ralph a naturalist, which is the strangest beast of all," added Peterkin' (52). Shortly afterwards, Peterkin's own simian nature is witnessed by a meeting with a monkey in which they repeat to each other 'O-o-o-oo-o' in a stereotypically comedic deployment of a non-human primate (54). The naturalist Ralph's identification as the 'strangest beast of all', however, includes him in a more complex classification that toys with the boundary between insider and outsider, the detached gaze and the object of scrutiny, the colonist and the brute. In terms that predict and partially construct the concerns of Fenn and Henty later in the century, the zoologist's hybrid nature is frequently connected with the flickering representations of violence as necessary task, sporting pleasure and the mark of savagery. Peterkin repeatedly teases Ralph with the air of restraint suggested by his vocation, exclaiming ironically as he lines up a shot at a giraffe that 'I *must* procure a specimen for you' (304) (original italics) and then later killing a frog apparently because he wishes Ralph to 'make a scientific inspection of it' (317). The line that Ballantyne takes in what would have been in 1861 the early stages of this debate is one of mutual interdependence: without the naturalist the hunter 'would degenerate into the mere butcher who supplies himself and his men with meat', while the naturalist would be condemned to linger in empty museums without the hunter's prey (192).

Ralph, indeed, appears to personally embody these twin roles. As a natural historian he complains as the travellers prepare to leave the gorilla country that 'I have not yet made nearly as many notes in regard to these monster-monkeys as I could have wished' (263). Yet earlier, his attention to a freshly killed specimen assumed a more visceral character, more akin to a butcher's interest in meat. Jack explains:

> As for Ralph, we must leave him to his note-book, I see there is no chance of getting him away from his beloved gorilla till he has torn its skin from its flesh, and its flesh from its bones. (220)

The enthusiasm with which Ralph is expected to undress the gorilla of its exterior focuses not so much on the notebook he diligently carries, but on the aggressive relish of the verb 'torn'. Like Henty's *By Sheer Pluck*, then, *The Gorilla Hunters* moves into and away from violence in a giddy balancing of contrary impulses that expresses the dual nature of man, both civilised and bestial, a bearer of civilisation who is also, radically, himself an animal, just as Jack and Peterkin are both adventurers and apes. Significantly, this interest in the boundary of man and beast in Ballantyne merges into concerns about the mouth as the portal of defilement and into the insistence on the eyes, the Foucauldian glance, as the origin of scientific knowledge. The gorilla controversy leads Ballantyne and his heroes not towards enlightenment, but into mud as, perhaps most surprisingly, the gorilla controversy comes to offer an intriguing perspective on Victorian waste management and on the intersections of ideas of species with anxieties about hygiene.

In the Mud

Ballantyne's interest in various species of muck and mire is a curiously recurrent facet of his writing and particularly of his imagining of tropical landscapes. Like terrestrial black holes, swamps and puddles seem to exert an irresistible pull on Ballantyne's heroes, contrasting very literally with R. L. Stevenson's summary of boy's literature as 'clean, open-air adventure'.[110] Such moments provide the punch line to a slapstick comedy basic, but also hint at darker and more complex possibilities.

Both Jack and Ralph in *The Gorilla Hunters* find their adventures upset not only by their monstrous quarry, but also, significantly, by dangers underfoot.

As the trio count up their victims to date, Peterkin recalls an undignified ending to one successful chase:

> 'You remember that enormously big, hairy fellow, that looked so like an ugly old man that Ralph refused point blank to fire at him; whereupon you fired at him point blank, and wounded him in the shoulder as he was running away?'
>
> 'We treated several big fellows in that way,' replied Jack; 'which of them do you allude to? – the one that roared so loud and terrified you so much that you nearly ran away?'
>
> 'No no; you know well enough which one I mean. The one that ran along the edge of the stagnant pool into which you tumbled as we were coming back.' (286–7)

Jack's unwitting and harmless plunge forms an uncertain celebration of the hunters' sporting victory. The new king of the African forest is anointed unceremoniously with stagnant water as he descends from the dignified status of the British adventurer, contaminated in his hour of triumph. The emphasis given to Jack's simian precursor at the pool's edge is central to the joke's significance. Jack's tumble appears as a response to the gorilla's presence, a materialisation of the ontological doubt inherent in his *fellow*ship with the 'big, hairy' brute.

The same movement from contact with a gorilla to human defilement is also apparent, although rather more dramatically, in the novel's final scene. Tracking a gorilla, 'the biggest we had yet seen' (418), alone through a 'muddy place' in which its footprints were 'deeply imprinted' (417), Ralph finds himself in hand-to-hand combat. Killing the gorilla with his hunting-knife he passes out until he returns to consciousness safe but still, literally, in a hole:

> On recovering, I found myself lying on my back at the bottom of what appeared to be a large pit. I must have lain there for a considerable time, for I felt cold and stiff [...] I knew, however, that I must certainly perish if I did not exert myself; so with much difficulty I crept out of the pit. The first object that met my eyes, on rising to my feet, was the carcass of my late antagonist [...] It must have died almost immediately after giving me the blow that had hurled me into the pit. I had not observed this pit, owing to the screen of bushes that surrounded it, but I have no doubt that it was the means of saving my life. (419–20)

In Ralph's climactic battle, the 'pit' appears oddly and conveniently from nowhere, as if the earth at the vital moment had opened and swallowed him up in consummation of a sudden, desperate wish. But as much as it provides vital protection, it also, importantly, constitutes a danger in itself: if Ralph can not scramble clear, the pit, as much as the gorilla, is certain death. Just as Jack finds his success unexpectedly dampened, so Ralph after his most glorious conquest wakes interred in the muddy ground with the gloomy ambience of gorilla stalking now darkened into even more sepulchral surrounds.

The interplay of comedy and potential tragedy, of peril and refuge in these two scenes may be read both in terms of the conventional forms and interests of the boy's adventure and in the light of the specific anxieties and excitements of their historical moment. This is not the first time Ralph has found himself in a sticky situation. At the outset of *The Coral Island*, his first steps as an infant see him fall into a 'pool of muddy water' in which he remains until his mother discovers him 'sweltering in the mud' and washes clean his 'dirty, little body'.[111] Broadly, such misfortunes emphasise, as in Fenn's *Nat the Naturalist*, the boy's opposition to a restrictive domestic regime of hygiene: for Ballantyne being a boy is about evading the female hand of cleanliness and getting as grubby as you like. Yet while this fascination for dirt is a relatively widespread generic enthusiasm, in 1861 and after the proximity of the primate adds an extra dimension that Ballantyne explored enthusiastically. Indeed, reading Jack and Ralph's muddy encounters with apes in relation to similar episodes in *Red Eric* and *Blown to Bits*, a pattern of human/ape relations emerges that elucidates Ballantyne's peculiar obsession, offers an interpretation of the oral and gustatory rhetoric of the du Chaillu controversy and asks profound questions of those who meet apes among dark forests.

Red Eric, Ballantyne's first novel of 1861 published just three months before *The Gorilla Hunters*, is a tale of shipwreck on the African coast that provides a more extended and striking consideration of the debasement that primates seem to usher the adventurer towards. Jim Scroggles, a sailor aboard the titular vessel, is walking 'alone in the depths of a lonely forest' when he is shocked to discover himself confronted with a large ape, not in this case a gorilla but *Trodlydytes Calvus*, or the nshiego mbouvé, a species named and described by du Chaillu, which, in a further twist to discussions of the Frenchman's scientific credibility, has never been seen or heard of since, although some natural historians have identified it with the bonobo. The result of the meeting is characteristically dramatic:

> Jim Scroggles' knees began to shake. He was fascinated with horror. The huge ape was equally fascinated with terror. It worked its wrinkled visage more violently than ever. Jim trembled all over. In another second the sheego displayed not only all its teeth – and they were tremendous – but all its gums, and they were fearful to behold, besides being scarlet. Roused to the utmost pitch of fear, the sheego uttered a shriek that rang through the forest like a death-yell. This was the

Figure 9. 'He was fascinated with horror'. R. M. Ballantyne, *Red Eric* (London: Nelson), 176.

culminating point. Jim Scroggles turned and fled as fast as his long and trembling legs could carry him.

The sheego, at the same instant, was smitten with an identically similar impulse. It turned, uttered another yell, and fled in the opposite direction; and thus the two ran until they were both out of breath. What became of the monkey we cannot tell; but Jim Scroggles ran at headlong speed straight before him, crashing through brake and bush, in the full belief that the sheego was in hot pursuit, until he came to a mangrove swamp; here his speed was checked somewhat, for the trees grew in a curious fashion that merits special notice. (167–8)

Typically, Scroggles and the ape find themselves in an elaborate game of similarity and difference that hinges on the semantic resonances and disparities of 'horror' and 'terror'. The fascination the pair 'equally' experience indicates an initial, impulsive attraction between them that is then counteracted by emotions that lead them intuitively to flight: for the ape a simple, if exaggerated, fear, the pure instinctive self-protection of an animal faced by a predator. Scroggles' 'horror', on the other hand, is, as befits the 'higher' species, a more complicated formulation. As the duo part, the opposite direction of their exits accentuates the specularity of the moment, as if a mirror had been placed along the threshold of their encounter. Their precipitate separation both expresses and aims to negate the realisation of their curious intimacy. The eerie attraction suggested by the verb 'smitten' represents the encounter through a kind of anti-narcissus complex, a self-recognition that utterly rejects what it sees.

The illustration of the scene (Figure 9) once again heightens the doubleness of man and ape with Scroggles and the sheego's eyes locked together, their bodies posed again as a mirror image. Again, the white adventurer's face is partially concealed, locating the scopic centre of the drawing in the sheego's troubling gaze. But in a rather different construal of the *Explorations*' prototype drawing, the sailor clearly lacks the firm-footed assurance of du Chaillu, his body resting for support against a tree trunk, his hands waving helplessly in front of him. Importantly, Linné's early description of the characteristics of *Homo sapiens* consisted merely of the dictum '*nosce te ipsum*' – 'know yourself', a formulation that allows Giorgio Agamben to conclude that '[m]an has no specific identity other than the *ability* to recognise himself'. '*Homo sapiens*,' Agamben continues, 'then, is neither a clearly defined species nor a substance; it is, rather, a machine or device for producing the recognition of the human.'[112] Scroggles' encounter with the sheego trades on the ambivalence of this constitutive process: the failure to discover a clear differentiation of what he is from what he is not. The narrative's sudden and unexpected attention to trees growing in a 'curious fashion that merits special notice' aims to re-install a colonial gaze self-confident in its empowered relation to its environment, but before this natural historical turn can gather momentum the ill-fated Scroggles' 'horror' and the uncertainty of his footing are manifested in yet more perilous circumstances.

The mangrove swamp surrounding these trees rises 'out of a sea of mud' that Scroggles is predictably unable to avoid. As he tries to negotiate this impediment he is startled anew by the 'gaze of a serpent' so that as he leaps for a branch he comes up short and finds himself 'up to the waist in the soft mud' (168) into which he begins rapidly and alarmingly to sink:

> Stretching out his hands to the root above his head, he found that it was beyond his reach. The sudden fear that this produced caused him to make a violent struggle, and in his next effort he succeeded in catching a twig; it supported him, for a moment, then broke, and he fell back again into the mud. Each successive struggle only sank him deeper. As the thick adhesive semi-liquid clung to his lower limbs and rose slowly on his chest, the wretched man uttered a loud cry of despair. He felt that he was brought suddenly face to face with death in its most awful form. The mud was soon up to his arm-pits. As the hopelessness of his condition forced itself upon him, he began to shout for help until the dark woods resounded with his cries. (169)

Scroggles' predicament is a yet more extreme version of the hygienic troubles endured by Jack and Ralph. Ballantyne's depiction of his hero's struggles, the partial extrications and re-immersions, and the markedly specific description of the 'thick adhesive semi-liquid', betray a touch of relish at the seemingly hopeless situation, but constitute also a moment of genuine existential anguish: 'face to face with death in its most awful form'. Death's personification reprises the composition of Scroggles' recent simian travails; the 'sheego' becomes this 'most awful form', the gatekeeper to a quagmire that threatens extinction until, in accordance with the expectations of the genre, Scroggles is rescued by his shipmates at the very last moment, just as Ralph is pulled by his companions from his grave-like pit.

The movement from vision to immersion that structures these encounters may be seen to offer a literal reading of the abyssal vacancy that Derrida figures in the gaze of his cat. Simian vision is metaphorised as a swallowing unguence that re-assimilates the human organism into the earth. Despite the discursive explosion around primate anatomy in the late nineteenth century, the ape appears to Ballantyne to announce a vacuum; the herald and embodiment of an appalling emptiness. To see the ape is suddenly, somehow to be lost, to enter what David Spurr describes in an analysis of Joseph Conrad and André Gide's depictions of central Africa as the 'psychic and metaphysical void designated by the name of horror'.[113] In a further renegotiation of du Chaillu's originary primates, the initial descriptions of the 'sheego' in *Red Eric* dwell more on the mouth than the eyes, contrary to the illustration's classic focus on vision. The animal's tremendous teeth and scarlet gums prefigure the sucking maw Scroggles goes flying into; yet it is still the eyes in Ballantyne's image that the reader sees, as if eyes and mouth were here interchangeable: as if these eyes were a devouring mouth. The primate in this context may be read not simply as the non-human or in evolutionary terms as the pre-human but also, most aggressively and problematically, as the anti-human, the horrifying negation of *Homo sapiens* exceptional status that resituates and redefines him (it) in the mud. The cries that resound from Scroggles around the 'dark woods' confirm his movement from the human towards the bestial as in his dire travails his voice occupies the space reserved conventionally for the animal's roar.

This relation of mud, apes and horror receives a further and more nuanced treatment later in the century in Ballantyne's Krakatoa novel *Blown to Bits*, particularly in its account of the hermit Van der Kemp's African servant Moses and his intriguing friendship with the eccentric Dutch naturalist Professor Verkimier. Here the place of gorillas is taken by orang-utans which play a much more marginal role in the excitement and provide a different kind of human/animal interaction from the belligerence of the gorilla hunters' African adventures. In the fulfilment of a well-remarked ambition in Victorian natural history, Verkimier has been able to train an orang-utan to a series of basic tasks, most notably gathering fruit for his master from high branches.[114] This structure of relations evidently has ramifications in terms of colonial and evolutionary politics: man naturally makes servants of inferior species, though fairly typically in Western representations of the East, the orang-utan is a lazy and ineffectual employee who causes Verkimier considerable vexation. When required to climb a Durian tree, the orang-utan shows itself at first unwilling until the professor expresses his authority in a rather surprising manner, donning a pair of spectacles, placing a hand on each knee and staring 'through the blue goggles into the animal's face'. As he then remarks, 'ven I bring my glasses to bear on him he always gives in' (187). Ballantyne's own illustration of the scene (Figure 10) once more follows a familiar pattern, the identical postures and matching expressions of surprise and wonderment by now a well-established trope. The professor's use of his glasses, however, offers a different perspective on eye contact between man and ape that anticipates and circumvents the horrifying vulnerability that overtakes poor Scroggles. Technology offers Verkimier a guarantee of mastery and a prophylactic against the abyssal gaze, turning the simian's goggle-eyed expression back against itself and illustrating a comforting human, visual domination that Kipling figures in *The Jungle Books* in his depiction of the impossibility of an animal meeting the gaze of his boy hero Mowgli.[115]

Figure 10. '"Do you hear?" said Verkimier sternly.' R. M. Ballantyne, *Blown to Bits* (London: Nisbet and Co., 1889 [1885]), 187.

But while *Blown to Bits* figures the adventurer overcoming the primate's ocular challenge, it still fails to keep him on his feet. Indeed, as the professor tirelessly scours the forests of the East Indies for objects of natural historical interest, Ballantyne summarises his project in terms that demonstrate a recognizable underside to his irrepressible determination: 'Verkimier had been absolutely revelling in this forest for several months – ranging its glades, penetrating its thickets, bathing (inadvertently) in its quagmires and maiming himself generally with unwearied energy and unextinguishable enthusiasm' (198). Time and again the professor's pursuit of Malay flora and fauna sees him come a cropper. After a day chasing rare and beautiful butterflies, he returns to camp 'drenched to the skin and covered with mud, having tumbled into a ditch' (196). Immediately, he rushes off once more in pursuit of a 'remarkable insect' with the undignified consequence of ending 'flat on the swamp' from which he emerges 'smiling though confused' (197). The perils of primate encounters from the African novels are thus broadened to encompass the natural historical expedition per se; Verkimier's privileged status as the proponent of the Western taxonomic mission is destabilised, a shift of his position that has profound implications not just for ideas of colonial power but more tellingly also for ideas of the human.

In an essay on 'Nature', the Victorian philosopher J. S. Mill underlines the implications of hygiene for larger questions of identity:

> Let us consider a quality which forms the most visible, and one of the most radical of the moral distinctions between human beings and most of the lower animals; that of which the absence, more than of anything else, renders men bestial; the quality of cleanliness.[116]

Mill's verdict reflects a commonplace signification of sanitation that was enshrined at the heart of nineteenth-century natural history and at the origins of serious zoological considerations of the great apes. Darwin in *The Descent of Man* contended that '[i]diots [...] resemble the lower animals [...] They are often filthy in their habits and have no sense of decency.'[117] In similar vein, Savage, with Wyman the father of the scientific gorilla, reflected in an aside on chimpanzees that:

> They are very filthy in their habits [...] It is a tradition with the natives generally here that they were once members of their own tribe, that for their depraved habits they were expelled from all human society, and, that through an obstinate indulgence of their vile propensities, they have degenerated into their present state and organization.[118]

Filth, then, as Henty would later reaffirm in his depictions of the squalid West African villages of *By Sheer Pluck*, is an evolutionary issue.[119] While the rational philosophical formulations of Mill would clearly stop short of positing the kind of literal transformation imagined by Savage's natives, hygiene still carries powerful significance concerning the ethical boundaries between man and beast. For Mill, grime evidences a mental if not an anatomical bestialisation. Accordingly, Ballantyne's recurrent dunkings and dirtyings toy with the category of the human and stigmatise Verkimier, despite his apparent conquest of the orang-utan, with the mark of the animal. For Ballantyne, it seems that there is never victory over and separation from apes, whatever feats of physical heroism or intellectual distinction his heroes perform. There is always in the end a pool of mud that obscures the superiority he labours to build. This association of primates and uncleanliness intersects with a number of more recent theoretical readings of filth. For Spurr, defilement 'marks the transgression of a crucial boundary between inside and out, between the self and that which it literally must exclude in order to maintain its difference from the other'.[120] Kristeva's formulation of abjection from *Powers of Horror* also provides a remarkably accurate summary of Ballantyne's puddles and pits. The abject is 'Imaginary uncanniness and real threat, it beckons to us and ends up engulfing us'; it ultimately derives its menace not from uncleanliness itself, but because it 'disturbs identity, system, order', upsetting in this context the location of man as taxonomically above and separate from apes.[121] 'The abject confronts us', Kristeva argues with clear significance for Ballantyne's muddy adventurers, 'with those fragile states where man strays on the territory of *animal*.'[122]

In the darkness of Ballantyne's abject spaces, it is worth reflecting on a key question of nineteenth-century primate studies that arose in concert with debates over the hippocampus but with rather less publicity. The hallux or big toe and the foot more generally was a far less glamorous subject for discussion than the brain, but, nonetheless, of vital importance in determining evolutionary relations between primates. As Christine Ferguson writes in an article on feet in George Du Maurier's *Trilby*, 'the foot in its Victorian discursive construction emerged as a perfect embodiment of the dilemma of founding a stable human identity'.[123] Huxley and Owen, as ever, found themselves in opposing corners on this vexed area of comparative anatomy. For Huxley, 'the resemblances between the foot of man and the foot of the Gorilla are far more striking and important than the differences'.[124] Owen, on the other hand (as it were), concluded that the 'innermost toe, the first to dwindle and disappear in the brute series, is, in Man, developed to a maximum size, becoming emphatically the "great toe", one of the most essential characteristics of the human frame'.[125] At issue in this aspect of the dispute was not just an academic point of osteological difference, but a far more evocative question of bearing, of whether man's upright gait, guaranteed by the structure of his feet, was an inalienable sign of human pre-eminence or just another vagary of species transmutation.[126] As *Punch* commented in the 1861 poem 'Monkeyana', simian posture was a fundamental aspect of their non-human identity:

> Then apes have no nose
> And thumbs for great toes,
> And a pelvis both narrow and slight;
> They can't stand upright
> Unless to show fright
> With Du Chaillu that chivalrous knight.[127]

The footing of the adventurer faced by the ape is therefore of more than passing significance. His tumbles constitute a movement down through space and backwards through time; away from the God his gaze is no longer able to look upwards towards. Ballantyne's heroes' recurrent pratfalls embody a literal descent of man that brings them down to the level of the apes, their feet ultimately insufficient to the task; a bestial indignity all the more poignant for the degenerate mess they are mired in. Rev. Spurgeon's introductory reference to Psalm 40 in his 1861 gorilla lecture reminding his listeners that 'the best way to lift up the lost and degraded from the horrible pit and miry clay, in a spiritual sense, is to preach Christ's cross' assumes in this context a far wider significance than the preacher perhaps realised.[128]

Ballantyne's tropical spaces thus perform a carnivalesque inversion of the priority of man. The authoritarian position of upright man and, in particular, of the scientist is fundamentally compromised as the paragon of animals finds himself down and dirty with the beasts. The Linnaean 'eye of God', the Foucauldian 'observing gaze', is left with nothing to see but the filth it is stuck in. Appropriately, mud appears not uncommonly as a metaphor for taxonomic confusion. Daniel Bivona writing on Victorian primatology in 2005 commented that the gorilla 'threatens to muddy taxonomic distinctions that should remain clear and unambiguous'.[129] Likewise, Darwin in a letter to the American botanist Asa Gray late in 1861, reflecting on the central question of design versus evolution, offered a striking image of his uncertainty:

> You say that you are in a haze; I am in thick mud; – the orthodox would say in fetid abominable mud. I believe I am in much the same frame of mind as an old Gorilla would be in if set to learn the first book of Euclid. The old Gorilla would say it was of no manner of use; & I am much of the same mind; yet I cannot keep out of the question.[130]

Mud operates as the opposite of knowledge, a trope that hinges on its obfuscation of sight, the privileged sense of learning and organisation and which leads Darwin towards the image of the gorilla, just as the image of the gorilla leads Ballantyne to mud.

While mud, then, carries the generalised significance of obscurity and debasement, *Blown to Bits* also conveys a more specific reading of filth that resonates markedly with the rhetoric of the gorilla controversy and with some extremely pressing matters of mid-century social welfare. As the catastrophic eruption accelerates, Ballantyne consistently depicts the volcano as a monstrous, macrocosmic human body that threatens the heroes with an overabundance of insalubrious discharges. Krakatoa is imagined variously as a mouth, throat or stomach. 'Clouds of smoke and steam [are] vomited forth' (94) like 'the very vomiting of Gehenna' (106); a lake sinks 'into its own throat' (303) and Moses anxiously suggests of the crater, 'de sooner we git off his lip de better lest we tumble into his mout"' (330). Conversely, Moses' body consistently provides images of the volcano's escalating violence: his 'cavernous yawns' (89) and 'crater-like smile' (108) give way to 'an explosive laugh' (264) that also appears as an 'earthquake on the negro's face' (90) or as the 'Splosions of Perboewatan' (125), the island the heroes find themselves on. In addition to illustrating the conflation of man and mountain, Moses' mouth in *Blown to Bits* is also both the stereotyped image of his alterity and the focal point for an interracial homoeroticism that recurs throughout the text.[131] At the first moment of Moses' introduction, the 'pout of his thick lips' and the 'gum-and-teeth-exposing' smile it expands into (52–3) draw the narrative gaze irresistibly, establishing a motif that variously finds expression in Moses' 'magnificent lips' (72) and his 'magnificent dental arrangements' (89). The curious combination of the body and the volcanic environment suggests, therefore, a compensatory recoil from the possibilities of same-sex attraction Moses evokes. Accordingly, it is Moses who is persistently the voice, the mouthpiece, of disaster. The intimation of a spectacular violence utterly destructive in its effects reverberates through the later stages of the text, always, significantly, as Moses' summation of events. In describing the immediate consequences of the eruption, Ballantyne refers to an area of over a mile of 'solid matter which as Moses expressed it, was blown to bits!' (376), while previously Moses had been led to conclude that 'we'll meet on Krakatoa no more, for dat place am blown to bits' (362). Likewise, Moses ends the novel with the reflection that 'de most happiest time as eber occurred to me was dat time when Sunda Straits went into combusti'n and Krakatoa was Blown to Bits' (438). The reiterated association of Moses with volcanic devastation assumes a yet more personal aspect when 'paddling with unreasoning ferocity' to escape the immediate surrounds of Krakatoa he gives 'vent at once to his feelings and his opinion in the sharp exclamation – "Blown to Bits!"' (342).

Rather than an isolated figure of menace, however, Moses is associated closely with the Dutch professor. Particularly, Verkimier and Moses share a robust enthusiasm for the enjoyment of food that attaches another aspect to the eroticised violence of the various human and geological mouths of Krakatoa. While Moses' consistent hunger adduces a familiarly pejorative association of the racial other with bodily appetites, Verkimier's comparable passion for eating signposts the inscription of science in *Blown to Bits* within discomforting somatic processes that Ballantyne seems unable to ignore. Sitting down with his colleagues to dine, Verkimier provides a figure that combines the imperatives of zoology with the pleasures of the table.

> 'It is *very* unfortunate,' he remarked with a sigh, which had difficulty in escaping through a huge mass of fish and rice. 'You see zee vonderful variety of ornizological specimens I could find here, and zee herbarium, not to mention zee magnificent *Amblypodia eumolpus* ant ozer booterflies – ach! – a leetle mor' feesh if you please. Zanks.' (240–41)

Ballantyne's intrusion of food into the sober reflections of science finds an echo shortly afterwards as Moses, responding to the professor, helps 'himself to coffee' before interrupting his reply with a request for the hero Nigel to '[p]ass de venison' (241). The excess of Verkimier's gourmandising, the 'huge mass of fish and rice' he consumes and the appeal for yet more, draws attention markedly to the considerable appetites of the professor which occupy Ballantyne on numerous occasions. At one point he even manages to dispose of a 'supper which it might have taxed a volcano's throat to swallow' (308).

If these images constitute a noticeable point of similarity between the two apparently antithetical figures, there is further evidence of a resemblance between them in their shared resistance to the formal conventions and idioms of language. The exaggerated accents they both exhibit provide a characteristic comic element in Ballantyne's text that hinges on a childlike pleasure in the sounds as much as the meanings of words. While it clearly intends to gratify his youthful readership, Ballantyne's amalgamation of science and baby talk (Verkimier's reiterated use of 'z' and 'v' sounds along with comically extended vowels, 'leetle' or 'booterflies') also, more significantly, subverts the elevated position of the professor as the privileged symbol of colonial authority, subordinating linguistic order to an infantile pleasure that rejects the responsibilities of adulthood and undercuts the systematising ambitions of imperial practices. With language constituting a key signifier of *Homo sapiens*' priority, Ballantyne's enthusiasm for these verbal games continues the problematisation of a fundamental human separation from the animal world.[132]

Among the more complex effects of the doubling of the professor and servant is an anxiety about the human body and its processes that resonates unavoidably with the depiction of Krakatoa's monstrously violent macrocosmic body. The 'hot mud' thrown into the sky by the eruption's first rumblings leaves the heroes 'mud-bespattered' (359) as if imperilled by the necessary outflow of their mountainous consumption. In *Blown to Bits* Ballantyne performs a complete digestive cycle that concludes with a scatological fixation between relish and disgust. The novel's metaphoric logic attaches eating to its abject double and leads to a perennial concern of Victorian Britain that was at its most worrying at the historical moment in which the gorilla controversy came to prominence. If du Chaillu's conquest of his 'hellish dream creature' allows him to cathartically purge himself of the taint of the animal, a more etymologically literal catharsis, the purging of the bowels rather than the emotions, appears as a perhaps unlikely ingredient in the gorilla controversy.

The 'great stink of London' that rose in the hot summer of 1858 brought a long-standing crisis in urban sanitation pungently to the attention of politicians in the Thames-side Houses of Parliament and necessitated the urgent construction of a network of sewers undertaken by Sir Joseph Bazelgette to alleviate the problem of human waste remaining untreated and unremoved in the city's homes, streets and river. As Stephen Halliday explains in his popular history of the stink, the Thames had become a 'fluid saturated with the impurities of fifty thousand homes – a dilute solution of animal and vegetable substances in a state of putrefaction – alike offensive to the sight, disgusting to the imagination and destructive to the health'.[133] Most dangerous was the possibility of another of the cholera epidemics that had periodically beset Britain since the 1830s. Importantly, it was partly Britain's emerging colonial interests that exacerbated the problem. Cholera was an unwelcome migrant from India and the ready and economical availability of guano from South America as a fertiliser meant that the traditional use of human excrement in agriculture was no longer practiced. By the mid-nineteenth century, the disposal of human waste in urban areas was a serious problem and an issue that consistently appears at the fringes of contemporary questions in primatology. Charles Kingsley's 1863 *The Water Babies*, a novel in which sanitation is a central focus, repeatedly makes a connection between metropolitan pollution and the image of an ape. Tom, the story's grimy hero, is a 'little black ape' or a 'small black gorilla' who even when removed from his urban setting still dirties 'everything terribly'.[134] Poor sanitation and national, even species degeneration thus form a combination of the most pressing significance that sees Kingsley end with the sage advice to his young readers: 'do you learn your lessons and thank God that you have plenty of cold water to wash in and wash in it too like a true Englishman'.[135] It is through hygiene that human superiority over the apes can be attested and vouchsafed.

Filth's degenerative potential naturally, then, designates the simian as unclean, an opinion that would have seemed entirely accurate to those unfortunate enough to encounter Britain's first full gorilla specimen. Spurgeon in his 1861 lecture describes the malodorous unveiling of the animal in 1858, a time when London evidently already smelt bad enough:

> At last a whole gorilla arrived in England preserved in spirits. Dr. Owen and Mr Bartlett of the Crystal Palace were present at the opening of the great tub; and when the lid was taken off, it yielded so fearful an effluvia that retreat was unavoidable. There was no great chance of standing against a gorilla of so highly offensive a character, and great indeed was the courage of Mr Bartlett, who determined to vanquish so strong an enemy. Feeling that it was a very rare animal and must not be lost, he took the gorilla away to try his best for its preservation. If any residents in Norwood should happen to be present, you may remember a very bad smell which annoyed you in 1858.[136]

In a parodic reference to du Chaillu's dramatic achievements, it is now filth that the heroic adventurer must set himself against, vanquishing the 'effluvia' that unavoidably resonates with the larger crisis in hygiene, the other 'very bad smell' of 1858. (In an intriguing coincidence, Norwood in South London was one of the locations of the outflow of Bazelgette's sewers, with construction well under way by the time of Spurgeon's address.)

Zoological engagement with primates, then, is connected to a spectrum of interlinked forms of hygiene. The textual sanitation required to prevent natural history being, in Waterton's words, 'swamped' by 'ignorance and fraud',[137] merges with anxious reflections on the human body, its own organic nature and its resemblance to the simian specimen. Contamination, while ostensibly coming from without in the form of du Chaillu, was also already within, both in a larger philosophical realisation of a human identity compromised by animality, and in the materialist crises of urban hygiene. The drive for mastery over animals through the various forms of colonial sport is stimulated in this context by an interweaving of fear and disgust that might be summarised by a passage from Walter Benjamin quoted by Fudge:

> The horror that stirs deep in man is an obscure awareness that in him something lives so akin to the animal that it might be recognized. All disgust is original disgust at touching [...] He may not deny his bestial relationship with animals, the invocation of which revolts him: he must make himself its master.[138]

The adjustment of human experience of animals from the scopic domain of natural history to the tactile and gustatory register that emerges around the gorilla controversy illustrates man's 'bestial relationship with animals' and the recognition of his own animal nature. The imperial drive towards mastery over and assimilation of animal others is as urgent politically as is it psychologically, but it is also deeply ambivalent. Human domination of the non-human world is complicated by the fetishisation of savagery in colonial trinketry, by uneven currents of violence and restraint in the boy's own adventure, and by recognition of the self in the other in the gorilla controversy. The idea of the coherent human subject at the heart of imperial ideologies emerges consequently as radically unstable. The story of the cultural construction of the gorilla is the story above all of the anxieties and uncertainties that accompany the designation 'human'.

As the nineteenth century progressed, questions of urban degeneration continued to add further layers of complexity to empire's structures of mastery and to considerations of the human/animal boundary, particularly through stimulating the imagination of two paradoxical forms of becoming animal. Like Kingsley's simianised urchin, the urban poor suggested the potential of human devolution back to a lower rung on the Darwinian ladder and exemplify another feature of the cultural history of gorillas. Paradoxically, the discourse of training and bodily fitness that emerged in response to this, and in which the imperial romance played an important part, appears as the embracing of a wild, animalised human subjectivity that despite its value to imperial militarism destabilises racial and zoological categories. Significantly, this pattern leads to an early and problematic form of environmentalism that illustrates the vital connections between ideas of species identity and ideals of ecological value in the context of the Victorian empire.

Chapter Four

WILD MEN AND WILDERNESS

Artificial Lives

In 1902 the American novelist and journalist Jack London, most famous for his canine tales *White Fang* and *The Call of the Wild*, embarked upon a journey into the depressed East End of London. Among the depiction of decay and hopelessness he presented in the following year's travelogue *The People of the Abyss* is a striking description of the bestial characteristics of Britain's urban poor. Unwisely walking the streets at night, London discovers a 'nightmare, a fearful slime that quickened the pavement with life, a mess of unmentionable obscenity that put into eclipse the "nightly horror" of Piccadilly and the Strand'. 'It was', he concludes in a metaphorical leap from this slippery opening, 'a menagerie of garmented bipeds that looked something like humans and more like beasts.'[1] In a moment that carries an echo of du Chaillu's confrontation with Africa's grotesque primates, he then adds zoological specificity to his image:

> They reminded me of gorillas. Their bodies were small, ill-shaped and squat. There were no swelling muscles, no abundant thews and wide-spreading shoulders. They exhibited, rather, an elemental economy of nature, such as cavemen must have exhibited. But there was strength in those meagre bodies, the ferocious, primordial strength to clutch and gripe and tear and rend. When they spring upon their human prey they are known even to bend the victim backward and double its body till the back is broken. They possess neither conscience nor sentiment […] They are a new species, a breed of city savages. The streets and houses, alleys and courts, are their hunting grounds […] The slum is their jungle, and they live and prey in the jungle.[2]

London's encounter with these eldritch beings illustrates a key aspect of concern for the consequences of Britain's rapid urbanisation throughout the nineteenth century and into the twentieth. Moral and bodily degeneration has resulted in the arrival of 'a new species' that identifies gorillas not only as the proto-human embodiments of an animal ancestry, but also as the post-human form of devolution. The slime London imagines quickening the pavements on which he discovers these eerie creatures reiterates the association of primates with an unsettling unguence that conveys a terrifying indistinctness: the dissolution of life-forms into an organic soup in which human and animal are indistinguishable. Importantly, the monstrous, hyperbolic aggression these specimens evince expresses the stakes of the discourse of restraint inconsistently apparent in Fenn's and Henty's narrations of natural history, while their physical atrophy reveals them as having descended beyond usefulness to any patriotic cause.

Such fears of a descent back down the Darwinian hierarchy were widely articulated around the *fin-de-siècle*. B. G. Johns in an article on 'The Literature of the Streets' in the *Edinburgh Review* warned of evolution that 'infinite peril lies in forgetting that the development may be for evil as naturally, as inevitably for good: upwards to the stars or downward to decay and death'.[3] Likewise, Darwin's friend, the surgeon Edwin Ray Lankester asserted in his 1880 *Degeneration: A Chapter in Darwinism* that 'we […] are as likely to degenerate as progress'.[4] Literary representations of this peril include Stevenson's 1886 novella of human duality *Dr Jekyll and Mr Hyde* and Conrad's 1907 tale of urban political and bodily corruption, *The Secret Agent*. In these depictions morality and species are intimately connected. As George MacDonald reminded readers of his 1883 fairy story *The Princess and Curdie*, 'it is always what they do, whether in their minds or their bodies, that makes men go down to be less than men, that is, beasts'.[5] Devolved specimens were liable, furthermore, to pass their deficiencies on to their children. The Hungarian Max Nordau, whose 1895 monograph *Degeneration* is perhaps the best known statement of the subject, commented on the 'new sub-species, which, like all others, possesses the capacity of transmitting to its offspring, in a continuously increasing degree, its peculiarities, these being morbid derivations from the normal'.[6] Only an increased incidence of sterility among these creatures, Nordau felt, prevented a perilous evolutionary future reaching disastrous proportions.

Degeneration theories comprise a significant element of the imperial discourse of species and environment in this era, particularly in the imagining of the complex relation of urbanised Britain to its geographical others. As metropolitan decline was charted, colonial wilds are depicted springing up in the heart of the civilised West. The publication of H. M. Stanley's bestselling narrative of the untamed regions *In Darkest Africa* (1890) was followed quickly by the founder of the Salvation Army William Booth's impassioned exposition of the predicament of slum-dwellers, *In Darkest England* (1890), in which he was lead to ask '[m]ay we not find […] within a stone's throw of our cathedrals and palaces similar horrors to those which Stanley has found existing in the great Equatorial forest?'[7] Under these testing environmental conditions human animality emerges, it seems, inevitably. Where London finds gorillas, Booth comparably encounters 'the human baboon', an even lowlier species on the animal ladder that represents a yet further descent from secure humanity.[8] Such images evince an uncomfortable intimacy between metaphor and biological process. The scandalised representation of a dehumanised metropolitan populace pivots on the possibility that a literal transformation is not, over time, unthinkable. The emotional response to this future is, like Scroggles' gut reaction to his animal doppelganger in *Red Eric*, one of horror, a position that merges ontological and geopolitical concerns. Assumptions regarding Britons' privileged national and racial identity appear untenable in the face of these 'new species' with all the questions they pose for the continuation of Britain's naturalised global domination. Without sturdy and civilised imperial servants, the ostensible biological basis of British hegemony disappears at the same time as the practical means of enforcing it.[9]

London's description of the East End's degraded denizens clearly indicates the intimacy of these debates with the preceding negotiations of humans and the great apes in the gorilla controversy. Gorillas both metaphorical and zoological were very much the front line of degeneration theory; the anxious bodily and sensory rhetoric they stimulated feeding into socially concerned reflections on Britain's cities. Johns' elucidation of an urban evolutionary trajectory 'downward to decay and death' recalls Ballantyne's interest in muddy matter underfoot, while General Booth's statement of his intended solution to the urban poor's situation repeats Spurgeon's biblical frame of reference in his 1861 address in support of du Chaillu. Reflecting on the slum-dweller's 'mad, desperate struggle' for life, Booth opines that the 'first thing to do is to get him at least a footing on firm ground' before the Salvationist can then pull 'him out of the horrible pit and miry clay in which he was sinking to perdition'.[10] Booth's good intentions pivot on a reading of failures in posture and, connectedly, hygiene as signs of a movement away from both God and a fully human identity. Significantly, despite the enormous improvements to urban sanitation conferred by Bazelgette's labours, the most depressed regions of the metropolis were still, as Booth and London record, mired in the most abject squalor. London's evocation of the 'fearful slime' quickening the city's pavements conflates the population with one of their most notable perils in a trope also seized upon by Booth in his imaging of the city as a 'human cesspool'.[11] In this rhetoric, urban degenerates are identified with their bodily products, illustrating the devolutionary stakes of sanitation and forming part of a wider, urgent and obsessive focus on digestive process that recalls both du Chaillu's travails and the debates surrounding the malign influence of penny dreadfuls.[12]

While poor nutrition was one of the key factors in the decline of the urban populace, it was also an important part of the metaphorical register of social improvement. Just as du Chaillu's prose seemed to his readers to taste all wrong, so the unsuitable reading matter that flooded the metropolis in the following years suggested to concerned commentators unpleasant and harmful eating habits. As Rev. Freeman Wills expressed it in the *Nineteenth Century*, an 'important part of the mental food – or rather poison – of the people is the penny novelette'.[13] Likewise, Johns condemned the 'nauseous mass' of 'penny dreadfuls' before extending his metaphor in a passage of purple prose and righteous ire that bemoans the literary diet of 'street Arabs and shopgirls':

> The feast spread for them is ready and abundant; but every dish is poisoned, unclean and shameful. Every flavour is a false one, every condiment vile. Every morsel of food is doctored, every draught of wine is drugged; no true hunger is satisfied, no true thirst is quenched; and the hapless guests depart with a depraved appetite, and a palate more than ever dead to every pure taste, and every perception of what is good and true.[14]

Johns' narrative of contamination illustrates an important, if complex, point of connection between the discourse of species as it emerges in the gorilla controversy and in degeneration theory and the development of the boy's own adventures of Fenn and Henty et al. Such nutritional disasters form part of an ambience of pollution that encompasses both eating and excreting. Indeed, London's description of the 'mess of unmentionable obscenity' he discovers conveys a significant double meaning: 'mess' as the outflow of the human cesspool, but also as a meal, albeit of the most disgusting savour. Consumption of the pernicious texts boy's own writing sets itself against incorporates the reader into a nexus of emesis, catharsis and degeneration that muddies the boundary, as in Ballantyne's *Blown to Bits*, between human and non-human, configuring a depraved bodiliness tainted by animality.

The ideological investments of boy's own adventures described in Chapter Two, then, comprise a form of literary hygiene that aims to lead the nation away from degradation and towards a re-installation of the human, and in particular the white, colonial human, un-imperilled by the degenerative effects of 'lower' forms of literature. Yet this movement is conflicted. The partial reliance of these texts on the kind of writing they sought to replace confuses the determinedly regenerative agenda they aspire to. Furthermore, while romance in this context appears as the (compromised) sign of national good health, it clearly had a markedly different signification to readers of du Chaillu: the sign of a negroid affectation and in turn, paradoxically, of textual debasement. Moral value is thus distributed unevenly across romance and adventure; humanity is both raised up by romance's celebration of a clean-living, vigorous imperial masculinity and shot down by the degenerative implications of du Chaillu and the penny dreadful that haunt its pages. While romance's violent confrontations with animal others police and enforce species boundaries, a contrary movement into animality operates through these hints of literary dissolution.

Romance's paradoxical relation to a human/animal binary is also inscribed in its involvement with an agenda of bodily improvement that responded to the kind of physical deterioration London observes in his urban gorillas deprived of 'abundant thews and wide-spreading shoulders'. London's diagnosis was an all too common verdict on the nation's fitness that advances an intricate involvement of body and environment. Writing in 1901, the essayist and Liberal politician C. F. G. Masterman meditated on the effects of a life without the 'fresh air and quieting influences of […] the fields':

> The result is the production of a characteristic *physical* type of town-dweller: stunted, narrow-chested, easily wearied; yet voluble, excitable, with little ballast, stamina or endurance – seeking stimulus in drink, in betting, in any unaccustomed conflicts at home or abroad.[15]

The rapid growth of an urban economy at the expense of Britain's rural traditions, then, creates a debased society of the ailing and the morally weak, born out of the airless claustrophobia of increasingly overcrowded conurbations. Metaphors of bodily decay and of unnatural bodily growth appear frequently in accounts of metropolitan and industrial expansion. The enlargement of the giant cities of the early twentieth century suggested to the architect Frank Lloyd Wright the development of 'a fibrous tumour', while Paris to Le Corbusier was a 'cancer'.[16] Buchan's gathered imperial savants in Carey's *Lodge* take a similar line. In the words of the financier Lowenstein, 'Industrialism has eaten us up, and […] become a morbid growth, taking our life's blood and giving us little back' (200); producing a 'sink of misery and crime' (201). In contrast to the ancient Athenian conception of the city as the privileged seat of learning and democracy, the industrial metropolis had become the locus of infection: the antithesis of nature and health.

Importantly, it was not only the working class inhabitants of slums who were exposed to the creeping degeneracy of town life. Baden-Powell was at pains to point out in *Scouting for Boys* that the 'sons of rich and well-to-do persons' were equally vulnerable to the adverse effects of the metropolis.[17] An opulent lifestyle of indolence and pleasure was every bit as sapping to the robust male body as the debilitating influence of indigence and disease. A generation of wealthy young men in George Gissing's phrase from his 1897 *The Whirlpool* 'coddling themselves in over-refinement' seemed destined to squander the virile birthright of an ascendant race and to run the risk of seeing a vigorous masculinity collapse into a hapless effeminacy.[18] Kingsley in *The Water Babies* images human devolution not just in the gorillarizing of the working-class Tom but also in an extended parable of the feckless Doasyoulikes whose idleness and taste for luxury eventually sees them regress until they are 'grown so fierce and suspicious and brutal that they keep out of each other's way, and mope and sulk in the dark forests'.[19] H. G. Wells' *The Time Machine* (1895) also imagines degeneration occurring across the social spectrum: the effete Eloi and the brutal Morlocks illustrating two distinct but equally perilous evolutionary declines. Moreover, if the slums reproduced in their congested alleys the moral conditions of an equatorial wilderness, the more apparently wholesome surroundings of the affluent urbanite could also in Buchan's *Lodge* suggest the unenlightened places of the earth. A London ball seems to Considine 'not the last word in civilisation but a return to a very early stage of barbarism' (134). Despite the vaunted company of 'royalty and ambassadors', the noise of the occasion merely evokes for the hunter 'the jabbering of monkeys in a Malayan forest' that differs from his recent experience of the Congo only in that the ballroom 'monkeys were caged instead of running wild on the tree tops' (133–4), a disparagement of urban leisure as the sign of bestiality that contrasts sharply with Buchan's life-long enthusiasm for country pursuits.

To counteract these gloomy prospects, Britons should return, it was felt by concerned commentators, to the land. Bodily and moral fitness hinged as Gail Low avers, on the 'conventional opposition between an urban, effeminate and overdeveloped culture of consumption and domesticity and the natural, masculine outdoor life of sport and warfare'.[20] Kingsley's muscular Christianity and later Baden-Powell's scout movement both express the value of outdoor activity in shaping bodies and minds appropriate to Britain's place in the world. This inter-implication of health and space constitutes what Low terms 'racial environmentalism', a conflation of the national and physical body that had implications for both British and colonial ecologies.[21] An idealisation of Britain's yeoman past underpinned campaigns for rural regeneration at home, while the extensive open spaces of the colonies provided a readymade solution. In advancing a way out of darkest England, Booth drew his reader's attention to the 'millions of acres of useful land [...] capable of supporting our surplus population in health and comfort', particularly in South Africa, Canada and Australia.[22] Bodily anxieties and ideals, then, share romance's investment in wilderness; physical regeneration maps onto a literary tradition of odyssey and testing to re-emphasise the (problematically) healthful world of adventure. Colonial legislation to conserve decreasing populations of fauna reflects and participates in this agenda as hunting enthusiasts insisted on the dichotomy of sport at home and abroad.

The historians of sport Mangan and McKenzie posit that 'emasculated' British sport was construed by members of the Shikar Club to be suffering from 'varying degrees of plutocratic excess, urban decadence, industrial encroachment and, for some, the debilitating presence of women'.[23] The increasing prominence of the *battue*, in particular, in which game was flushed from its hiding places by beaters, was often cited as evidence of lacking prowess and manly endeavour. To Baden-Powell, compared with the feral allure of the colonial chase, fox hunting, rapidly emerging in the second half of the nineteenth century as the preferred relaxation of the British countryman, had become 'a more artificial pastime with less real sport in it'.[24] Likewise, at the outset of his 1863 *African Hunting*, W. C. Baldwin stagnating in Scotland, traditionally Britain's most testing sporting region, determined to 'cast about me for some land of greater liberty' and to find an arena befitting his indomitable masculine spirit.[25] As the Cape millionaire Lawson argues in Buchan's short story 'The Grove of Ashtaroth' before turning to the immensity of the South African uplands, 'I hate shooting little birds and tame deer.'[26] Accordingly, as the colonial chase was marketed as the ideal activity for those seeking a true challenge to and expression of their masculinity, it was also identified as an antidote to the many hazards of metropolitan life. Captain Shakespear opens his *Wild Sports in India* (1860) with a promise to British parents that hunting will keep their sons from taking to 'the gaming table, or to an excess of feasting, rioting, or debauchery', contending in a delighted imagining of the honed boyish frame that 'the active form, the muscular arm, the sinewy hand, the foot whose arched instep betokens its spring and elasticity […] were not given […] to waste their activity, strength and lightness in frivolous pursuits or effeminate pleasures'.[27] Hunting and the entry into the wild environment it provides, appears as a powerful bodily restorative. Overseas among the ample uncultivated spaces and prodigious populations of truly savage beasts, Britons could hone and regenerate their racial potency and save themselves from the bestial fate of the city man.

This questioning of the effects of civilisation corresponds to a simultaneous idealisation of the racial other as the bodily image of a wild-born health untroubled by metropolitan perils. Ballantyne in *Hunting the Lions* (1869) provides an impassioned statement of this theme as the hero Tom Brown offers his black servant a detailed inventory of urban dangers that both indicates the vital medical necessity of the hunting expedition for the British city-dweller and elevates the African in a hierarchy of bodily fitness:

> Ah! Mafuta […] you're a happy man! The fact is, that we civilised people lead artificial lives, to a large extent, and, therefore, require a change sometimes to recruit our energies – that is, to put us right again, whereas you and your friends

live in a natural way, and therefore don't require putting right […] For instance, we want clothes, and houses, and books, and tobacco, and hundreds of other things, which cost a great deal of money, and in order to make the money we must work late and early, which hurts our health, and many of us must sit all day instead of walk or ride, so that we get ill and require a change of life, such as a trip to Africa to shoot lions, else we should die too soon.[28]

The damage engendered by the materialistic cycle of employment, expenditure and consumption pivots most tellingly on the identification of Mafuta as a 'happy man' living in a 'natural way' unharmed by the stifling ambience of the 'artificial lives' of the town-bred. These urban shortcomings and the African's contrasting prowess are clearly exemplified by Ballantyne at the beginning of the story when Tom and his fellow lion-hunters, faced with the potentially deadly appearance of a panther tempted into camp to prey on a dog, are effectively disabled by an ingrained metropolitan softness:

Pearson flung his knife and fork at it […] The major hurled after it a heavy mass of firewood. Hardy and Hicks flung the huge marrow bones with which they happened to be engaged at the time. Tom Brown swung a large axe after it, and Wilkins, in desperation, shied his cap at it! But all missed their mark, and the panther would certainly have carried off his prize had not a very tall and powerfully built Caffre […] darted at it an assegais.[29]

While Tom displays a certain manly, if ineffectual, endeavour in his use of an axe, his comrades are stymied by their urban indulgences. The 'firewood', 'huge marrow-bones', 'knife and fork' and 'cap' they incompetently employ in their defence evoke an atmosphere of easeful indoor repose: warmth, overeating and sartorial correctness that stand in stark opposition to the determined and successful actions of the 'tall and powerfully built Caffre'. Ballantyne presents, therefore, an initial inadequacy among the hunters against which their, and particularly Tom's, subsequent exploits in the field can be measured, purposefully illustrating the value of diligent training and the transformational possibility of the colonial setting. While this pattern hinges on a racially stereotyped fetishisation of the black body, it also underlines the ambivalence of empire's dominatory hierarchies. London pointedly quotes T. H. Huxley's conclusion from his time as a 'medical officer in the East End of London' that '[w]ere the alternative presented to me, I would deliberately prefer the life of a savage to that of those of Christian London'.[30] The idea of a stable, British (and human) identity is consistently problematised by the menace of degeneration and by the discourse of bodily well-being that it stimulated.

Buchan's *Lodge* provides a purposeful response to the problems engendered by Britain's urbanised and industrialised landscape that offers a similar hypothesis to Ballantyne's in his depiction of the lion-hunters. A sharpened awareness of metropolitan Britain's social problems is a recurrent aspect of Buchan's text that is addressed at one moment in shocking terms. Lady Warcliff asserts in a Draconian aspiration towards social hygiene that 'I want to see these hordes of thriftless, degenerate, scrofulous pariahs treated as what they are, irredeemable outcasts from society, and compelled by the state to keep their noxious influence away from the saner parts' (205). Elsewhere, the tone is more moderate. Hugh Somerville argues:

> We live, most of us, in gardens which are very pleasant and well-watered, but sleepy and not over-wholesome. And we grow old and stale before our time – the old age of decay, not the honest old age of being worn down with the friction of life. (89)

In turn, Mrs Deloraine uses the same metaphor to articulate her antipathy towards the 'petty life' that besets the modern world: 'We have grown deplorably urban in our civilisation. We still talk of nature but it is a garden-nature' (262). The entropic restrictedness of metropolitan life finds, furthermore, a more bitterly condemnatory image than the garden in Lady Flora's envious summary of the possibilities open to the colonial male: 'if they find the shades of the prison-house closing on them, they can put their packs on their shoulders and shake the dust of civilisation off their feet' (90).

Set against the memory of the homeland's enervating atmosphere, the immense East African wilderness around Carey's country house offers a powerful critique of the urban and suburban state that produces a contradiction in the context of the wider imperialism. Empire's aim of 'creat[ing] industries' and 'build[ing] cities' (136) appears at odds with the celebration of the wild the text continually returns to and which is vividly evoked in Buchan's close attention to the body of the hunter Considine:

> [His] long lean figure on a blue roan seemed wholly in keeping with the landscape. He wore an old khaki suit and a broad-brimmed felt hat, and sat his horse as loosely as a Boer. He leaned forward, peering keenly about him, whistling some catch of song. In civilised places he looked the ordinary far-travelled sportsman, a little browner and tougher, perhaps, than most. But the Considine of the Turf Club and the Considine of the veld were different beings. The bright eyes, set deep in the dark face, and the sinewy strength of his pose gave him the air of some Elizabethan who had sailed strange seas to a far country. To Hugh at the moment he seemed the primal type of the adventurer. (120)

Tanned, muscular and keenly alert, the hunter represents the apogee of British manhood and the *sine qua non* of colonial rule. Considine's soldierly bearing in his 'old khaki suit' and the portentous 'sinewy strength of his pose' offer a guarantee of continuing imperial supremacy but his bodily virtue, however, pivots problematically on resemblance and transformation. Sitting his horse like a Boer, Considine assumes a new being away from the civilised environs of the Turf Club, merging with the landscape to become 'the primal type of adventurer'. While as an Elizabethan he evokes a uniquely British, culturally sophisticated boldness in distant regions, this 'primal' identity and even perhaps the darkness of his face, a 'little browner' than most, disrupt evolutionary categories. Indeed, the consanguinity of the white hunter and the indigene is a notable and recurrent theme in hunt literature. Although Buchan's familiarly racist position in the *Lodge* contests that the African 'represents the first stage of humanity' well beneath 'the level which we roughly call our civilisation' (183), such developmental hierarchies become difficult to sustain with reference to a practice that repeatedly subverts a straightforwardly polarised disjunction of the civilised and the primitive. Romance, furthermore, and especially the African romances of Rider Haggard, figure racial transformations blurring into species transformation as the environmental antidote to dehumanising urban degeneration appears paradoxically as another kind of becoming animal.

Metamorphosis

While Considine represents an idealised figure honed by years of hard-living adventure to a keen physical fitness, the younger Hugh Somerville, by contrast, appears in need of training. In the first hours of a hunting trip he realises that he is, like Ballantyne's lion hunters, 'still soft from civilised life' and confesses to 'some nervousness lest he might show up badly in a tight place, having never before faced anything more dangerous than a sleepy Norwegian bear' (122). The early morning air, however, effects an almost immediate transformation in a passage that blends a romanticised depiction of a South African terrain much beloved by Buchan with a narrative of sharpening bodily prowess:

> [O]ver the crest of the far downs came a red arc of fire, and the heavens changed to amethyst and saffron, and last of all, to a delicate pale blue, where wisps of rosy cloud hung like the veils of the morning. They were near the western edge of the escarpment, and, looking down into the trough, Hugh saw over the great sea of mist the blue fingers of far mountains rising clear and thin into the sky. The air was bitter cold and the cheeks tingled with the light wind that attends the dawn [...] He realized that his senses had become phenomenally acute. His

eyes seemed to see farther, his ears to mark the least sound of the bush, while the scents of the morning came to his nostrils with a startling freshness. (119–20)

The dramatic improvement in Hugh's bodily acuteness is framed by the wide perspective of the African morning. Surrounded by a seemingly limitless vista, a 'great sea of mist' and mountains rising 'into the sky', his senses expand into the generous environment. Later, camping at night, he reflects that 'never had he felt his mind more serene or his body more instinct with life' (128). The enlivenment of his form suggests that, like the 'primal' Considine, Hugh is undergoing a metamorphosis in the sporting arena that replaces an urbane, cultured identity with a more purely somatic being in tune with its own primitive nature. Buchan imagines his colonists infused and energised by the landscapes they traverse; Carey, indeed, Hugh later avers, 'has the wilds so much in his soul, and he lives so entirely among elemental things, that he has the same *aura* as this land' (233, original italics). This possession of the human by the natural arises through a long period of what might be described in a term of central importance in much ecocritical thought as 'dwelling'.

Developed from the philosophy of Heidegger, 'dwelling' implies, in the words of Greg Garrard in *Ecocriticism*, the 'imbrication of humans in a landscape of memory, ancestry and death, of ritual, life and work'; a relation of 'duty and responsibility' that Carey with his farming interests to some extent encapsulates, despite his arrival in Africa as a colonial outsider.[31] In caring for the land, Carey is conversely enriched and nurtured by it, although his extensive investment in mining and forestry would be unlikely to win him much favour with environmentalists today. This imagining of harmonious dwelling and masculine rejuvenation in the Cape is underpinned by the vexed notion, not uncommon in this period, that South Africa is *by nature* a 'white man's country', inherently fitted to European polity and rule. Considine, for example, opines in a brief consideration of Africa's diverse geography from 'Lake Nyasa and the Congo to the Cape' that 'some of these are white men's countries, and in time are going to be colonies' (155).[32] Such speculation of an innate affiliation between racial identity and colonial environments is deeply problematic and illustrates a conscription of ecological dwelling into repressive regimes that Garrard explores in a different context in a section on 'dwelling' in Nazi environmental ideology.[33] But while racial characteristics predispose Britons to the kind of ecologically improved bodies Buchan reveals in Carey and Considine, this form of training and development paradoxically stimulates a reimagining of the white man as the savage. The racial implications in colonial discourse of bodily transformations, only vaguely attached to Considine with his dark face, are explicitly evoked with reference to Hugh as, fully hardened by the great outdoors, he appears 'tanned like an

Indian' in 'clothes so stained and ragged that he looked like some swagman' (229). Physically adjusted to the wilderness, Hugh allows the garments of the civilised man to fall into disrepair, casting him in the guise of a disreputable itinerant as he begins to inhabit a form that both hints at class degeneration in the image of a 'swagman' and disturbs the clear distinction of the colonist and the colonial subject in the image of the Indian.

Indeed, the abandonment of formal, European attire frequently operates in hunting narratives as an important indicator of the hunter's position on the imperial axis of civilisation and primitivity. W. C. Baldwin celebrates the deliverance of the sportsman from the cumbersome injunctions of nineteenth-century fashion, revealing that in the African bush '[w]e do just as we like, and wear what is most convenient. When on foot a blue and white shirt and a short pair of gaiters, with the addition of a cap and shoes, are all that I burden my body with.'[34] Likewise, Ballantyne's Tom Brown, revelling in life 'far away from the haunts of civilised men, – alone with primaeval Nature' is seen to 'throw open his vest and bare his broad bosom to any breeze that might chance to gambol through the forest'.[35] The physical form liberated from an excess of clothing in an 'untrammelled, open-air life' encouraged the hunters Stigand and Lyell in an early twentieth-century manual of African hunting to make a connection of the huntsman to an originary human: 'I suppose we inherit it from our ancestors who lived in caves and under stars. To be rid of stiff collars and starched shirts and all the tiresome formalities of life in a civilised country is a pleasure in itself.'[36] As the white hunter leaves behind the vestments of his urban identity, he returns to a primal, inherited self completely comfortable among the African wilderness.

The involvement of Rider Haggard with issues of degeneration, the body and ecology was long-standing and voluminous. His famous boast at the outset of his most successful novel, *King Solomon's Mines* that 'there is not a petticoat in the whole history' not only removes his text from a debilitatingly feminised literary culture, but also, more literally, expresses his opposition to nineteenth-century urban fashions and more broadly to an enervating urban civilisation.[37] Rather, Haggard prefers the rough-and-ready garb of the adventurer, a point he forcibly illustrates when later in the same text the retired naval man Good finds himself perilously restricted in his movements by an inappropriate sartorial pernicketyness that nearly sees him trampled by a bull elephant.[38] In the introduction to *Allan Quartermain*, Haggard provides perhaps his clearest disparagement of modern civilisation, eulogising the eponymous hero's 'hunter's simplicity' while bemoaning a metropolitan milieu which has 'fail[ed] us utterly'.[39] Furthermore, beyond his extensive output of fiction, Haggard also addressed contemporary social, and relatedly environmental, concerns in a number of nonfictional treatises on the state of the nation. The

1902 *Rural England* was an exhaustive and impassioned two-volume account of agricultural decline and rural depopulation that exhorted a substantial reinvestment in the British countryside. 1905 saw him produce *The Poor and the Land*, in which he reflected on the success of the Salvation Army's colonies in the United States, while *Regeneration* (1910) drew attention to General Booth's social work closer home, in Britain's ailing urban centres.

Haggard's fascination for Africa, stimulated like Buchan's by a stint as a colonial administrator, expresses his antipathy towards Western industrial civilisation as it idealises a more 'natural' human existence in the wilds. Quartermain in his eponymous novel provides a powerful avowal of the attractions of Africa compared to the stifling atmosphere of Britain:

> I longed once more to throw myself into the arms of Nature. Not the Nature which you know, the Nature that waves in well kept woods and smiles out in cornfields, but Nature as she was in the age when creation was complete, still undefiled by any sinks of struggling, sweltering humanity. I would go again where the wild game was, back to the land whereof none know the history, back to the savages, whom I love.[40]

Quartermain's enthusiasm for Africa pivots on an environmental hierarchy: from the malodorous atmosphere of metropolitan decay in the 'sinks of struggling, sweltering humanity' at the bottom, through the image of a harmonious rural Britain in the 'well-kept woods' and smiling cornfields, to the African apogee of primal, capitalised 'Nature'. His intention to go 'back' illustrates his personal desire to return to the theatre of his youthful adventures, but might also be read as a wider reactionary celebration of a pre-modern wilderness long overlaid by development in Britain: the atavistic impetus of romance discussed in Chapter One. The movement 'back to the savages' is a signal part of this environmental agenda and comprises a racially stereotyped insistence on indigenous populations as far more intimately connected with the natural world than their Western counterparts. As Garrard avers, 'Since the sixteenth century at least, "primitive" people have been represented as dwelling in harmony with nature, sustaining one of the most widespread and seductive myths of the non-European "other".'[41] Haggard's depictions of Africans are unavoidably linked to both racial and ecological discourses and inform a recurrent interest in shifting identities and acts of cultural cross-dressing through which he imagines escape from the restrictive environs of Britain.

While his almost thirty tales of Africa contain numerous examples of the white adventurer's assumption or enactment of a savage nature in the wilderness, the 1892 *Nada the Lily* offers a slightly different, and perhaps more complete, embodiment of Haggard's fixation with the 'primitive'.[42] Rare among his works in containing only the most marginal European presence through a travelling white man who frames the narrative before disappearing from it entirely, the composition of *Nada the Lily* involved, as Haggard explained in his preface, the challenge to 'forget his civilisation, and think with the mind and speak with the voice of a Zulu' (21–2). In one regard, the ventriloquial narrative of African history that follows clearly functions, as Laura Chrisman contends, as 'an exercise in self-legitimation and vindication, to be achieved through donning the garb of Zulu history' that deliberately produces black savagery in order to justify white invasion.[43] Accordingly, Haggard's dedicatory address to his imperial mentor Sir Theophilus Shepstone, an influential figure in colonial South Africa, in the respectful Zulu term 'Sompseu', master or steward, attempts to naturalise British authority into African tradition and to gloss over the unsettling historical actualities of British imperial rule. A comparable version of this ideologically charged insertion of an imperial elite into indigenous culture appears in *King Solomon's Mines* when the three white heroes adopt Zulu names in their proto-colonial mission into the African interior, as if they might govern organically from within rather than as an unwelcome and alien power.[44]

This imperialist undercurrent is an incontestable element of Haggard's writing, yet the agenda of colonial domination it supports when read in the broader context of degenerationist and species discourse is uneasily upheld. The narrow-chested, atrophied creatures of London's abyss whose grievous bodily failings imperilled Britain's global future are deliberately countered by Haggard's at times rather overexcited depictions of black, male bodies. Describing the Zulu tyrant Chaka called upon to settle a bloody dispute among the tribe, Haggard glories in his honed physique:

> He stalked up; and he was a great man to look at, though still quite young in years. For he was taller by a head than any round him, and his chest was big as the chests of two; his face was fierce and beautiful, and when he grew angry his eye flashed like a smitten brand. (53)

Haggard's zeal for the Zulu consists of both an aesthetic and a utilitarian dimension. The appreciation of Chaka's beautiful face and hyperbolically broad chest implies an enjoyment that often verges in Haggard's works, and elsewhere more obviously in Buchan's representation of the pan-Africanist insurgent Laputa in *Prester John*, on the homoerotic.[45] Allied to this admiring attention is an approval of the soldierly value of such bodies, accentuated by the belligerent demeanour Chaka reveals in his flashing eye. Zulus, indeed, were eulogised by the British as a 'higher' form of African, constituting, as

Chrisman argues, an 'African "aristocracy"' that rendered them appropriate subjects for idealising Western fantasies.[46] Importantly, this Zulu 'noble savagery' is consistently situated within a restoratively ecocentric discourse of animal vitality and natural aggression. As Haggard in his preface eulogises the 'Zulu military organisation, perhaps the most wonderful the world has seen', he introduces a celebration of an African warlike spirit that promulgates a brutal harmony in this 'wild tale of savage life' (21), and constitutes, paradoxically in the wider scheme of *fin-de-siècle* debates, a wilfully degenerationist project.

In Chaka's movement towards the argument outside his kraal, he significantly adopts the gait of a hunter, *stalking* up to his tribesmen and subtly identifying this human conflict with a wider, and wilder, context of violence against and between animals. Consistently, as the novel develops through a series of battles and insurgencies against Chaka's tyrannical rule, Haggard clothes violence in an organic rhetoric of predator and prey that denies any sense of impropriety to his bloodthirsty excesses. Baleka, a wife of Chaka, delineates the king's growing discontentment with an image of feline predation: 'he does but play with me as a leopard plays with a wounded buck' (111). The witch doctor Noma's aggressive intentions identify him as 'cunning as a jackal and fierce like a lion' (39), while, in escaping him his rival in medicine, Mopo flees 'like a buck when the dogs wake it from sleep' (41). In Haggard's pre-colonial African wilderness, warfare is conducted with a wild vigour that blends harmoniously with the fluctuations of the environment: spears flash 'like lightnings' (232) and shields are heard 'roaring' like a wave 'fallen on the beach' (234) as the murderous excitement of the narrative unfolds as the elemental overflowing of an untamed planet. The deposed Halakazi chief Galazi surveys this organic violence as he observes his friend Umslopogaas, 'The Slaughterer', lead an assault against the Swazi:

> [T]he lines of the warriors sprang up as a wave springs, and their crests were like foam on the wave. As a wave that swells to break they rose suddenly, like a breaking wave they poured down the slope [...] Galazi heard the thunder of their rush; he looked round, and as he looked, lo! The Slaughterer swept past him running like a buck. (233)

Haggard's mixed simile of waves, thunder and a running buck naturalises the ensuing, typically exaggerated *coup-de-grâce* of two Halakazi chiefs 'cleft through' by Umslopogaas' mighty axe, constructing 'the battle and its joy' (234) as a part of Africa's natural savagery. As Monsman argues, 'Haggard not only believed the shedding of blood is in man's savage roots, but he embraced this animalistic wildness.'[47]

If Chaka's body and extended treatments of warfare illustrate an enthusiasm for savage masculinity, Haggard's movement away from European civilisation and into 'animalistic wildness' take a further step in the representation of Umslopogaas and Galazi as the 'wolf-brothers'. Exiled from his tribesmen on the mysterious Ghost Mountain, Galazi, in a supernatural turn characteristic of Haggard, becomes king of the 'ghost-wolves', not wolves per se but 'evil ghosts of men who lived in ages gone, and who must now live till they be slain by men' (130).[48] When Umslopogaas later joins him in the wilderness, the two men mimic this metempsychosis as they don wolf skins for a night of hunting that operates as a gesture of wild fulfilment:

> So Umslopogaas took the grey wolf's hide and bound it on with thongs of leather, and its teeth gleamed upon his head and he took a spear in his hand. Galazi also bound on the hide of the king of the wolves, and they went out on to the space before the cave. Galazi stood there awhile, and the moonlight fell upon him, and Umslopogaas saw that his face grew wild and beastlike, that his eyes shone, and his teeth grinned beneath his curling lips. He lifted up his head and howled out upon the night. (138)

The ritual metamorphosis of man into wolf through the wearing of a skin clearly exhibits the connection of clothing and identity: the garment as the emblem of becoming that eases the human into his transformed shape but which also symbolises an inner nature that has existed all along. Clearly, the easy assumption of an animal form by these Africans is underpinned by and buttresses Victorian racial hierarchies. The ostensibly porous boundary of Zulus and animals imagined in the wolf brothers also emerges prominently in Haggard's article 'A Zulu War Dance' (1877) in which an elaborate spectacle of Zulu warriorhood sees the dancers move through a series of apparent transformations, their war-cry 'now [...] the snorting of a group of buffaloes, now the shriek of an eagle as he seizes his prey, anon the terrible cry of the "night-prowler", the lion'; their movements in turn 'like a panther' and 'like a snake'.[49] Yet rather than operating as a form of racial disparagement, these similitudes function as a peculiarly problematic celebration of the wild man's brute prowess that Haggard uses to question the value of Western civilisation. Indeed, such emphasis on a natural affiliation between man and beast is reflected later in both Kipling's Mowgli from the *Jungle Books*, inspired by *Nada the Lily*, and in Edgar Rice Burroughs' *Tarzan on the Apes* (1912) and following adventures. These feral humans illustrate the complex interplay of kinship and difference, of dwelling and domination that emerge in Haggard's Africa and which complicate readings of colonial ecology and subjectivity.

Unsurprisingly, the transformation of Galazi and Umslopogaas into their totemic shapes facilitates Haggard in a series of visceral descriptions of animal violence. Dogs are torn 'to fragments' (145) and a Zulu regiment is left 'smitten, torn, mangled, dead, hidden under the heaps of the bodies of wild beasts' (301). Violence to Haggard appears as a fundamental attribute of wolfhood: Galazi exultantly asserts that 'I have become a wolf-man. For with the wolves I hunt and raven' (137); Umslopogaas, similarly belligerent in his new apparel, experiences 'but one desire – the desire for prey' (139). The automatic association of animals with violence that the wolves illustrate forms a crucial part of the imperialist discourse of animality and a key element of the rhetoric of the imperial hunt. Hunting narratives often prelude or accompany the main excitement of the adventurer engaging with his animal quarry with depictions of animal-on-animal violence that set the tone for what is to come. In *King Solomon's Mines*, for example, Haggard intersperses the excessive depredations of the three adventurers 'burning for slaughter'[50] with an image of inter-animal predation that validates and interprets their activities. As Quartermain observes 'a sable antelope bull […] quite dead, and transfixed by its great curved horns […] a magnificent black-maned lion, also dead',[51] Haggard evokes an inherent, natural African destructiveness that Ballantyne also employs earlier in the century to introduce the central human adventures of *The Gorilla Hunters*:

> In another moment the thick wall of underwood […] was burst asunder with a crash, and a wild buffalo bull bounded into the plain and dashed madly across. On its neck was crouched a leopard which had fixed its claws and teeth deep in the flesh of the agonised animal. In vain did the bull bound and rear, toss and plunge. At one moment it ran like the wind […] then it reared, almost falling back; anon it plunged and rushed on again, with the foam flying from its mouth, and its bloodshot eyes glaring with the fire of rage and terror, while the woods seemed to tremble with its loud and deep-toned bellowing. (57)

Ballantyne's insistence on the elemental fury of the moment, the flight 'like the wind' and the 'fire of rage', involves the ensuing indulgences of the sportsmen with a natural order of bloodshed that identifies them as just another species of predator, participants in the ancient facts of life in which a creature must kill to eat or to protect its territory. This common trope, termed by MacKenzie the 'chain of destruction',[52] pivots, significantly, not only on the restoration of enervated British manhood in savage Africa and a wider discourse of racial environmentalism, but more simply on pleasure. Ballantyne's minute realisation of the marks and effects of violence displays an instinctual gratification that simulates the gory gusto of the predatory beast, positioning the narrative gaze as close as possible to the ravening jaws and facilitating an instinctive enjoyment of the animal's glory that is also a notable component of Haggard's bloodthirsty *Nada the Lily*.

The enthusiasm for violence beyond scientific or dietary necessity that these texts reveal provides further evidence of the compromised restraint disseminated by Fenn's and Henty's boy's own responses to the perilous excesses of the penny dreadful. While romance on the one hand set about endeavouring to manage textual, moral and physical degeneration through a discourse of strict self-control and discipline, it also aimed to free itself from the strictures of civilisation in the re-enactment of a primal evolutionary inheritance. As Haggard protests in the opening to *Allan Quartermain*, 'supposing [...] we divide ourselves into twenty parts, nineteen savage and one civilised, we must look to the nineteen savage portions of our nature, if we would really understand ourselves'.[53] Vitally, the combination of the insistence on creating distance from and returning to and embracing a savage selfhood comprises a restless movement simultaneously away from and back into animality. If the transforming bodies of the urban poor necessitated the reassertion of the human through a carefully controlled programme of improvement in which the measured, dominatory regime of natural history played a significant role, they also demanded a re-entry into a truly wild ecology, conspicuously absent from the industrialised homeland. Colonial environments are thus categorised and ruled but also, significantly, inhabited; 'the animal' is the other but also, crucially, the self.

Haggard's celebration of the savage, therefore, enacts and refers to a widespread interest in the duality of civilised human consciousness that was often a suggestive subtext of sporting culture. The hunter and soldier J. G. Millais in *Great Hours in Sport* (1921), a volume of reminiscences edited by Buchan, explicitly addresses the binary structure of the modern mind:

> All men have a contemplative or poetic side to their character as well as the elements of the primeval savage. Stevenson first came near the truth in his Dr. Jekyll and Mr. Hyde creation. Man is such a strange mixture of what some would call primitive brutality and exquisite sentiment.[54]

Not unlike the elaborate furnishings of Buchan's Musuru, the modern hunter is both the brute and the sophisticate, blending social accomplishment with a raw visceral brio that implicitly values an untamed nature, signalling an empathy that cherishes the wilds and discovers in them a deeper and more ancient self absent from the polite routines of civilisation. Introducing a 1957 edition of *Nada the Lily*, Edward Boyd argues that Haggard was able to realise in composing his Zulu tale 'a literary catharsis for his "natural gift of savagery" [that] enabled him to wade up to his Id in blood' (14). Clearly, this conceptualisation of a polar self reproduces, as Boyd intimates with regard to Haggard's text, the classic Freudian psychic structure of conscious and unconscious, torn between the cultured habits of the urbanite and the libidinal impulses of the inner barbarian, contesting the social decorum of the ego with the feral longings of the body.

This pattern has long provided, and continues to provide, hunting with one of its most prominently reproduced justifications. Hunting, by this argument, is a fundamentally natural aspect of a human animal nature. Garry Marvin writing in the Animal Studies Group's *Killing Animals* states that 'all forms of hunting involve a movement toward the animal and an entering into the habitat of the animal'.[55] While doubtless accurate in a straightforward geographical sense, the existential implications are more complicated. The implicit assumption that hunting confers ontological entry into a generalised animality involves an anthropocentric representation of 'the animal' that strategically exaggerates the role of violence in animal behaviour: being an animal does not necessarily and automatically entail aggression. Even top predators such as big cats are not always on the hunt and, of course, herbivores never at all (although they may exhibit aggression in the protection of territory or their young). The deployment of animality as an aspect of human sporting experience at least to some extent facilitates a mystification of hunting that legitimates the pleasures of violence through a tenuous quasi-spiritual, ecocentric rhetoric. Roger Scruton, a philosopher and a vigorous apologist for the chase claimed in 1999 in the heated lead-up to the 2004 Hunting Act that '[p]lanted in us, too deep for memory, are the instincts of the hunter-gatherer [...] The experience of the hunter involves a union of opposites – absolute antagonism between individuals resolved through a mystical identity of species.'[56] Scruton's position is in essence remarkably similar to Haggard's (super)naturalisation of violence through Umslopogaas and Galazi; men transformed into beasts in consummation of an ancient human birthright, encapsulated in the hyperbolically savage wilderness of pre-colonial Africa.

The animalistic aggression that Haggard and others found so attractive in their imagining of Africa may be comprehended, therefore, as a complex validation of colonial domination: soldiers and hunters as wild men, violence as healing the effects of human encroachments on the natural world, empire as survival of the fittest. Interestingly, Matt Cartmill in sketching an image of the hunter in his cultural history of hunting *A View to a Death in the Morning* quotes Friedrich Nietzsche's illustration of the mentally healthy from *The Genealogy of Morals* in a passage that evokes some of the problems of this ideological investment in animal violence:

> They revert to the innocence of wild animals: we can imagine them returning from an orgy of murder, arson, rape and torture, jubilant and at peace with themselves […] Deep within all these noble races there lurks the beast of prey, bent on spoil and conquest. This hidden urge has to be satisfied from time to time, the beast let loose in the wilderness.[57]

The key note in Nietzsche's depiction is an interplay of innocence and excess that sees 'conquest' as the natural expression of the inner beast and expresses a trajectory in his work that Jennifer Ham summarises as the contention that 'to take the animal out of the human is to render the human inhuman'.[58] This representation of human health through a bestiality taken to correspond directly with violence is forcefully reminiscent of Haggard's affirmation of savage Africa, but also corresponds with the ideal of the hunter presented in Buchan's *Lodge*. Indeed, Buchan makes specific reference to Nietzsche. Lord Appin suggests of Considine that he 'worships, with Nietzsche, the Superman' (52), an allusion reprised later when the hunter remarks, '[t]hat Nietzsche fellow Appin was chaffing me about the other night has got the right end of the stick' (137). Though Buchan's seemingly throwaway citations may be difficult to interpret precisely in the light of the breadth and subtlety of Nietzsche's work, relish in an instinctual violence recurs in Buchan's representation of his adventurer's expeditions across the East African wilderness. Hugh, 'shaken and blood-stained' after killing his first lion, is thrilled with an 'insane jubilation' (124–5) that transports him from the controlled clear-mindedness of urban normalcy to an impulsive existence at one with an unrepressed nature. Comparably, Considine's tan becomes finally 'deepened into a Mephistophelian duskiness' (235) as the hunt taints him with a demonic otherness. While Buchan's heroes enact Nietzsche's supposition that violence forms a natural, healthy aspect of human subjectivity, Hugh's temporary insanity and Considine's devilishness introduce another commonly represented facet of the hunter's experience: the entry not only into an organic realm of bodily well-being, but also simultaneously into a distinct psychic domain that adds another layer to the stratifications of ecology, the body and colonial power that accumulate around depictions of brutality against exotic animals and in images of the hunter's transformations.

A Perpetual Fever

Although ideas of domination are conceptually central in adventure fiction's representations of colonial contacts, the relationship of imagined masculine identities to this mode are intricate. As we have seen, the involvement of human subjectivity with a discourse of animality is a particular point of complexity and ideological instability in this regard. On the one hand, the fetishisation of a supposedly ecocentric savagery utilises animality to naturalise imperial violence. Conversely, in other ways, discourses of animality unsettle domination. The pervasion of an animal self beyond the allocation of an inferior nature to disenfranchised groups and into the privileged form of the adventurer unwittingly undercuts hierarchical depictions of species and races. Animality's paradoxical deployment in degenerationist theory as both the mark of evolutionary descent and the sign of recovery besets human sovereignty with a war on two fronts: a bestial inheritance that emerges in sickness and in health. This compromised boundary of human and animal is intimately involved with ecological questions. The value of wilderness to the re-instigation of human well-being degraded by the animalising influences of the teeming metropolis informs an environmentally sensitive attitude to the natural world: a vision of the natural man dwelling in the wilds, whose habitation of them, nonetheless, is ultimately destructive in character, as the environmental histories narrated in the introduction to this study indicate.

The recurrent imaging of hunting as madness or sickness provides another strand to the negotiation of human identity in violent engagements with animal others. If the sporting field's brutality comprises a natural violence that brings man back into harmony with the savage force of the wild while also symbolising imperial confidence, it also often constitutes for the hunter the assumption of an alternate state of consciousness. The *coup-de-grâce*, in particular, the precise moment of an animal's death, supplies a pathway into an other-worldly psychic arena in which the sportsman becomes a stranger to himself, exiled from his everyday, mundane mind. As Stigand and Lyell comment in similar rhetoric to Buchan's identification of Hugh's 'insane jubilation': 'Big game shooting is like a perpetual fever – once it has been enjoyed, one always goes back to it with the same zest as before.'[59] When, in the common sporting terminology, 'the blood is up', the hunter becomes lost in his actions: febrile and uncertain, transported into an eidetic experiential realm blurring fact and fancy and, crucially, encompassing fantasies of both domination and passivity. As Harry Storey confessed with deliberate but suggestive evasiveness following a description of a hunter with 'slaughter in his heart, quivering with excitement', 'It is almost impossible to analyse the feelings of a sportsman.'[60]

Such ecstasies, in the literal etymological sense of standing outside oneself, evoke what Foucault termed 'limit experiences', moments of 'desubjectivation' that have the 'function of wrenching the subject from itself, of seeing to it that the subject is no longer itself'.[61] The narrative tradition of the romance as, in many instances, a dreamlike textual location reinforces such adjustments of human subjectivity. Indeed, the dream is often an integral component of the narration of hunting in colonial romance, both reprising the sportsman's adventures and returning in wakefulness to add its peculiar ambience to his continuing exploits. Ballantyne's African romances are particularly noteworthy in this context, not just in their engagement with the oneiric form of the gorilla, but more generally in their insistence on the hallucinatory qualities of African wilderness and of the giddying act of predation. As Peterkin reflects on the adventurers' first arrival in the African jungle in *The Gorilla Hunters*, 'it seems [...] like a dream, or a romance' (35), or, as Ralph later reaffirms, the forest is 'like a vivid dream, instead of a reality' (110).

Such insistence on the connection of the inner and the material worlds in the unfolding of the sportsmen's expedition evidently invites speculation concerning unspoken motivations behind the satisfactions of the imperial chase. The idea of the hunt as a displaced fulfilment of other, repressed impulses is a persuasive and prevalent mode of analysis of the culture of colonial sport that emerges particularly strongly in eco-feminist analyses. Although Ballantyne did not hint, as Haggard did, at the unconscious content of his romances, his remarkably prolific output, sometimes running to four or five novels a year produced from largely uncorrected manuscripts, reveal a literary sensibility every bit as chary of editorial revision as Haggard's. His works, perhaps unsurprisingly, demonstrate a tendency towards bizarre and psychoanalytically compelling digressions and speculations that convey some troubling undercurrents, especially in relation to gender.

Importantly, domination in its Latin root *dominus* or master is a specifically gendered term that extends of patterns of ecological and colonial violence into forms of sexual violence. As Northrop Frye summarises in a reflection on the role of hunting in the romance, the 'hunt is normally an image of the masculine erotic, a movement of pursuit and linear thrust, in which there are sexual overtones to the object being hunted'.[62] Andrea Dworkin's trenchant study of male sexual violence in her seminal work of feminist criticism *Pornography* offers, accordingly, a vigorous and influential reading of hunting as an integral aspect of patriarchal power's pervasive brutality. Hunting, for Dworkin and other eco-feminists, more than a vivid metaphor for patriarchal abuses is a common, material symptom of a violence that directs its abuses to women and animals alike.[63] Pornography, as Dworkin demonstrates, at times explicitly utilises images of the hunt to structure gender relations in the relentlessly dominatory terms of predator and prey. A photograph from an American soft-porn magazine cited by Dworkin exemplifies a widespread sexualisation of violence driven by the 'perpetuation, expansion, intensification and elevation' of male power.[64] Naked and tied tightly to a Jeep, a model is displayed as the quarry of two men who sit behind her: 'The Beaver Hunters', in hunting gear, holding rifles, their triumph expressed in the accompanying caption:

Western sportsmen report beaver hunting was particularly good throughout the Rocky mountain region during the past season. These two hunters easily bagged their limit in the high country. They told HUSTLER that they stuffed and mounted their trophy as soon as they got her home.[65]

Hustler's coarse conflation of hunting and sexual sadism is clearly a commonplace and successful element of such publications' strategies. Brian Luke draws attention to the routine imaging of the pin-up model as prey in titles such as *Playboy*, *Musclemag* and *Sports Illustrated*.[66] Environmental and sexual violence in this context become inseparable and, accordingly, Dworkin's analysis of 'The Beaver Hunters' identifies the magazine's model with a wider ecological context: 'She is an animal, think of deer fleeing the hunter, think of seals clubbed to death, think of species nearly extinct. The men will stuff and mount her as a trophy; think of killing displayed proudly as triumph.'[67] The helpless female body at the mercy of *Hustler*'s 'Beaver Hunters' and the clubbed bodies of seals or of 'species nearly extinct' testify in like manner to a masculine aggression comprehensive in its victims and devastating in its effects. Women to 'man as hunter' are merely 'part of the wildlife to be plundered for profit and pleasure, collected, used'.[68]

At the root of these multiple abuses for Dworkin is a conception of manhood that celebrates and mythologises the deployment of force and the subjection of other beings:

> With the rise of social Darwinism in the nineteenth century [...] Man-the-Aggressor is at the apex of the evolutionary struggle, king of the earth because he is the most aggressive, the cruellest. Male-supremacist biology [...] is, in fact, an essential element in the modern legend of terror that man spews forth celebrating himself: he is biologically ordained (where before he was God's warrior) to terrorize women and other creatures into submission.[69]

Ideals of the biologically or spiritually 'natural' man, familiar from Haggard's glorification of a restorative or cathartic masculine violence, are inserted by Dworkin into a wider narrative of cruelty. The savage communion of the huntsman-hero of the imperial adventure as he reaches the Darwinian apogee in the colonial wilds operates in these terms as the consummation of a broader and darker urge. Tellingly, Dworkin goes on to argue that '[t]he power of men in pornography is *imperial* power, the power of sovereigns who are cruel and arrogant' (my italics).[70] Acts of colonial domination, then, however masked as an organic emblem of dwelling are ultimately saturated, Dworkin's argument implies, with a libidinal agenda in which the key note is 'the pleasure of power and the power of pleasure'.[71]

The connection between hunting and sexual aggression is, as Frye's analysis implies, nothing very new. MacKenzie in *The Empire of Nature* notes that 'the sexual analogue of the gradual building-up of the chase and the orgasmic character of the kill had long been recognised in writings about and pictorial representations of the hunt'.[72] The archaic 'venery' designates both hunting and the sexual act and signals a longstanding correlation that clearly, in most instances, casts the female as the animal victim. In Shakespeare's *Titus Andronicus*, Marcus' depiction of the raped and mutilated Lavinia identifies the dishonoured woman with the hunted beast: 'O thus I found her, straying in the park, / Seeking to hide herself, as doth the deer / That hath receiv'd some unrecuring wound.'[73] *Hustler*'s puns and allusions, then, rather than an unseemly appropriation of an entirely unrelated discourse, articulate an established involvement of hunting with a rhetoric of sexual violence that evidently may be read into the colonial hunting tale.[74] Moreover, Britain's tropical colonies, conventionally typecast as the locus of an erotic freedom, add a further charge to the psycho-sexual dynamics of predation in their distance from the ostensibly more restrained and genteel atmosphere of the homeland. The mountains of animal remains that irresistibly draw the narrative eye in the masculine form of hunting literature evince, therefore, a profoundly problematic consummation. Like pornography, hunting narratives facilitate a scopophilic interrelation of power and the gaze that pivots on the objectification of the victim and the ecstatic enactment of dominatory impulses that relish suffering as the exultant affirmation of the self.

Despite the pervasiveness of these predatory erotics in the culture of the imperial hunt, it is important to resist oversimplification. As the complex and fluctuating significations of violence in Fenn's and Henty's narrations of the value of natural history indicate, masculine brutality is not just a straightforward and unproblematic expression of interior urges, but also a complex cultural phenomenon. Neither is masculinity, as the depiction of the naturalist as outsider reveals, a unitary marker of identity that comprises a consistent level of aggression. Without contesting the overarching premise of eco-feminist criticism, close readings of colonial romance allow a more nuanced interpretation of the ostensibly straightforward dominatory heterosexuality re-enacted in the sporting field. As Val Plumwood suggests, the 'recognition of a more complex dominator identity is [...] essential'.[75] Ballantyne's *The Gorilla Hunters* in particular represents an uncertain and nebulous sexuality that complicates the erotic dichotomy of predator and prey with a colonial sensibility paradoxically haunted by fantasies of vulnerability. The involvement of the environment and male desire in the imperial hunt ultimately far exceeds the trope of domination and draws attention to the deep-seatedly ambivalent psycho-dynamics of the chase that infuse human/animal interactions.

Sporting masculinities, for example Wilson's intended deployment of the hunting trophy in his failed seduction and the nervous debility of the epicene, anti-huntsman Bathurst in Henty's *Rujub*, identify the hunt as the commonly understood mark of manly and heterosexual achievement through which the boy becomes the man. Conceptions of gendered space, the manly wilds and the emasculating metropolis are an important aspect of this process. *The Gorilla Hunters*, accordingly, provides a robust dramatisation of a metropolitan crisis of gender identity that utilises hunting in a program of masculine self-improvement, hinging on the steady repudiation of feminine traits that have tainted the hero in his urban sojourn. While Jack exhibits his manliness from the very start of the novel, Ralph, appears at the outset as an effete and somewhat girlish figure, physically callow and out of bodily condition: in Ballantyne's vernacular, a 'muff'. Peterkin remarks on meeting his friend after many years that 'you were rather a soft green youth then and don't seem to be much harder or less verdant now' (12) and Jack observes he seems to have 'grown so much stouter' (27) in the intervening time. In a fracas that follows the three comrades' reunion, Ralph, rather embarrassingly, seizes an 'old woman's umbrella, as the only available weapon' (26), offering a parodic reflection of the other men's soldierly virtue that recurs throughout the text. Ralph is forced to admit that he is not so 'powerful or active' as Peterkin (51), unable to 'depend on his nerves' (97) and prone to an unmanly neglect of duty that sees him fall asleep during his watch (43). Most shamefully, when Jack and Peterkin plan for battle, Ralph 'arranges [the] hut and makes things comfortable' (330) as he is disparagingly assigned a female role in recognition of his failings as a man. The text stages Ralph's anxiety at his own inadequacy, his sense of dishonour and disappointment in himself; yet Ballantyne's didactic intentions pivot on his resolution to lay the 'lesson to heart' (47). As Ballantyne asserts, 'muffs may cure themselves' (71).

Importantly, Ballantyne's rejection of the taint of effeminacy throughout the course of his tale necessitates a violent reaction towards the few women that infringe into this determinedly homosocial text. The novel opens with an allusion to a seemingly innocent dispute between Ralph and his landlady Agnes concerning the exact time of Peterkin's arrival at the house of his old friend. Ralph sternly insists that 'Agnes may say what she pleases, – she has a habit of doing so; but I know for certain […] that it was exactly five o'clock in the afternoon, when I received a most singular and every way remarkable visit' (9). The assertion of male authority over an unwelcome female interference takes a more physical form when Peterkin's hurried departure from the room is 'followed by a clatter and a scream from old Agnes, whom he had upset and tumbled over' (20). Agnes' mishap embodies a forceful warning to a woman who, eavesdropping at the door perhaps, threatens to intrude on or compromise their male togetherness (although the ambiguity of the verb 'tumbled', referring potentially to either Peterkin or Agnes' loss of balance, implies a confusion of subject and object that, as we shall see, is a feature of Ballantyne's writing). Similarly, Tom Brown's landlady in *Hunting the Lions*, significantly named Mrs Pry, receives a pointed caution when Tom casually remarks 'when you make up the bill don't forget to charge me with the tumbler I smashed yesterday'.[76] This simmering, nonchalant and ostensibly accidental aggression cleanses the male from a malign feminine influence, safeguarding the homosocial unit from the meddling of women who oppose and undermine the cultivation of a thorough masculinity; releasing the virile male from his domestic straitjacket and, in the light of his ensuing predatory adventures in the African forest, reinforcing eco-feminist readings of the transferability of violence.

Such constitution of male identity through violence against women takes its strangest form in *The Gorilla Hunters* in Peterkin's narration of an extraordinary dream of hunting elephants:

> The biggest elephant had on a false front of fair curls and a marriage ring on its tail. Stay; was it not the other one had that? No, it was the biggest. I remember now, for it was just above the marriage ring I grasped it when I pulled its tail out. I didn't pull it off, for it wouldn't come off; it came out like a telescope or a long piece of india-rubber. Ha! and I remember thinking how painful it must be. That was odd, now, to think of that. The other elephant had on crinoline […] Well, let me see. What did I do. Oh yes, I shot them both, that was natural – but it wasn't quite so natural that the big one should vomit up a live lion which attacked me with incredible fury. (112–13)

Peterkin's fantastic vision assassinates the conventional image of domestic British womanhood, deploring the world of curls, marriage rings and crinoline in favour of the manly life of the big-game hunt that assumes in this context a deeply misogynist significance. The elephants' strange apparel shadows the daily business of the hunter in the African forest with a curious, brutal suggestiveness. Peterkin's insistence on pulling the tail 'out' rather than 'off' and his exclamatory recollection of the pain of this procedure illustrate a cruel erotic impulse that is addressed simultaneously to both women and animals. Concluding with the offhand 'I shot them both; of course, that was natural', Peterkin shows hunting both denouncing and replacing a conjugal sexuality, satiating libidinal desire in the 'natural' and liberated arena of the sporting field where men can be men without a woman's intervention.

Through Peterkin's dream, then, Ballantyne's text conceives of hunting as an overtly, and aggressively, heterosexual act unsure of its object. Ralph's transformation into the image of the virile hunter in the novel's closing sequence unsurprisingly, therefore, assumes a notably phallic form. In desperate combat with a gorilla at close quarters, he finally discovers a weapon more fitting than a woman's umbrella:

> When within ten yards of me I could restrain myself no longer. I raised my rifle, aimed at its chest and fired. With a terrible roar it advanced. Again I fired, but without effect, for the gorilla rushed upon me. In despair, I drew my hunting knife and launched it full at the brute's chest with all my might. I saw the glittering blade enter it as the enormous paw was raised to beat me down. (419)

Ballantyne's depiction of the novel's final kill culminates evocatively in the drawing of the blade, 'glittering' to encourage the gaze towards itself against the last, helpless gesture of the 'enormous paw'. Significantly, this victorious performance of domination is too much for Ralph. Fading into emotional exhaustion he declares 'I felt as if I were falling headlong down a precipice; the next, I became unconscious' (419). He awakes in a 'state of dreamy uncertainty' that soon slips into a 'state of delirium' (420); the force of the moment is too much to bear, a gratification so concentrated it is almost as if he had been asleep all along, acting in some hallucinatory realm of fantastic excitement. The incident is fraught with tensions. Ralph's metamorphosis into the successful hunter is juxtaposed by his descent 'headlong down' towards the devolutionary pit that marks the indistinctness of the species boundary between man and ape. The subject and object of domination appear subtly entwined.

Yet, while the relationship of predator and prey is far from straightforward, superficially at least the febrile intensity of Ralph's phallic accomplishment buttresses readings of the hunt that privilege the dominatory psychosexual aspect. The prominence of the weapon in Ralph's reimagining of his success comprises perhaps the most consistent element of the numerous instantiations of the colonial *coup-de-grâce* and the one most easily reduced to a violent eroticism. Indeed, in general terms, the colonial hunting narrative prospers through the intimacy it establishes between the gun and the pen, as the sights of the rifle and the gaze of the narrator are united in the trajectory of the prose, tracing the flight of the bullet from the hunter to his victim. A commonplace preface to recollections and imaginings of the hunt reflects on this intimate association of the weapon and the pen. Allan Quatermain in *King Solomon's Mines* begins his tale by asserting that 'I am more accustomed to handle a rifle than a pen',[77] while Gordon Cumming had previously confessed in similar terms in the introduction to his *Five Years of a Hunter's Life* that '[t]he hand, wearied all day with grasping the rifle, is not best suited for wielding the pen'.[78] Beyond a conventional authorial modesty, the substitution of the pen for the rifle entices the reader with a hint of what is to come: writing that fixes on the quarry, unabashed by the violent and the visceral. As Ritvo suggests, 'as the animal was reduced to its component parts [...] the hunter became embodied in his rifle and ammunition';[79] the weapon becomes part of the self, the embodiment of a hyperbolically potent masculinity.

For Haggard in *Nada the Lily*, the quest for the perfect weapon provides an integral aspect of the constitution of his African heroes' fierce masculinity. The powerful appeal of the club 'Watcher of the Fords' that 'destroys all who stand before it' (119) fills Galazi with a 'great desire [...] to possess it' (120) that does not balk at the prophecy that 'he who owns it [...] dies by the assegai' (121). To Umslopogaas the 'iron chieftainess', the great axe 'Groan-Maker', is an object of longing more seductive than the charms of love: after a meeting with a beautiful young Zulu woman 'Umslopogaas thought rather of axe Groan-Maker than of Maid Zinita; for ever, at the bottom, Umslopogaas loved war more than women' (152). In an exaggerated version of Ballantyne's cherished homosociality, the club and axe provide for the wolf brothers a metonymic realisation of an indomitable violence that replaces marital love. Umslopogaas, reflecting to Galazi on the destructive influence of wives, hopes '[m]ay we one day find a land where there are no women, and war only' (299). Haggard's delight in these weapons reconfigures a prominent aspect of colonial hunting narratives demonstrative of the hunter's investment in his weapon and inscribed in copious appendices, digressions and asides on the intricacies of ballistic technology.

The now little-known Victorian adventurer F. Vaughan Kirby in his shocking 1896 *In Haunts of Wild Game* is particularly explicit in his descriptions of the intimate impacts of his rifle. Reporting the kill of a leopardess, Kirby enthuses that 'the 360-grain hollow Metford bullet raked her from behind, tearing through her heart and lungs, the butt lodging in her throat – another score for a modified form of Express rifle!'[80] The triumph of his gun is vividly attested by the comprehensiveness of the raking and tearing of the beast, facilitated by a specific entry point of the bullet that seems to have fascinated Kirby. Earlier in the narrative, a shot at a buck, 'entering just below the tail', had 'completely raked him, cutting the left lung in its course, and passing out between the neck and shoulder' as he demonstrates his relish at a particularly lascivious violation of his prey.[81] In similarly frenzied vein, Kirby records his assault on a reedbuck ram:

> It ran straight towards us, dogs full cry after him, and so close I dare not fire; and went away down the spur with long steady bounds, his fanlike tail spread out very prettily. I made a lucky shot, bringing him down in his tracks, the solid 590-grain bullet going through him from end to end.[82]

The flickering of Kirby's interest between the buck's grisly fate and the technophilic narration of ballistic detail illustrates this technology as an implement and emblem of environmental mastery, inhabited by the hunter's destructive appetite. Such figuring of the *coup-de-grâce* in sporting literature as a penetration of an animal body insistently exhibits the quasi-erotic charge of the kill. With obsessive regularity the lethal gun shot is followed through the prey, generating a series of macabre and visceral images relentless in their *schadenfreude*. In *The Gorilla Hunters* Ralph kills a leopard with 'two bullets right between its two eyes' (63) and Jack, firing at a lion observes that his bullet 'went in at his mouth and smashed its way out at the back of his skull' (313). Peterkin later congratulates Ralph when he remarks with casual colloquialism after his friend takes a shot at a rhino 'you have blown out his eye [...] I do believe' (383). In *Hunting the Lions* in a reversal of the direction of Kirby's 'raking' of his victim, Tom's shot at a lioness had 'hit her just behind the head, and travelling along the spine, had stuck near the root of the tail'.[83]

These displays of agency indicate the hunter fulfilling the self through the infliction of pain, living through the weapon and in the delight of its effects. An important part of the frisson of such moments is the subtle figuring of the prey's imagined willingness to receive the predator's agonising penetrations. The ram's tail in Kirby's depiction, spreading prettily before his eyes, advertises itself to the hunter, as if the beast were complicit in its own destruction, feigning the determination to escape yet all the while craving the lethal bullet that will rake it 'end to end'. Often the hunter imagines an animal posing itself for his pleasure, eschewing flight in favour of a violent demise. Captain H. Shakespear, for instance, portrays an Indian tiger that 'sprang to his feet and exposed his broad, left side to me', seemingly only too eager to receive the *coup-de-grâce*.[84] The grammatical construction of such platitudes of sporting commentary recurrently stresses the beast's silent clamouring for death: facing a buffalo, Kirby enthuses 'I let him have it square in the shoulder.'[85] Storey, after a bear in Ceylon, concludes the excitement with 'I [...] gave it another shot to make sure.'[86] The bullet as gift constructs non-human animals welcoming human dominion: a theme, again, with a long history. The pheasant, Ben Jonson wrote in the seventeenth-century country house poem 'To Penshurst', for example, is 'willing to be kill'd'.[87] Positioning animals in this way clearly has significance for eco-feminist analyses of hunting. Collard and Contrucci write of a patriarchal conceptualisation of feminised Nature that 'she beckons and invites hooks and guns in the same way women are said to lure men and ask for rape'.[88] Dworkin, correspondingly, in *Pornography* quotes the psychologist of sex Havelock Ellis' insistence that 'the primary part of the female in courtship is the playful, yet serious, assumption of the role of a hunted animal who lures on the pursuer, not with the object of escaping, but with the object of finally being caught'.[89] This projection of agency onto the passive victim evidently has implications for the wider procedures of imperial hegemony. David Spurr argues of the struggles of the colonial situation that '[a]uthority is in some sense conferred by those who obey it'.[90] In offering its body to the predator, the animal meekly accepts the dominance of the hunter and confirms his role as colonial sovereign, facilitating a thrilling spectacle of male power replayed over and again: a fantasy both erotic and ideological.

Yet if the pleasure of the text for the readers and narrators of the imperial hunting narrative exists in the imagining and reimagining of self-empowerment, Ballantyne's *The Gorilla Hunters*, as much as it is structured around the conversion of Ralph into the image of the heterosexual hunter, is pervaded by images of vulnerability and submissiveness that run counter to the overarching dominatory agenda. Particularly, Ralph's relative weakness next to the masculine perfection of his companions provides not only the starting point for a conventionally didactic narrative of male transformation, but also indicates a keen fascination with disempowerment, effeminacy and the homoerotic. In the novel's opening chapter, Ballantyne depicts his sportsmen playfully representing their friendship in the terms of a conventional heterosexual romantic association. Writing to Jack, Peterkin's emotions overflow with an unmanly expression of amity: '"B'luv'd Jack" – will that do to begin with? eh! I'm afraid it's too affectionate; he'll think it's from a lady friend' (20). Ralph's reunion with Peterkin, meanwhile, configures their relationship as a contrast between the meek and powerful:

> I am not prone to indulge in effeminate demonstration, but I am not ashamed to confess that, when I gazed on the weather-beaten, though ruddy countenance of my old companion, and observed the eager glance of his bright blue eyes, I was quite overcome, and rushed violently into his arms. I may also add that, until that day, I had had no idea of Peterkin's physical strength, for during the next five minutes he twisted me about and spun me round and round my own room until my brain began to reel. (13)

Ralph's spontaneous indulgence in an 'effeminate demonstration' is stimulated by his apprehension of the body of his old friend: 'overcome' by Peterkin's 'weather-beaten', 'ruddy' face and 'bright blue eyes', Ralph becomes the passive, emasculated recipient of his 'eager' friend's masculine virtues. 'Twisted' in Peterkin's arms, Ralph is held like a plaything, resolutely mastered, his reeling brain signalling the dizzy exhilaration of the moment. The violence marking their embrace, while referring to the wider culture of combat and hunting that informs their bonding, also displays a radical ambivalence at the moment of contact, the sense of a clandestine fulfilment that inevitably wrestles with itself.

Although Africa functions as the revitalising, homosocial zone that offsets the feminised and feminising metropolis, as the adventurers begin their expedition Ralph continues to reveal a colonial subjectivity that contrasts sharply with the kind of belligerent energy apparent in Kirby's writing. Gazing into the dense jungle his poetic imagining of the foliage depicts a complex and conflicted masculinity:

> Rich luxuriance of vegetation was the feature that filled my mind most [...] Thick tough limbs of creeping plants and wild vines twisted and twined round everything and over everything, giving to the woods an appearance of tangled impenetrability; but the beautiful leaves of some, and the delicate tendrils of others, half concealed the sturdy limbs of the trees, and threw over the whole a certain air of wild grace, as might a semi-transparent and beautiful robe if thrown around the form of a savage. (31)

Ralph structures his appraisal of the forest around two linked but contrasting moods. While the '[t]hick tough' branches suggest a sturdy masculinity, these limbs are both threatening and sensual. Initially, Ralph is struck by the uncanniness of the tropical fecundity, dismayed at a sinister growth that in its twisting and twining signals the monstrosity of this profusion yet also reveals a fascination that causes him to linger in his description of it. Menace then slips into attraction as the leaves' delicacy and beauty that half conceals the limbs suggests 'a semi-transparent and beautiful robe if thrown around the form of a savage'. The reiterated incompleteness of the covering draws attention suggestively to the imagined savage body, teasingly veiling and evoking its nakedness and tempering a conventional, primitive manliness with a flimsy, effeminate garment.

Furthermore, the twisting of the wild vines returns Ralph to the twisting he experienced previously in Peterkin's arms, while the 'rich luxuriance of vegetation' that begins his reverie also reprises an earlier episode. Describing Jack's appearance at their reunion, Ralph notes that his companion's hair had 'been allowed to grow luxuriantly' (27) before moving to a more detailed appreciation of his friend's physique, admiring his 'great length of limb' and 'immense breadth of chest and shoulders' (28). Ralph's vision of the woods relives his delight in the fit, male body and dramatises a sense of disquiet that accompanies it. The 'impenetrability' of the woods cordons off the alluring body, dampening his voyeuristic pleasure with a hint of danger. Ballantyne's text, then, both hints at and retires from a homoerotic undercurrent to the homosocial and demonstrates an inconsistent distribution of and attitude to masculine power. Ralph's relative weakness next to the sinews of his companions and the limbs of the trees is both a source of shame and a location of pleasure; the ambivalent, eidetic atmosphere of the hunting expedition in *The Gorilla Hunters* conceals a polymorphous and ambiguous sexuality that requires a more qualified approach to the unconscious motivations of environmental domination. Encoded in Ballantyne's depiction of Ralph's alternate masculinity is a hegemonic heterosexist alignment of femininity and homosexuality with passivity. Evidently, such patterns trade on the interplay between different categories of masculinity in the Victorian empire. Ralph's characterisation as the effete, disempowered naturalist next to Peterkin, the vigorous ex-serviceman, constitutes the same conflict that informs Henty's and Fenn's representations of colonial natural history, especially regarding the culturally sensitive balance of restraint and aggression. Ballantyne's exploration of these themes, however, is characteristically more emotionally intense.

Most significantly in terms of representations of human/animal interaction, Ballantyne's delineation of Ralph as a passive and docile figure expresses a subtle intention not just to dominate animal others, but to imagine experiencing the effects of this domination. If the obsessive narration of animal suffering facilitates human self-assertion through a powerful portrayal of agency, Ballantyne also troubles the directness of this dominatory trajectory through a readjustment of the narrative perspective to encompass an imagining of victimhood. Watching by moonlight 'a beautiful little antelope' and its 'little fawn' drinking at a pool, Ralph lingers on the animals' activity:

> The two looked timidly round for a few seconds, and snuffed the air as if they feared concealed enemies, and then, trotting into the water, slaked their thirst together. I felt as great pleasure in seeing them take a long satisfactory draught, as if I had been swallowing it myself, and hoped they would continue there for some time. (300)

Ralph's pleasure pivots on a slippage from observation to vicarious experience that seems at first innocent enough: a natural relish in the most basic bodily need. Yet the instant also contains a faint, but significant air of peril. The 'swallowing' that is the focus of Ralph's vision shifts the hunting narrative's conventional interest in the internal experience of animals from agony to satisfaction in a moment that is nonetheless haunted by aggression in the suggestion of the 'concealed enemies' to which the antelopes are exposed. 'Snuff' (to 'sniff', but also to 'extinguish') intrudes a further deathly hint into the scene, so that inhabiting the animals' fulfilment at the water-hole, Ralph allies himself also to their potential suffering; the weakness he previously experiences in the masculine arms of his companions evolves into identification with the weakness of prey before the predator. In his perception of the vulnerability of the quarry, Ralph envisions himself absolutely mastered by the prowess of his companions, rather than affirming himself as the master of empire's animal others.

On one level, the nexus of fear, vulnerability and pleasure that underpins Ballantyne's representation of the antelopes at the pool merely adds a frisson to the pornographic self-empowerment of the hunter: another version of the bullet as gift that enhances a brutal delight in animal suffering through the imagining of the victim's complicity. But alongside this dominatory trajectory, the text's investment in Ralph's disempowered subject position also hints at a culturally long-standing tradition of the hunter becoming his *own* victim that disturbs as much as reinforces this agenda. As Frye recalls, 'the image of the hunter pursuing an animal is never far from metamorphosis, or the actual changing of the hunter into the animal'; or, in the question posed in Shakespeare's *As You Like It*, 'What shall he have that kill'd the deer? / His leather skin and horns to wear.'[91] Like Actaeon in Ovid's *Metamorphoses* transformed into the likeness of a deer and torn apart by his own hounds, violence eventually is turned on its perpetrator, the power dynamic reversed, the hunter exposed to his own aggression. Ralph's association with the objects of masculine domination, both through his vicarious experience of the antelope and his feminised role in the group, identifies him as the clearest embodiment of this Actaeon complex, also subtly apparent in the chaffing identification of Jack as the gorilla and Peterkin as the monkey.[92] Through this pattern, the animal bodies upon which the hunter inscribes his agency, through which empire enacts its rule, also testify to a complex mutual involvement of subject positions, of dominator and dominated, human and animal that, in conclusion, offer a further image of the instability of these boundaries and a point of central relevance to the global ecological future.

CONCLUSION

Imperial romance expresses human involvement with the natural world, and indeed the term human itself, as beset by paradoxes. To glance back over the adventures of this study, as much as Henty and Buchan in *Rujub the Juggler* and *A Lodge in the Wilderness* seek to regulate and domesticate animal others as an emblem of the assimilation of racial others, they also retain an ideological and aesthetic investment in otherness as a core ingredient of their narrative practices and as a sign of a culture and a masculinity infused with virility. The naturalist's craft for Fenn and Henty while involved in the Euro- and anthropocentric ordering of the world, constructs an ambivalent human subjectivity that fails to marshal its own savagery. Gorillas provide an illustration *par excellence* of the uncertainty of the species divide and of the instability of literary categories: the embodiment of an ontological doubt that muddies human priority. The discourse of the human body, particularly here the male body, both in degeneration and at its peak, further disturbs the absoluteness of the human/animal divide; while Ralph's meeker, disempowered sensibility illustrates the complexity of the psychic thrills that inhere in such texts' obsessive interest in violence towards animals.

These patterns reveal imperial romance's presentation of non-human animals as a multifaceted and conflicted textual experience that requires a reconsideration of a crudely reductive reading of the genre as simple escapism. Images of the natural man, the degenerate, the ape, the victim and the savage indicate the human as a designation porous at many points and destabilise a hegemonic logic that ostensibly abjects animality as the sign only of the disenfranchised other. While imperial romance's continual recourse to animality, to the apprehension and embracement of an animal self, forms a central part of a discourse of colonial power, it also, ironically and uncomfortably, constitutes its logical limit. These arguments foreground the *ontological* ambivalences of *Homo sapiens* in a Victorian, imperial context: the contingency of the most profound question of species being. At the same time, however, this analysis has significant ramifications for *ecological* issues, for our conception of being-in-the-world and the variety of complex relationships that constitute this. Who we think we are inevitably determines how we think we should live.

Perhaps most importantly, these adventure fictions (in some cases against the grain of their intentions) reveal the collapse of what Val Plumwood describes as a 'hyper-separated' model of human habitation of the biosphere through which humanity is defined as radically apart from other species and from our environments. 'Hyper-separation', in Plumwood's analysis, operates as a form of 'differentiation that is used to justify domination and conquest' through stigmatising the other as 'both inferior and radically separate'.[1] Rather, for Plumwood, the 'ecological self' is the 'self-in-relationship', a conceptualisation that facilitates a 'movement beyond self/other dualism' and towards a 'non-instrumental mode' of human environmentality that includes 'respect, benevolence, care, friendship and solidarity'.[2] The implications of this model are clear for both postcolonial reconfigurations of international relations in terms more intimately connected with global social justice and for a more radical ecological consciousness. Plumwood's idealistic aspiration aims to counter abusive and exploitative worldviews by insisting on the fallacy behind them. Imperial romance's myriad breakdowns in depicting a hyper-separated humanity corrode the logical basis of imperial and ecological violence and the construction of subaltern others. In adventure fiction, the basis of dualistic thought, the 'master identity' that Plumwood summarises as the 'incorporating, totalising, or colonising self', is, at times unwittingly, at times deliberately, expressed in intimate relation to the other it seeks to denigrate, exclude or appropriate.[3] Optimistically, this movement away from Manichean structures of thought enables a movement towards a more cooperative, less instrumentalist ethos. But a key question remains: how to move from an apprehension of the failures of dualism to an environmental practice of respect and nonviolence?

Evidently, throughout this study human animality has appeared as a cause of or enticement to aggression rather than as a moderating influence that might stimulate a move beyond hierarchical thinking. Plumwood's paradigm of the 'master identity' can inhere even in ontological models that purposively contest hyper-separation. The recognition of the animal self to those encountering great apes necessitates a forceful, but inevitably disappointed, purgation of that trace; or, to Haggard and Buchan, the expression of human animality functions as a brutality which in turn feeds into the military machine of colonial rule. Likewise, aesthetic appreciation of non-human animals, as in Fenn's depiction of Nat's oscillation between admiration and destruction of his specimens, is shadowed by a violence that automatically reinstates the separation of human and animal. As Barbara Noske writes in addressing a recurrent validation of hunting among deep ecologists such as Gary Snyder and Aldo Leopold, '[h]unters profess to feel an at-oneship: a closeness to the animal individual they are hunting; but curiously they then proceed to take away precisely that which makes them feel close in the first place: movement, behaviour, *life*' (original italics).[4] Indeed, Uncle Dick's reflection on his quarry in *Nat the Naturalist* that '[n]o stuffed specimens of ours will ever reproduce a hundredth part of their beauty' testifies to the self-defeating logic of a belligerent affiliation.

Violence, nonetheless, remains a component of the romance tradition and a part of the restless negotiation of the human/animal boundary and of the relational and hyper-separated self in the imperial milieu. More broadly, approaches to violence remain central to the ongoing (relative) dis-alignment of ecocriticism, animal studies and postcolonial studies. The vegan abolitionist position closely involved with much work in critical animal studies which aims for an end to all animal exploitation appears unavoidably and irreconcilably in conflict with, for example, traditional forms of subsistence hunting that many ecocritics valorise. There are, indeed, telling geographical factors underlying the possibility or impossibility of veganism in many parts of the world. Indigenous Arctic communities, for example, that have relied for centuries on whales, seals and walruses for food and other utilities in a region of, at best, severely limited agricultural potential, evidently live in a way that is incompatible with animal liberationist ideals, although compatible with the ideals of sustainability. While of course many vegans would not insist on abstaining from meat as an absolutist ethical position in this context, this example nonetheless reminds us of the unresolved tension between animal and ecological ethical priorities. At root, this is a problem of the decidability of environmental violence. In an era in which environmental policy decisions are increasingly debated at a global level, the question remains: who may kill what and for what reasons? And beyond this, perhaps even more pressingly, who decides and for what reasons? If it is not possible to reject all forms of violence against animals across the board, then it is at least possible to bring vigilance, critical intelligence and respect for cultural diversity to the analysis of these forms.

In approaching the knotted strands of this issue in our contemporary moment, the preceding analysis of Victorian and Edwardian imperial adventures may be of present relevance, at least to some aspects of the debate. As we have seen, the historical development of Western environmentalism has been nourished by ideas of wilderness and heroic testing that have been intimately associated with the colonial arena. This link further evokes the collision of ecology and ontology; it is because the primal appeal of wilderness hunting supposedly connects us with a deep sense of 'who we are' that it has proved so influential in the formation of arguments in favour of conservation. The seduction of this trope still resides in a kind of evolutionary katabasis that depends on the familiar motifs of 'going native' and by extension theriomorphism: becoming like an animal as a return to a biological inheritance. As such, there remains an, albeit unstable, sense of hierarchy, or of evolutionary gradation, in this environmental imaginary that is far from helpful to the dual progression of ecological and social justice. Those who have entered modernity and civility, the supposition runs, return to what they have ostensibly become separated from, entering into violent contact with wild animals that, as the lines from Noske quoted above expose, is routinely, but problematically, imagined as a relationship of equality or mutual participation rather than domination. If adventure fiction and its imperialist contexts teach us anything, it should be a wariness towards the occluded ideological undercurrents and political inequalities implicit in and facilitated by Western defences of violence against animals, and the narrative of the 'natural' man they unfold.

The result is that the destabilisation of the human/animal boundary and a scrupulous unravelling of the anthropos behind anthropocentrism are clearly not, on their own, enough to allow for a thorough decolonisation of the environmental movement. Nonetheless, the convergence of animal studies and postcolonial studies with ecocriticism and, more widely, with questions of environmental policy provides an important set of tools for decision making, the value of which is determined precisely by their disparity of interests. This tense multiplicity of perspectives offers fruitful ground for a deeply reflexive and self-critical environmentalism, attuned to the divergent ethical priorities that inevitably arise in the complexity of our ecological emergency. This critical coalition may suggest significant ways to move, as Leonard Lawlor writes in a different context, towards 'a lesser violence, even the *least* violence' (original emphasis).[5]

Despite the cautionary note concerning the promise of the destabilisation of the human for the formation of a nonviolent ecological consciousness, imperial romance's narrations of ambivalent species identity do also support some other important conclusions of wider ecological significance. The relational self relies for Plumwood on the recognition of both kinship (to avoid the 'radical exclusion' of others) and difference (to counteract the 'incorporation' of the other into the self)[6] and this interplay of self and other is crucially manifested in this study in relation to text as well as to species. Derrida in 'The Animal That Therefore I Am' coins the term 'fabulation' to express the containment of non-human animals in human symbolic economies at the expense of representations that aim towards the 'real'. 'We know', he writes, 'the history of fabulation and how it remains an anthropomorphic taming, a moralizing subjection, a domestication. Always a discourse of man.'⁷ In talking about his cat, Derrida emphasises the tension between real and symbolic animals:

> I must make it clear from the start, the cat I am talking about is a real cat, truly believe me, *a little cat*. It isn't the *figure* of a cat. It doesn't silently enter the room as an allegory for all the cats on the earth, the felines that traverse myths and religions, literature and fables.⁸

The insistence on a discontinuity between real and symbolic seems ethically vital, but in terms of literary analysis, philosophically fraught. How is it possible to *read* a 'real' cat, despite Derrida's avowal that he is writing about one? Ballantyne's *The Gorilla Hunters* is perhaps an unlikely source for theoretically current considerations on animals and representational politics, but as Ralph gazes into the African jungle at the outset of his adventures in the wilds he offers a suggestive summary of the coexistence of the uneasily related modes of the fabulous and the real:

> There was something inexpressibly delightful, yet solemn in my feelings as I gazed into that profound obscurity where the great tree stems and the wild gigantic foliage nearest to me appeared ghost-like and indistinct, and the deep solitudes of which were peopled, not only with the strange fantastic forms of my excited fancy, but, as I knew full well, with real wild creatures, both huge and small, such as my imagination had not fully conceived. I felt awed, almost oppressed with the deep silence around. (42)

Ralph's acknowledgement of a discontinuity between the 'strange fantastic forms of [his] excited fancy' and the 'real wild creatures' beyond his conception may be taken as an important reminder of the limits of anthropomorphism: its approach towards but ultimate failure to reach non-human animals. But recognising this gap, there remains, decisively, some involvement of fancy and the real. Ralph's qualification that the creatures were 'such as my imagination had not *fully* conceived' indicates, if not yet even a partial success in reaching the animal real, then at least a sense that imagination is not entirely and irrevocably detached from other species. Indeed, the epistemological complexities of humanity's engagements with its species others need not necessarily deny the potential for imagination to engage meaningfully with other beings.

Like Ralph, we know 'full well' that 'real wild creatures' exist and the representation of them should not be taken simplistically as an incorporation of 'the animal' into 'the human', but to some extent, in some environmentally engaged textual forms (even those saturated with ideologies of violence), as a participation in the non-human. Romance looks out towards the wilderness, as well as in towards its own fancies; towards, to return to Buchan's Musuru, 'the glamour of the unknown' (37). It is the entry into what is beyond the domesticated, anthropocentric world that fuels romance's narrative drive; as much as the wilderness is assimilated both imaginatively and politically, its partially apprehended otherness infiltrates back into the anthropomorphising imagination. To take a metaphor from Philip Armstrong of far broader relevance than the fictions considered here, animals leave their 'tracks' in these texts.[9] The model of kinship and difference that underpins relationality is paralleled by a textual interdependence of the anthropomorphic effects of human representation and the apprehension of real animals that necessarily, if unevenly, informs these representations.

One final point remains to be made about the uneasy sense of the co-constitution of human and animal apparent in imperial romance's recurrent anxiety over the human body and its products. The slime that Jack London figures on the city's streets metaphorises fears of an indistinctness between organisms: an undifferentiated organic nature that includes humans and their species others. Human metamorphoses and playful doublings of man and ape enact this supposition of a shared bodiliness: transformations and resemblances made possible by the common and continuous material of biospheric life. The sensory movement of this book from the ocular Foucauldian glance to the tactile, olfactory and gustatory experiences produced in engagements with great apes demonstrate a significant shift from distance to intimacy. The gaze relies on a space between subject and object that facilitates classification, connoisseurship and objectification; yet smell, touch and taste situate subject and object in a proximity that problematises such differentiation. The interplay of these modes of experience, particularly in the narration of natural history and the progression from the gaze to the mud, offers a more complete portrayal of the human sensorium in which the hero discovers himself far less able to tell himself apart from his animal others.

If the experience of a shared, or at least related, bodiliness leads to a recognition of the interpenetration of self and other, the inevitable susceptibility of this bodily nature and its embeddedness in the biosphere points also to a shared fate. In this regard the Actaeon complex as figured in Ralph's excited fancy may provide a compelling metaphor. The psychological investment in victimhood he represents stands to receive an unimagined consummation as the velocity of environmental degradation proceeds unabated. Violence will return eventually to its perpetrators; the hunter's destructive energy is turned back towards him. Self-evidently in destroying the planet we destroy ourselves and as humanity prosecutes its holocausts with no declining impetus, Ralph's concluding remark in his apprehension of the African forest may offer a poignant conclusion. 'I felt awed, almost oppressed by the deep silence around' suggests both the depth of human affiliation to the natural world that permeates even the most insistently and violently hyper-separated discourse and an image, potentially, of the consequences of that violence. Oppressed by the quiet, we can imagine Ralph inhabiting a dystopic global future, empty of both 'real wild animals' and the 'excited fancy' they inspire. This prospect surely encourages a deeper sense of ecological responsibility in which the analysis of literature and other arts has an urgent role to play as a complement to scientific and public policy debates. Adventure fiction encapsulates the paradoxical coexistence of a profound sense of environmental value with a determined legitimation of environmental and political injustice that illustrates the need to understand our ecological crisis as a facet of our collective cultural and imaginative lives and, connectedly, a question (in part) of who we think we are.

NOTES

Introduction

1 Ballantyne, *The Gorilla Hunters*, 106–7.
2 Ballantyne, *Six Months at the Cape*, 42.
3 Ballantyne, *The Settler and the Savage*, 149.
4 The Animal Studies Group, *Killing Animals*, 4, 50.
5 Mukherjee, *Postcolonial Environments*, 17.
6 O'Brien, 'Articulating a World of Difference', 141. Lawrence Buell remarks that although 1978 saw the introduction of the term 'ecocriticism', environmentally informed criticism can be discovered well before this. Buell cites as examples Leo Marx's *The Machine and the Garden* (1964), Raymond Williams' *The Country and the City* (1973), Norman Foerster's *Nature in American Literature* (1923) and Ralph Waldo Emerson's *Nature* (1835). See Buell, *The Future of Environmental Criticism*, 13–14.
7 Young, *Postcolonialism*, 15.
8 O'Brien, 'Articulating a World of Difference', 142.
9 Glotfelty, *The Ecocriticism Reader*, xix; Said, *Culture and Imperialism*, 5.
10 Nixon, 'Environmentalism and Postcolonialism', 233, 235.
11 Soper, 'What is Nature', 124. For a fuller account of environmentalist disapprobation of 'postmodernism' see Soulé and Lease (eds), *Reinventing Nature* and in particular Paul Shepard's trenchant essay, 'Virtually Hunting Reality in the Forests of Simulacra' in which he concludes with bitter eloquence that 'Lyotard and his fellows have about them no glimmer of earth, of leaves or soil' (20).
12 Huggan, '"Greening" Postcolonialism', 703. Comparably, however, some critics of postcolonial studies have pointed out that despite its avowed ethical commitment to the non-Western world, many of postcolonialism's most influential figures are based in the English-speaking academies of the metropolitan West. As Simon Gikandi claims, 'postcolonial theory doesn't make sense to literary and cultural scholars outside English' (cited in Watts, 'Towards an Ecocritical Postcolonialism', 252).
13 Watts, 'Towards an Ecocritical Postcolonialism', 252.
14 Mukherjee, *Postcolonial Environments*, 46.
15 Armstrong, 'The Postcolonial Animal', 413.
16 James, 'Review', 113.
17 Armstrong, 'The Postcolonial Animal', 413.
18 Garrard, *Ecocriticism*, 139–40.
19 Ibid., 148; Tiffin, 'Unjust Relations', 31.
20 Lundblad, 'From Animal to Animality Studies', 497.
21 See Ballantyne, *Lost in the Forest*.

22 See Midgely, *Animals*, 14, Ritvo, *The Animal Estate*, 249–52 and MacKenzie, *Empires of Nature*, 46
23 See Ritvo, *The Animal Estate*, 250–51.
24 See Beinart and Hughes, *Environment and Empire*, 68; Pringle, *Narrative of a Residence*, ch. 8.
25 Harris, *The Wild Sports of South Africa*, xviii.
26 For an exhaustive listing of early African hunting texts see Czech, *An Annotated Bibliography*. For a bibliography of Indian narratives see Burton 'A Bibliography of Big Game'.
27 Indeed, as Ritvo points out, to some outside the ranks of sporting enthusiasts the late nineteenth century's proliferation of largely formulaic hunting narratives was a rather vexing literary development. See Ritvo, *The Animal Estate*, 255–6.
28 Ballantyne, 'Hunting the Lions', 25.
29 Du Chaillu's work will be considered in detail in Chapter Three. For an account of Livingstone's ambivalent attitude to hunting see MacKenzie, *The Empire of Nature*, 104 and Donald, *Picturing Animals*, 177.
30 Selous, *Sport and Travel*, 143.
31 Major-General Bisset summarised the young Prince's achievement as 'that glorious day when we killed six hundred head of game, all larger than horses' (Bisset, *Sport and War*, 180). For details on Selous and Cumming see respectively MacKenzie, *The Empire of Nature*, 124 and Ryan, *Picturing Empire*, 203.
32 Rangarajan, *India's Wildlife History*, 26, 32.
33 See Ritvo, *The Empire of Nature*, 283–4 for more detail on the fate of quaggas.
34 MacKenzie, 'Empire and Ecological Apocalypse', 223.
35 North America offers further evidence of indigenous environmental impacts that undercut a colonial tendency in some regions to romanticise the 'native' as a harmless and harmonious presence in nature. While John Muir suggested that 'Indians walked softly and hurt the landscape hardly more than the birds and squirrels', there are clear indications that pre-colonial America was, as Gary Paul Nabhan writes, 'dramatically shaped by Native American management practices'. See Soulé and Lease (eds), *Reinventing Nature*, 88.
36 See Rangarajan, *India's Wildlife History*, 11–14 on Mughal hunting; 35–8 on hunting in independent princely states during British rule. To add further nuance to the impacts of pre and post colonial hunting compared with colonial hunting, Susie Green in her cultural history *Tiger* describes Indian independence as having a perhaps surprisingly negative impact on tiger populations (see Green, *Tiger*, 21).
37 While concern for some domestic species intensified with the development of the RSPCA early in the nineteenth century, exotic species and wild British species still attracted little concern. See Chapter Two for a fuller discussion of these issues.
38 Haggard, *Allan's Wife*, v.
39 Storey, *Hunting and Shooting in Ceylon*, xvi.
40 Buchan, *The African Colony*, 168.
41 Ibid., 172.
42 For a fuller discussion of the influence of the industrial revolution on the environment see Guha, *Environmentalism*, 4 and Armstrong, *What Animals Mean*, 1. The theme of industrialisation and in particular its perceived effects on the male body are taken up in more detail here in Chapter Four.
43 Shakespear, *Wild Sports of India*, 175.
44 For an appendix listing the various acts of game legislation across the British Empire see MacKenzie, *The Empire of Nature*, 312–13. See also Ritvo, *The Animal Estate*, 284.

45 Storey, *A Ceylonese Sportsman's Diary*, 1.
46 Buchan, *The African Colony*, 185.
47 The formation of game reserves such as at Sabi in Transvaal in 1898, the forerunner of the Kruger national park, and in the same year at Yala in Ceylon, to this day Sri Lanka's most biologically diverse region, are two high profile examples of how colonial hunting constructed the spaces for later conservation. For a more wide-ranging, historically detailed consideration of the relation of empire and conservation, see Grove, *Green Imperialism*.
48 For his description of the three stages of hunting see MacKenzie, 'Chivalry, Social Darwinism and Ritualised Killing', 41–57. While helpful in identifying the key functions of hunting and depicting the inextricable link of human and non-human histories, MacKenzie's tripartite division is to an extent simplistic. As Beinart and Hughes suggest, hunting was never so neatly demarcated: the commercial hunt was not, for example, without a symbolic charge and the mercantile utilization of animals continued long after sport became established as a leisure pursuit (nor indeed were ritualistic sport hunters averse to profit). See Beinart and Hughes, *Environment and Empire*, 68.
49 MacKenzie, *The Empire of Nature*, 164.
50 Ibid., ix.
51 Beinart and Hughes, *Environment and Empire*, 16.
52 Stigand and Lyell, *Central African Game*, 3.
53 By way of comparison with this apparent convergence of environmentalism and racism, Grove cites early French colonial conservationists in Mauritius who were also early opponents of slavery. See Grove, *Green Imperialism*, 9 (fn).
54 O'Brien, 'Articulating a World of Difference', 144. For more detail on evictions of indigenous peoples from national parks see Adams, *Against Extinction*, 110–15.
55 Guha, 'Radical American Environmentalism', 75.
56 Adams, 'Nature and the Colonial Mind', 41.
57 Huggan, '"Greening" Postcolonialism', 702.
58 The Animal Studies Group, *Killing Animals*, 3.
59 For a full consideration of the contributions of Singer, Regan and others to animal ethics see Plumwood, *Environmental Culture*, 143–66.
60 Cited in Fudge, *Perceiving Animals*, 47.
61 Cited in Lippit, 'Magnetic Animal', 1119.
62 Derrida, '"Eating Well"', 112.
63 Baudrillard, *Simulacra and Simulation*, 131, 133.
64 Spiegel, *Dreaded Comparison*, 32.
65 See particularly the works of the schoolmaster, literary critic and key influence on Gandhi's vegetarianism Henry Stephens Salt, especially *Seventy Years among Savages* (1921) and *Animals' Rights: Considered in Relation to Social Progress* (1892).
66 Twine, *Animals as Biotechnology*, 9.
67 Ahuja, 'Postcolonial Critique', 558.
68 Ibid., 558.
69 Tiffin, 'Unjust Relations', 31.
70 Cited in Cavalieri, *The Animal Question*, 47.
71 Friends of the Earth, http://www.foe.co.uk/campaigns/biodiversity/index.html (accessed 17 October 2008).
72 See the Deep Ecology Platform, http://www.deepecology.org/platform.htm. For a richer and more nuanced account of deep ecology than is possible here, see Buell, *The Future of Environmental Criticism*, 102–4.

73 Cilano and DeLoughrey, 'Against Authenticity', 72.
74 Loomba, *Colonialism/Postcolonialism*, 104.
75 Mukherjee, *Postcolonial Environments*, 48.
76 Morton, *The Ecological Thought*, 38.
77 Adams, *Against Extinction*, 234.
78 See Mukherjee, *Postcolonial Environments* especially 42–58 for the most detailed discussion to date of the relationship of deep and social ecological positions in the negotiation of postcolonial studies and ecocriticism.
79 Buell, *The Future of Environmental Criticism*, 10–11.
80 Derrida, 'The Animal That Therefore I Am', 402.
81 The question of whether domestication, or indeed, to return to Spiegel's terms, mastery, is necessarily morally undesirable is not straightforward. The work of Vicki Hearne and Paul Patton on animal training has been especially influential in this regard. See particularly Patton's 'Language, Power and the Training of Horses' in Wolfe (ed.), *Zoontologies*, 83–99.
82 Fudge in her 2002 *Animal* also prefers to retain the singular 'the animal'. Fudge intends to 'make the word "animal" in all of its singularity an uncomfortable one' arguing that 'the abstract term is exactly what is both necessary, and deeply problematic in a culture where meat eating, pet ownership and anthropomorphic children's books all sit comfortably together' (Fudge, *Animal*, 164).

Chapter One: Otherness and Order

1 Green, *Dreams of Adventure*, 3.
2 Lyall, 'Novels of Adventures and Manners', 551.
3 Salmon, *The Literature and Art of Empire*, 1.
4 Salmon, *Juvenile Literature As It Is*, 203.
5 White, *Joseph Conrad and the Adventure Tradition*, 42.
6 Henty has attracted one monograph (Logan, *Narrating Empire*) and frequent but very brief mentions in broader works on Victorian children's literature. Recent work on Ballantyne is confined to two journal articles: Robert Irvine's 2007 study of Ballantyne's *Gascoyne the Sandalwood Trader* 'Separate Accounts: Class and Colonisation in the Early Stories of R. M. Ballantyne' in the *Journal of Victorian Culture* and my 2008 essay in the *Victorian Review*, 'Adventures in the Volcano's Throat: Tropical Landscape and Bodily Horror in R. M. Ballantyne's *Blown to Bits*'. Recent substantial criticism on du Chaillu is constituted by McCook, '"It May be Truth"', Mandelstam, 'Du Chaillu's Stuffed Gorillas' and Grant, '"Interior Explorations"'.
7 For gender readings of Haggard see McLintock, 'Maidens, Maps and Mines', Sheick, 'Adolescent Pornography' and Bunn, 'Embodying Africa'. Work with a more postcolonial focus includes, for example, Stiebel, *Imagining Africa* and Chrisman, *Rereading the Imperial Romance*.
8 MacDonald (ed.), *John Buchan Revisioned*.
9 Dryden, *Joseph Conrad and the Imperial Romance*, 2. It is perhaps also of some significance that two recent studies, Dryden's and White's, harness their consideration of the imperial adventure to an analysis of Conrad, a mainstream figure whose canonical status offsets the relative unimportance of the genre.
10 Graham Law in an article on 'The Romance of Empire: John Buchan's Early Writings' offers a similarly reductive judgement to Dryden's when he avers that adventure romances performed a 'very simple and specific ideological function' (4).

11 For a succinct and readable account of Bhabha's key ideas see Huddart, *Homi K. Bhabha*.
12 In the first decades of the nineteenth century it seems that literature specifically for boys was rare. As Fenn writes in his biography of Henty, 'to go back to, say 1830, there were hardly any books for a boy to read' (Fenn, *G. A. Henty*, 333).
13 Frye, *Anatomy of Criticism*, 186.
14 Ibid., 187; Green, *Dreams of Adventure*, 23.
15 Ibid., 37.
16 Lewis, 'On Stories', 93. Likewise, writing on an unsatisfactory film adaptation of Haggard's *King Solomon's Mines*, Lewis avers that there 'must be a pleasure in such stories distinct from excitement' (Ibid., 92). The absence of an appetite for such pleasures is a theme he returns to elsewhere, lamenting that 'the taste for romance seems in our age to be dead, and the very corpse mutilated and mocked' (Lewis, *English Literature*, 330).
17 Green, *Dreams of Adventure*, 203.
18 Cited in Fuchs, *Romance*, 1.
19 Frye, *Anatomy of Criticism*, 306.
20 Hulme, *Colonial Encounters*, 182–3.
21 Young, *Colonial Desire*, 167.
22 For Haggard's depictions of Quartermain's ivory trading adventures see particularly *King Solomon's Mines* (1885), *Maiwa's Revenge* (1888) and *The Ivory Child* (1916). For Ballantyne's sandalwood traders see *Gascoyne* (1864).
23 For a materialist reading of *King Solomon's Mines* that connects Haggard's novel to the development of South African diamond mining see McClintock, *Imperial Leather*.
24 White, *Joseph Conrad and the Adventure Tradition*, 44.
25 Lyall, 'Novels of Adventures and Manners', 535.
26 Ibid., 551. The disapprobation of realism in the late nineteenth century was a campaign prosecuted with vigour by several eminent literary figures: R. L. Stevenson and Andrew Lang as well as Haggard. This mistrust encompassed, as Peter Keating summarises, both the French Naturalism of Emile Zola and the more psychologically inflected works of Henry James and involved the association of such texts with 'introspection, unmanliness and morbidity' against which romance promised a 'fresh wind [that] blows away morbidity and brings a return to health' (Keating, *The Haunted Stud*, 345).
27 Frye, *Anatomy of Criticism*, 186. In his later study of romance, *The Secular Scripture*, Frye comments in terms that anticipate Green's judgement that 'the adventure stories of Rider Haggard and John Buchan and Rudyard Kipling [...] incorporate the *dreams* of British Imperialism' (my italics) (Frye, *The Secular Scripture*, 57).
28 Monsman, 'Of Diamonds and Deities', 281.
29 Cited ibid., 281
30 Haggard, *King Solomon's Mines*, appendix 4, 273.
31 Cited in Monsman, 'Of Diamonds and Deities', 293. Both Freud and Jung were interested readers of Haggard's early romances and were particularly drawn to *She*, a text that Freud appropriately described as a 'strange book, but full of hidden meaning'. See Etherington, *Rider Haggard*, 38–9, 51–5, and Cohen, *Rider Haggard*, 112–13 for a full account.
32 Lang, 'Realism and Romance', 690.
33 Ibid., 689.
34 Buchan, *The Runagates Club*, 13.
35 Low, *White Skins, Black Masks*, 3.

36 Norquay (ed.), *R. L. Stevenson on Fiction*, 53.
37 Haggard, *Allan Quartermain*, 11, 13.
38 Buchan, *Memory Hold-the-Door*, 13–14.
39 Cited in Love, *Practical Ecocriticism*, 28.
40 Buchan, *Memory Hold-the-Door*, 283–4.
41 See Law, 'The Romace of Empire', for a further discussion of the interplay of romance, empire, industrialisation and the environment in Buchan's work.
42 Lang, 'Realism and Romance', 691.
43 For Buchan's autobiographical account of his time with Milner, see Buchan, *Memory Hold-the-Door*, 96–125. See also Smith, *John Buchan*, 106–40.
44 Page references to primary works discussed at length will be incorporated into the main body of the text.
45 The theme of the neo-Elizabethan imperialist as a designation of intrepid but cultivated masculinity is one that Buchan returns to elsewhere, notably in his depiction of his friend and fellow South African colonial administrator Basil Blackwood in *Memory Hold-the-Door* (107). It also features later in the *Lodge* in the portrayal of the hunter Considine (see Chapter Four).
46 The legendary figure of Prester John, reportedly a Christian ruler in the midst of a savage region variously located in Asia or Africa, in fact appears more than once in the *Lodge*. Carey, for example, remarks in the first chapter that, 'Here we are in Prester John's country' (38), while later Lady Flora, the niece of a Duchess optimistically suggests, 'Let us visit Prester John and demand tea' (88). The seeds of the novel are thus clearly sown in the earlier text.
47 Arnold, *Held Fast for England*, 100.
48 Bristow, *Empire Boys*, 147.
49 Lewis, 'On Stories', 93.
50 Cited in Fenn, *G. A. Henty*, 62.
51 Frye, *Anatomy of Criticism*, 187.
52 Buchan's interest in environmental contrasts often revolves, as at Musuru, in the land around a country house and, in particular, the point at which the husbanded garden meets the wilds. In an African setting the short story 'The Grove of Ashtaroth' from the collection *The Moon Endureth* (1912) offers an interesting comparison to Musuru in the depiction of the Southern African dwelling of mining magnate Lawson with its 'lawns and rose-gardens' landscaped among 'stark savagery' (Buchan, 'The Grove of Ashtaroth', 102).
53 Donald, *Picturing Animals*, 161.
54 Ibid., 76.
55 Danahay, 'Nature Red in Hoof and Paw', 101.
56 MacKenzie, *The Empire of Nature*, 180.
57 The comparative status of tigers and lions in western symbolic economies is an intriguing, complex and historically long-standing issue. In the imperial context, this feline dichotomy is neatly, and rather curiously, summarised by Ballantyne in an unpublished account of 'The Defence and Relief of Lucknow'. 'All men', he writes, 'are capable of tiger-like ferocity, but only those are capable of what we call lion-like courage, whose spirits have been fostered in an atmosphere of Christianity.'
58 MacKenzie, *The Empire of Nature*, 180.
59 Cited in Donald, *Picturing Animals*, 185.
60 As the first Inspector General of the Indian Forest Service concluded, in MacKenzie's summary: 'No government would dare to conserve such a dangerous animal'

(MacKenzie, *The Empire of Nature*, 182). Relatedly, Sigmund Freud in *Civilisation and its Discontents* contended that civilisation was the condition 'in which wild and dangerous animals have been exterminated' as the absence of animals provides a powerful symbol of human success in a variety of discourses (cited in Malamud, *Reading Zoos*, 4).
61 Pandian, 'Predatory Care', 81.
62 Cited in MacKenzie, *The Empire of Nature*, 11.
63 Alderson, *Pink and Scarlet*, vii.
64 Ballantyne, *The Gorilla Hunters*, 17–18.
65 Buchan, *The Half-Hearted*, 308.
66 Ibid., 317; cited in MacKenzie, *The Empire of Nature*, 195.
67 Baden-Powell, *The Matabele Campaign*, 417.
68 It is worth noting that while the metaphor of the tiger was widely used by the British in its own pro-imperial terms, it has also been much used by insurgents themselves, from the eighteenth-century Indian revolutionary Tipu Sahib, the self-styled 'tiger of Mysore' to the modern Sri Lankan Tamil independence movement the Liberation Tigers of Tamil Eelam (LTTE), commonly known as the Tamil Tigers. Tipu's most significant contribution to the political iconography of the tiger was the life-size model of a British serviceman being consumed by a tiger that was to become, in Maya Jasanoff's words, 'one of the most eye-catching museum pieces of the British Empire', and which fostered British symbolisation of tigers as images of Indian revolutionary activity. See Jasanoff, *Edge of Empire*, 177.
69 Pandian, 'Predatory Care', 79.
70 Pandian cites the establishment of the Imperial Forest Department in 1864 and the 1878 Indian Forest Act and their aim of facilitating what he describes as the 'regulated resource extraction' central to colonial governmentality. For a full account of Britain's exploitation of India's forest resources see Gadgil and Guha, *This Fissured Land*, 122–34.
71 Logan, *Narrating Empire*, 82. Logan's reading of Henty's masculinity is also questioned in Chapter Two in my consideration of *By Sheer Pluck*.
72 Bathurst's self-development also relates to other turn-of-the-century texts concerned with the restoration of honour, following an early misfortune. See particularly Buchan's *The Half-Hearted* (1900) and A. E. W. Mason's *The Four Feathers* (1902).
73 For a more detailed discussion of the commercial uses of elephant anatomy see Beinart and Hughes, *Environment and Empire*, 67.
74 For a detailed and fully theorised account of the role of feathers and other animal products in ladies' fashion from the 1860s see Tolini, '"Beetle Abominations"'.
75 Richards, *Commodity Culture*, 1.
76 Ibid., 3. Shukin, *Animal Capital*, 5.
77 Marx, *Capital*, 163.
78 Ibid., 163–4.
79 Ibid., 165.
80 Alongside stuffing animals on a commission basis to clients who brought their own skins, taxidermists also acquired skins under their own initiative to feed Britain's growing attraction to such ornaments.
81 See MacKenzie, *The Empire of Nature*, 44. Comparably, Haggard's Allan Quartermain begins his eponymous narrative in a vestibule decorated with 'about a hundred pairs' of horns and the guns which shot them (Haggard, *Allan Quartermain*, 11).
82 For a fuller discussion of the long-standing association of hunting and sexual desire, see Chapter Four.

83 Fitzgerald, 'Animal Furniture'.
84 Storey, *Hunting and Shooting in Ceylon*, 109–10.
85 Ibid., 106, 108.
86 Ibid., 110.
87 Fitzgerald, 'Animal Furniture', 273.
88 Ibid., 273.
89 Ibid., 275.
90 Comparable usage of 'clearing' as a euphemism for environmentally destructive activities still occurs today, often with reference to woodland designated for development, the supposition being that organic growth is removed to return land to an appropriate, even, conversely, naturally, 'clear' state on which building may easily commence.
91 Ward's text was first published in 1892 and despite his death in 1912 it has continued, under various editorships, to be a popular volume in the sporting fraternity. Ward is also cited in Fitzgerald, 'Animal Furniture', as a pioneer in animal furniture.
92 Donald, *Picturing Animals*, 280.
93 Buchan, *The Leithen Stories*, 28. See also 'Foutainblue' in *The Watcher in the Threshold*, 228 and *Huntingtower*, 116.
94 MacKenzie, *The Empire of Nature*, 47.
95 Buchan, *The Prince of the Captivity*, 167.
96 Donald, *Picturing Animals*, 180.
97 Wolfe, *Zoontologies*, 105.
98 Contrastingly, the recent revival of the consumption of offal especially in high-end restaurants may be read as a backlash against such a Baudrillardian menu of culinary simulacra.
99 Bilig, 'Commodity Fetishism and Repression', 313.
100 Shukin, *Animal Capital*, 171.

Chapter Two: Scientists and Specimens

1 Baudrillard, *Simulacra and Simulation*, 129–30.
2 Ibid., 137.
3 Akeley, 'Gorillas Real and Mythical', 429.
4 Baudrillard, *Simulacra and Simulation*, 137.
5 For a case study on the relation of museum and church architecture, see Mark Girouard's *Alfred Waterhouse and the Natural History Museum*.
6 Inauthentic taxidermic specimens, on the other hand, were not uncommon during the nineteenth century, most famously in Charles Waterton's 'nondescripts', fantastic animals assembled from parts of several different species.
7 For an account of the diorama's uneasy location between serious science and populist spectacle see Wonders, *Habitat Dioramas*, 10.
8 Haraway, *Primate Visions*, 38–9.
9 Foucault, 'Of Other Spaces', 26.
10 Quinn, *Windows on Nature*, 8.
11 See Baratay and Hardouin-Fugier, *Zoo*, 118.
12 See Rothfels, *Savages and Beasts*, for an account of Hagenbeck's animal transport business.
13 See Baratay and Hardouin-Fugier, *Zoo*, 118.
14 Ritvo, *The Animal Estate*, 211.

15 Ibid., 211.
16 See Baratay and Hardouin-Fugier, *Zoo*, 134.
17 Farber notes that admission to London zoo was originally gained in the early nineteenth century only through the invitation of a Society member. Among the most notable sensations provided by these gardens after access became easier was the arrival of the Society's first hippo in 1850, an event that, as Farber describes, 'drew extensive crowds and captured the imagination of the press' (*Finding Order in Nature*, 95). Yet, despite this populist appeal, menageries remained, in Donald's words, 'symbols of discordant heterogeneity, folly or disorder' (*Picturing Animals*, 167). For a full discussion of the relation between the zoo and the menagerie see Ritvo, *The Animal Estate*, ch. 5.
18 Owen, *On the Extent and Aims*, 115.
19 The general public was first admitted to the gardens in 1847 on Mondays and Tuesdays only at the cost of a shilling. A year later the price was down to sixpence and the restrictions relaxed. The Queen, meanwhile, praised these efforts towards the 'diffusion of intellectual recreation […] among the great masses of the people'. See Scherren, *Popular History of Animals*, 96–7.
20 Baratay and Hardouin-Fugier, *Zoo*, 134.
21 Although Americans William Gregory and Henry Raven were able to secure permission to shoot gorillas in Congo as late as 1937, attitudes to the hunting of large game had been becoming less favourable for some time, led not only by a developing conservationist agenda, but also in response to the carnage of the First World War. Akeley, indeed, confessed to feeling something like a murderer on his specimen collecting expeditions (*In Brightest Africa*, 114).
22 For many naturalists in this period, the only tragedy of extinction inhered in the possibility of a species dying out before specimens had been obtained. As long as exhibits were safely secured, extinction only added glory to the taxidermist's art. As Owen wrote, '[n]o triumph of science has appeared more marvellous to the intelligent mind than the reconstruction of a form of life that has passed away long years ago' (Owen, *On the Extent and Aims*, 67).
23 Owen, *On the Extent and Aims*, 12.
24 Drayton, *Nature's Government*, 171.
25 McCracken, *Gardens of Empire*, 2.
26 Flower, *Essays on Museums*, 175. Ostrich farming in the Cape benefitted by a method of artificially incubating ostrich eggs developed by the British doctor and scientist William Atherstone in the 1860s. See Beinart and Hughes, *Environment and Empire*, 72.
27 Cited in Scherren, *Popular History of Animals*, 13.
28 Farber records that by 1900 Germany boasted 150 natural history collections, Britain and America 250 and France 300, *Finding Order in Nature*, 91.
29 Owen, *On the Extent and Aims*, 126.
30 Cited in Macgillivray, *Lives of Eminent Zoologists*, 264.
31 The development of encyclopaedias in the eighteenth century may be seen as a comparable product of an Enlightenment quest for completeness of knowledge.
32 Ritvo, *The Platypus and the Mermaid*, 51.
33 For a discussion of opposition to Linné's system see Donald, *Picturing Animals*, 32.
34 Koerner, 'Carl Linnaeus', 157. Another Biblical reference of relevance to Linné is the later verse of 1 Kings 4:33, in which Solomon appears as an early natural historian: 'And he spake of trees, from the cedar that is in Lebanon even unto the hyssop that

springeth out of the wall: he spake also of beasts, and of fowl, and of creeping things, and of fishes.'
35 The sentimentalist involved is Miss Twamley whose *The Romance of Nature* is cited in Allen, *The Naturalist in Britain*, 75.
36 Cited in Farber, *Finding Order in Nature*, 13.
37 Foucault, *The Order of Things*, xxi.
38 Ibid., 144.
39 For a discussion of postcolonial/ Foucauldian analyses of power and classification see Loomba, *Colonialism/Postcolonialism*, 61. Another influential account may be found in Mary Louise Pratt's *Imperial Eyes* in which she posits natural history writing in contrast to overtly expansionist imperialism as a form of 'anti-conquest' narrative that nonetheless aims at 'territorial surveillance, appropriation of resources, and administrative control' (39).
40 For a fuller consideration of Raffles' contribution to natural history see Ritvo, 'The Power of the Word', 5.
41 Spurr, *The Rhetoric of Empire*, 163.
42 Conversely, Gary Lease writes 'the plant taxonomies of aboriginal societies are virtually always the same in structure as […] modern scientific ones' (in Soulé (ed.), *Reinventing Nature*, 9).
43 MacKenzie, *The Empire of Nature*, 36.
44 Ritvo, *The Animal Estate*, 205.
45 Cited in Brantlinger, 'Victorians and Africans', 195; see Spivak, 'Can the Subaltern Speak?' for her full delineation of epistemic violence.
46 See Ritvo, *The Platypus and the Mermaid*, 58.
47 Waterton, *Essays on Natural History*, 2.
48 Ritvo, *The Platypus and the Mermaid*, 86.
49 Huxley, 'Darwin on the Origin of Species', 8.
50 Foucault, *The Order of Things*, xx.
51 Gosse, *The Romance of Natural History*, v.
52 Noakes, 'The *BOP*', 153–4.
53 Cited in Dunae, 'Penny Dreadfuls',139.
54 For a full discussion of the relation of the *BOP* to the numerous other boys' magazines established from the 1850s on, see Drotner, *English Children*.
55 Cited in Noakes, 'The *BOP*', 154.
56 *Times*, Friday, 5 May 1899.
57 Salmon, *Juvenile Literature As It Is*, 185–6.
58 Ballantyne had initially hoped to found a magazine to be titled *Ballantyne's Magazine* to fill the purpose later taken up by the *BOP*, but he was unable to gain the support of a publisher.
59 Huxley, *Lay Sermons*, 102–3.
60 Gladstone, *Teaching of Natural History*.
61 Baden-Powell, *Scouting for Boys*, 118.
62 Ibid., 104.
63 Wood, *Boy's Own Natural History*, iv.
64 Wood, 'On Killing, Setting and Preserving Insects', 431.
65 Wood, *The Illustrated Natural History*, 46.
66 Ibid., 149.
67 Buchan, *Great Hours in Sport*, 279, 287.

68 Schell, 'Tiger Tales', 231.
69 Anon., *Some Remarks on Cruelty to Animals*, 73.
70 Cited in Ritvo, *The Animal Estate*, 135.
71 Ibid., 132. See also Armstrong, '*Moby-Dick* and Compassion', 29.
72 Salmon, *Juvenile Literature As It Is*, 35.
73 Stables' remarks on 'break-jaw Latin' and its unwanted reminder of the schoolroom are cited in Noakes, 'The *BOP*', 160.
74 Salmon, *Juvenile Literature As It Is*, 55.
75 Dunae, 'Boys' Literature and the Idea of Empire', 108. See also Bristow, *Empire Boys*, 47. An interesting counterpart to these debates on the interaction of higher and lower forms of literature in the context of boy's own literature can be found in Frye's analysis of romance. Frye writes that any 'serious discussion of romance has to take into account its curiously proletarian status as a form generally disapproved of, in most ages, by the guardians of taste and learning, except when they use it for their own purposes' (Frye, *The Secular Scripture*, 23).
76 For an account of Henty's involvement in various boy's own type publications, see Arnold, *Held Fast for England*, 11.
77 *Academy* 550, 18 November 1882, 361.
78 See Fenn, *G. A. Henty*, 2–3 for an account of Henty's 'leanings towards natural history'.
79 For a full discussion of the relation of Henty to Victorian self-improvement narratives and in particular the work of Samuel Smiles, see Richards, 'Spreading the Gospel of Self-Help'.
80 See Allen, *The Naturalist in Britain*, 170 for a discussion of the role of field clubs in the UK.
81 Rudler, *On Natural History Museums*, 6.
82 Leighton and Surridge, 'The Empire Bites Back', 249. See also Kipling's 'The Undertakers' from *The Jungle Books* and its crocodile anti-hero, the 'blunt-nosed Mugger of Mugger-Ghaut […] the demon of the ford […] murderer, man-eater and local fetish' (237).
83 For an account of the use of images of animal suffering in the animal welfare movement see Ritvo, *The Animal Estate*, 141–2.
84 As Leighton and Surridge write, 'The image of animals in the Victorian period was deeply fissured along the axis of violence. Certain animals, such as cats and dogs, even though they had teeth and claws that could scratch and bite, were designated as symbols of peace and companionship. Other animals, especially apes and tigers, were assigned to a more primitive and violent past and were thus ascribed to a space against which the domestic, both on the level of the home and the nation, could be defined' (Leighton and Surridge, 'The Empire Bites Back', 104).
85 Henty's enthusiasm that boys should have no qualms about violence is supported by Fenn who comments in his biography of his friend that 'He had a horror of a lad who displayed any weak emotion and shrank from shedding blood, or winced at any encounter' (Fenn, *G. A. Henty*, 334).
86 Bristow, *Empire Boys*, 47.
87 In common with the majority of hunting narratives, both Henty and Fenn's texts contain lengthy asides on ballistic technology and detailed descriptions of the young adventurers' first efforts with their weapons. See *By Sheer Pluck*, 109 and ch. 8 of *Nat the Naturalist*.

88 Wallace, *The Malay Archipelago*, 460.
89 Ibid., 460.
90 Ballantyne, *The Fugitives*, 179. An interesting comparison with Moses antipathy to science can be found in Ballantyne's 1887 tale of Madagascar *The Fugitives*, in which the stock African Ebony rather surprisingly emerges as a natural history enthusiast. For a fuller consideration of science and scientists in *Blown to Bits* see Miller, 'Adventures in the Volcano's Throat'.
91 Cited in MacKenzie, *The Empire of Nature*, 40.
92 A contrast to this stereotyped racial incompetence in preserving natural history specimens can be found in Darwin's *Autobiography* in which he describes his relationship with John Edmonstone, a 'negro [living] in Edinburgh, who had traveled with Waterton and gained his livelihood by stuffing birds, which he did excellently; he gave me lessons for payment, and I used often to sit with him, for he was a very pleasant and intelligent man' (51).
93 Perhaps unsurprisingly neither Henty nor Fenn shows any serious interest in any deeper signification of animals within African or Indonesian cultures. The disapprobation of sartorial usages of animals may also reflect a generic dislike of the feminine most famous in Haggard's boast in *King Solomon's Mines* that 'there is not a *petticoat* in the whole history' (42).
94 See Haggard, *King Solomon's Mines*, ch. 11.
95 Chrisman, *Rereading the Imperial Romance*, 6. For a further discussion of the technologies involved in natural history, see Pratt, *Imperial Eyes*, 29.
96 Pratt, *Imperial Eyes*, 33.
97 MacKenzie, *The Empire of Nature*, 36.

Chapter Three: The Animal Within

1 Haraway, *Primate Visions*, 10.
2 Fudge, *Animal*, 129; Haraway, *Primate Visions*, 11.
3 Cited in Lippit, 'Magnetic Animal', 1112.
4 Cited in Rupke, *Richard Owen*, 270.
5 Cited in Janson, *Ape and Ape Lore*, 13.
6 Darwin, *The Descent of Man*, 405. Although he was later to lose his faith, Darwin was diligent in framing his research with the religious tradition of which he was a part. By his choice of epigraphs to the *Origin*, Darwin immediately includes a divine presence in a scientific schema that has continued to the present day to attract allegations of Godlessness. Quoting W. Whewell's judgement that 'events are brought about not by insulated interpositions of Divine power, exerted in each particular case, but by the establishment of general laws', Darwin sought to reorientate rather than remove theism from the creation of species and in the final pages of his work offered the theologically resonant conclusion that 'all the organic beings which have ever lived on this earth have descended from some one primordial form, into which life was at first breathed' (*Origin*, 455). For an account of Darwin's spiritual 'evolution' see his *Autobiography*, (85–93).
7 Cited in Jensen, *Thomas Henry Huxley*, 72. Reports vary as to the precise details of the exchange. Jensen provides several alternative contemporary versions of Wilberforce's attack.
8 Owen, *Classification and Geographical Distribution*, 103.

9 For a detailed consideration of the symbolic significance of apes in the Middle Ages and the Renaissance, see Janson, *Ape and Ape Lore*.
10 Haraway, *Primate Visions*, 11.
11 The importance of the hippocampus in comparative anatomy provided the novelist Charles Kingsley with an irresistible opportunity for satire. As he wrote in his 1863 children's tale *The Water Babies*, 'You may think that there are other more important differences between you and an ape, such as being able to speak, and make machines, and know right from wrong, and say your prayers, and other little matters of that kind. But that is a child's fancy, my dear. Nothing is to be depended on but the great hippopotamus test' (Kingsley, *Water Babies*, 109).
12 Owen, *Classification and Geographical Distribution*, 103. Owen had in fact offered the same conclusion to his 1848 'Osteological Contribution to the Natural History of the Chimpanzee' as his work demonstrated trenchant consistency. He explains his antipathy to Darwin's theory most fully in an essay in the *Edinburgh Review*, April 1860, 487–532.
13 Cited in Rupke, *Richard Owen*, 273.
14 *Edinburgh Review*, April 1863, 548.
15 Huxley, *Man's Place in Nature*, 153.
16 It is worth noting, however, that scientific apprehensions of the anatomical intimacy of humans and apes were well-established by the Victorian era, with Linnaeus commenting that he hardly knew 'a single distinguishing mark which separates man from the apes, save for the fact that the latter have an empty space between their canines and their other teeth'. Cited in Agamben, *Open*, 24.
17 Rupke, *Richard Owen*, 314.
18 Only three articles to date are devoted solely to the controversy: Bucher, 'Canonization by Repetition', Mandelstom, 'Du Chaillu's Stuffed Gorillas' and McCook, '"It May be Truth"'. A number of longer works provide brief summaries of the events. See particularly Browne, *Darwin* and Rupke, *Richard Owen*.
19 *Times*, 3 March 1861.
20 Cited in Rupke, *Richard Owen*, 316.
21 Unpublished letter from du Chaillu to Owen, 21 December 1860 in the library of the Natural History Museum, London.
22 Cited in Mandelstam, 'Du Chaillu's Stuffed Gorillas', 231.
23 *Proceedings of the Royal Geographical Society*, 25 February 1861, 111.
24 *Times*, 28 May 1861, 12.
25 Buckland, 'The Naturalist', *Field*, 2 March 1861, 179.
26 *Field*, 3 August 1861, 101.
27 Savage and Wyman, 'Trodlydytes Gorilla', 420.
28 For a detailed account of the early gorilla from Hanno to Savage and Wyman see Yerkes and Yerkes, *The Great Apes*. A more creative take on early rumours of large anthropoid apes in Africa can be found in Kipling's story 'The Knights of the Joyous Venture' (*Puck of Pook's Hill*, 45–61).
29 See Agamben, *The Open*, 25–6 for a discussion of the place of Tyson's work in natural history.
30 Waterton, *Essays on Natural History*, 14.
31 Ibid., 40.
32 Unpublished letter Waterton to Ord, 29 April 1861, Glasgow University Library.
33 For a discussion of the rather gruesome unpacking of Owen's first gorilla specimen, see Gott '"It's Lovely to be a Gorilla"', 207–8.

34 Buckland, 'The Naturalist', *Field*, 2 March 1861, 179.
35 Lamont, 'The Gorilla Controversy', 4.
36 Browne, *Darwin*, 157.
37 Bhabha, *The Location of Culture*, 81.
38 Derrida, 'The Animal That Therefore I Am', 372.
39 Ibid., 381.
40 Simmons and Armstrong, *Knowing Animals*, 37.
41 McCook, '"It May be Truth"', 186.
42 Gray, 'M. du Chaillu's African Discoveries', 10.
43 Gray, 'The New Traveller's Tales', 663; *Field*, 11 May 1861.
44 Gray, 'The New Traveller's Tales', 662.
45 *Morning Advertiser*, 23 May 1861, 4.
46 Ibid., 4.
47 See Zgórniak. Kapera and Singer, 'Fremiet's Gorillas', 226 for an account of gorilla specimens in the French natural historical establishment. For a contemporary Victorian account of gorillas in France, see also Owen, *Memoir on the Gorilla*, 4–5.
48 Gray, 'M. du Chaillu's African Discoveries', 10.
49 Murray, 'The Gorilla War', 20.
50 Spurgeon, 'The Gorilla', 4.
51 *Morning Advertiser*, 1 June 1861, 3.
52 See Vaucaire, *Paul du Chaillu*, 127–30 for a discussion of Kneeland's supposed involvement.
53 Gray, 'Dr Gray of the British Museum', 3.
54 Ord to Waterton, 21 July 1861, unpublished letter, Library of American Philosophical Society, Philadelphia.
55 Cited in McCook, '"It May be Truth"', 190.
56 Gray, 'The Gorilla', *Athenaeum*, 21 September 1861, 373–4.
57 *Athenaeum*, 8 June 1861, 766.
58 *Morning Advertiser*, 25 May 1861.
59 Waterton to Ord, 14 September 1861, unpublished letter, University of Glasgow library.
60 Gray, 'The Gorilla', *Athenaeum*, 21 September 1861, 373.
61 Ibid., 373.
62 Gray, 'Zoological Notes', 64–5.
63 *Gardener's Chronicle*, 22 June 1861. For a discussion of the relation of the gorilla controversy to Museum politics see Rupke, *Richard Owen*, 319.
64 *Morning Advertiser*, 16 June 1861; *Athenaeum*, 14 December 1861, 807. Numerous volumes of tall tales purportedly from the German Baron Karl Friedrich von Münchhausen appeared in the eighteenth and nineteenth centuries, most notably those by Erich Raspe.
65 Darwin to Tegetmeier, 28 May 1861, http://www.darwinproject.ac.uk/darwinletters/calendar/entry-3164.html (accessed 3 August 2012).
66 Huxley, *Man's Place in Nature*, 36.
67 Ibid., 71–2.
68 McCook, '"It May be Truth"', 179.
69 *Morning Advertiser*, 29 May 1861.
70 Cited in Buckland, 'The Naturalist', *Field*, 27 April 1861, 357.
71 *Gardener's Chronicle*, 8 June 1861, 528.
72 Gray, 'The Gorilla', *Athenaeum*, 12 October 1861, 479.
73 *Morning Advertiser*, 16 June 1861, 5.

74 Du Chaillu, 'The New Traveller's Tales', 694.
75 *Morning Advertiser*, 3 July 1861, 4.
76 Haggard, *The Holy Flower*, 143; Kafka, 'A Report to an Academy', 128.
77 Ord to Waterton, 21 July 1861, unpublished letter, American Philosophical Society Library, Philadelphia.
78 An interesting comparison to the incident at the Ethnological Society, and further evidence of imperial salivary anxiety can be found in John Buchan's *The Three Hostages* (1924) in which Richard Hannay after his enemy Medina spits in his face describes the act as a 'filthy Kaffir trick', 106.
79 'The Latest from Africa', *Punch*, 13 July 1861, 19.
80 Ord to Waterton, 20 October 1861, unpublished letter, American Philosophical Society library, Philadelphia. A 'mustee' in Victorian racial models was someone one-eighth of black African descent.
81 See Clodd, *Memories*, 71 and Bucher, 'Canonization by Repetition', 16–17.
82 Du Chaillu while delivering a lecture at Wakefield had sought an audience with the distinguished Yorkshire naturalist only to be turned away brusquely from the door.
83 Clodd, *Memories*, 72.
84 Wallace, 'Monkeys', 441.
85 Reade, *Savage Africa*, preface.
86 Ibid., 212.
87 Ibid., 197.
88 Ibid., 226.
89 Ibid., 587.
90 Du Chaillu, *Journey to Ashongoland*, v.
91 Ibid., vi.
92 Ibid., ix.
93 Ibid., 356.
94 Du Chaillu, *Stories of the Gorilla Country*, 1.
95 Du Chaillu, *Wild Life Under the Equator*, 53, 54.
96 Du Chaillu, *Stories of the Gorilla Country*, 1.
97 Ibid., 259.
98 Du Chaillu, *Wild Life Under the Equator*, 192.
99 Akeley, *In Brightest Africa*, 239.
100 Waterton, Letter to the *Gardener's Chronicle*, 8 June 1861, 552.
101 *Gardener's Chronicle*, 29 June 1861, 602.
102 Reade, 'Notes on the Derbyan Eland', 172.
103 Owen, *Classification and Geographical Distribution*, 89.
104 *London Illustrated News* 34 (1859), 348.
105 Owen, *Classification and Geographical Distribution*, 89.
106 Cited in Owen, *The Life of Richard Owen*, 116.
107 Waterton, Letter to the *Gardener's Chronicle*. 30 March 1861, 288. Diana Donald records an orang-utan of comparable tendencies at the early nineteenth-century menagerie at Exeter 'Change in London, in the 'habit of kissing those who gave it fruit' (Donald, *Picturing Animals*, 171).
108 *Morning Advertiser*, 17 December 1861, 3.
109 See Young, *The Idea of English Ethnicity*, 11–40 for a discussion of the significance of 'Saxon' as a marker of an ostensibly stable English ethnicity.
110 Norquay, *R. L. Stevenson on Fiction*, 154.

111 Ballantyne, *Coral Island*, 12.
112 Agamben, *Open*, 26.
113 Spurr, *The Rhetoric of Empire*, 95.
114 Du Chaillu's unsuccessful attempts to partially civilise primates, for example, may be read in the *Explorations*, ch. 8.
115 See particularly 'Mowgli's Brothers' and 'Kaa's Hunting'. As the panther Bagheera remarks of Mowgli in the latter story, 'above all he has the eyes that make the Jungle-People afraid'. Kipling, *Jungle Books*, 63.
116 Mill, *Three Essays*, 48.
117 Darwin, *The Descent of Man*, 53.
118 Cited in Huxley, *Man's Place in Nature*, 61.
119 Swift in *Gulliver's Travels* offers a similar paradigm of the relation of hygiene to questions of species and moral priority in his depiction of the Yahoos whose sanitary degeneracy emerges perhaps most powerfully in their medical cure-all of forcing a 'mixture of dung and urine' down the sufferer's throat (309). As Freud summarises in *Civilisation and its Discontents*: 'the use of soap' might be 'an actual yardstick of civilisation' (30).
120 Spurr, *The Rhetoric of Empire*, 81.
121 Kristeva, *Powers of Horror*, 4.
122 Ibid., 13.
123 Ferguson, 'Footnotes on *Trilby*', 127.
124 Huxley, 'Professor Huxley on Man's Place in Nature', 127.
125 Owen, *Classification and Geographical Distribution*, 94.
126 Relatedly, as Simmons and Armstrong comment, 'Bipedality – walking, running, standing on two legs is often casually cited as the prime evolutionary adaptation that distinguishes the human from other animals' (Simmons and Armstrong, *Knowing Animals*, 6).
127 *Punch*, 18 May 1861, 206.
128 Spurgeon, 'The Gorilla', 2.
129 Bivona, 'Human Thighs', 84.
130 Darwin to Asa Gray, 11 December 1861, http://www.darwinproject.ac.uk/darwinletters/calendar/entry-3342.html (accessed 27 December 2008).
131 For a full account of the homoerotic in *Blown to Bits* see Miller, 'Adventures in the Volcano's Throat'.
132 For more detailed discussions of the role of language in questions of species identity see Agamben, *Open*, 33–5 and Fudge, *Animal*, 117–28.
133 Halliday, *The Great Stink of London*, 21.
134 Kingsley, *Water Babies*, 19, 23, 36.
135 Ibid., 246.
136 Spurgeon, 'The Gorilla', 8.
137 Waterton to Ord, 14 September 1861.
138 Cited in Fudge, *Animal*, 7–8.

Chapter Four: Wild Men and Wilderness

1 London, *People of the Abyss*, 283–4.
2 Ibid., 284–5.
3 Johns, 'The Literature of the Streets', 64.
4 Cited in Pick, *Faces of Degeneration*, 217.
5 MacDonald, *The Princess and Curdie*, 220.
6 Nordau, *Degeneration*, 16.

7 Booth, *In Darkest England*, 11–12. A similar metaphor is deployed by Buchan in his 1924 *The Three Hostages* when Richard Hannay cautions: 'London is like the tropical bush – if you don't exercise constant care the jungle, in the shape of the slums, will break in' (77).
8 Booth, *In Darkest England*, 12. Another significant deployment of apes as an image of racial deterioration occurs in the representation of the Irish. Reporting on a visit to Ireland Kingsley wrote with familiar horror, 'I am haunted by the human chimpanzees I saw along that hundred miles of horrible country.' '[T]o see white chimpanzees is dreadful' (cited in Loomba, *Colonialism/Postcolonialism*, 109).
9 For a consideration of the effects of urbanisation on Britain's military see Baden-Powell, *Scouting for Boys*, 184.
10 Booth, *In Darkest England*, 45.
11 Ibid., 63.
12 An eloquent example of the potential consequences of London's ongoing sanitary problems can be found in Richard Jeffries' 1885 novel *After London* in which the now submerged city transforms the water above it into a potentially lethal poison.
13 Wills, 'Recreating Evening Schools', 112.
14 Johns, 'The Literature of the Streets', 65.
15 Masterman, *The Heart of Empire*, 8.
16 Cited in Sutcliffe, *Metropolis*, 12. See also for a later representation of this theme Lewis Mumford's 1938 description of the diseased giant cities of the USA: 'ravaged landscapes, disorderly urban districts, pockets of disease, patches of blight, mile upon mile of standardized slums, worming into the outlying areas of big cities, and fusing with their ineffectual suburbs. In short: a general miscarriage and defeat of civilized effort' (Mumford, *The Culture of Cities*, 8).
17 Baden-Powell, *Scouting for Boys*, 184.
18 Gissing, *The Whirlpool*, 14.
19 Kingsley, *Water Babies*, 175–6.
20 Low, *White Skins, Black Masks*, 30.
21 Ibid., 16.
22 Booth, *In Darkest England*, 93.
23 Mangan and McKenzie, 'Radical Conservatives', 185.
24 Baden-Powell, *Pig-Sticking*, 30.
25 Baldwin, *African Hunting*, 3.
26 Buchan, 'The Grove of Ashtaroth', 99.
27 Shakespear, *The Wild Sports of India*, 2.
28 Ballantyne, 'Hunting the Lions', 120–21.
29 Ibid., 38–9.
30 London, *People of the Abyss*, 316.
31 Garrard, *Ecocriticism*, 108.
32 See also Buchan, *The African Colony*, 91.
33 Garrard, *Ecocriticism*, 112.
34 Baldwin, *African Hunting*, 58.
35 Ballantyne, 'Hunting the Lions', 42.
36 Stigand and Lyell, *Central African Game*, 4. For a comparable discussion of the involvement of a degenerationist discourse with Victorian debates on footwear, see Christine Ferguson's article on literary foot fetishism. Ferguson concludes that, 'Bare feet, typically viewed as a sign of a subordinate class or racial status, might in fact encourage the physical regeneration of the nation' (Ferguson, 'Footnotes on *Trilby*', 131).

37 Haggard, *King Solomon's Mines*, 42.
38 Ibid., 78–9.
39 Haggard, *Allan Quartermain*, 12, 14.
40 Ibid., 15. An earlier version of this passage occurs in Haggard's first published work, the article 'A Zulu War-Dance' which appeared in the *Gentleman's Magazine* in 1877. Here Haggard writes of a journey into Natal, 'It was like coming face to face with great primeval Nature, not Nature as we civilised people know her, smiling in corn-fields, waving in well-ordered woods, but Nature as she was on the morrow of the Creation.' See appendix B3 of Haggard, *King Solomon's Mines*, 260.
41 Garrard, *Ecocriticism*, 120. See also Val Plumwood's *Environmental Culture* in which she asserts that in 'the colonising, racial supremacist version, it is inferior and "barbarian" others who are closer to nature, an earlier and more primitive stage of our own rational civilisation' (21).
42 Perhaps Haggard's most famous vision of cross-cultural disguise appears in the doubling of Sir Henry Curtis and the Zulu warrior Umbopa from *King Solomon's Mines* in which the two men's matching physiques convey a comparably vigorous masculine energy. Curtis' apparent descent from Vikings provides Haggard with the racial lineage behind this comparison and illustrates a fixation with the Norseman as a white savage that recurs in Haggard's work, most notably in his Viking saga *Eric Brighteyes* (1891).
43 Chrisman, *Rereading the Imperial Romance*, 102. A different reading of Haggard's relation to Zulu history is offered by Monsman who described *Nada the Lily* in the title of a 2004 article as 'A Triumph of Translation' while condemning 'overly-determined readings derived from programmatically selective citations' often dismissive of Haggard's novel (Monsman, '*Nada the Lily*: A Triumph of Translation', 374).
44 Haggard, *King Solomon's Mines*, chs 4 and 5.
45 For a discussion of homoeroticism in Buchan's *Prester John* see Craig Smith, 'Every Man Kills the Thing He Loves'; for a consideration of Haggard and the homoerotic see Low, *White Skins, Black Masks*, 53–5, 61.
46 Chrisman, *Rereading the Imperial Romance*, 12. For a detailed discussion of the specific function of Zulus in the British colonial imagination see ibid., 75–99.
47 Monsman, '*Nada the Lily*: A Triumph of Translation', 378.
48 Intriguing examples of Haggard's interest in the paranormal may be found in his two gorilla novels, *The Holy Flower* (1915) and *Heu-Heu* (1923) where telepathy, prophecy and the most supernatural of apes depict an Africa resolutely opposed to Western rationality.
49 Haggard, *King Solomon's Mines*, appendix B3, 266.
50 Haggard, *King Solomon's Mines*, 74.
51 Ibid., 75.
52 MacKenzie, *The Empire of Nature*, 149.
53 Haggard, *Allan Quartermain*, 14.
54 Buchan (ed.), *Great Hours in Sport*, 113.
55 The Animal Studies Group, *Killing Animals*, 24.
56 Scruton, *On Hunting*, 73–4.
57 Cartmill, *A View to a Death*, 157.
58 Ham and Senior (eds), *Animal Acts*, 158.
59 Stigand and Lyell, *Central African Game*, 4.
60 Storey, *Hunting and Shooting in Ceylon*, 210.

61 Foucault, 'Interview With Michel Foucault', 241.
62 Frye, *The Secular Scripture*, 104.
63 For further eco-feminist readings of hunting see Andree Collard and Joyce Contrucci *The Rape of the Wild* and Marti Kheel 'License to Kill: An EcoFeminist Critique of Hunter's Discourse' in Adams and Donovan (eds) *Animals and Women*.
64 Dworkin, *Pornography*, 25.
65 Ibid., 26.
66 Luke, 'Violent Love', 640.
67 Dworkin, *Pornography*, 27–8.
68 Ibid., 29.
69 Ibid., 16.
70 Ibid., 223.
71 Ibid.
72 MacKenzie, *The Empire of Nature*, 42–3.
73 *Titus Andronicus*, 3.1.89–91.
74 Indeed, 'The Beaver Hunters' is in some ways quite explicitly linked to the colonial culture of big-game hunting. Its title reprises such popular Victorian narratives as Ballantyne's *The Gorilla Hunters* or *The Walrus Hunters* and Mayne Reid's *The Giraffe Hunters* or *The Wild Horse Hunters* and the crude suggestiveness of stuffing and mounting the trophy evidently recalls the developing popularity of taxidermy.
75 Plumwood, *Feminism and the Mastery of Nature*, 5.
76 Ballantyne, 'Hunting the Lions', 15.
77 Haggard, *King Solomon's Mines*, 40.
78 Cumming, *Five Years of a Hunter's Life*, x.
79 Ritvo, *The Animal Estate*, 265.
80 Kirby, *In Haunts of Wild Game*, 261.
81 Ibid., 34.
82 Ibid., 39.
83 Ballantyne, 'Hunting the Lions', 64.
84 Shakespear, *The Wild Sports of India*, 62.
85 Kirby, *In Haunts of Wild Game*, 166.
86 Storey, *A Ceylonese Sportsman's Diary*, 13.
87 Cited in Fudge, *Animal*, 77.
88 Collard and Contrucci, *The Rape of the Wild*, 46.
89 Dworkin, *Pornography*, 148.
90 Spurr, *The Rhetoric of Empire*, 11.
91 Frye, *The Secular Scripture*, 105.
92 The idea of an Actaeon complex was initially suggested, though only briefly developed, by Jean-Paul Sartre in *Being and Nothingness* (1943). Sartre's complex forms part of an intricate exploration of sexuality, the alimentary, assimilation and knowledge and also involves the conceptualisation of a 'Jonah complex' to evoke the 'dream of a non-destructive assimilation' (579).

Conclusion

1 Plumwood, *Feminism and the Mastery of Nature*, 102, 101.
2 Ibid., 154–5.
3 Ibid., 157.

4 Noske, *Beyond Boundaries*, xii.
5 Lawlor, 'Animals Have No Hand', 44.
6 Plumwood, *Feminism and the Mastery of Nature*, 155.
7 Derrida, 'The Animal That Therefore I Am', 405.
8 Ibid., 374.
9 Armstrong, *What Animals Mean*, 3.

BIBLIOGRAPHY

Academy. 'Gift-Books'. No. 550. 18 November 1882, 360–61.
Adams, Carol J. *The Sexual Politics of Meat: A Feminist Vegetarian Critical Theory*. London and New York: Continuum, 2000.
Adams, Carol J. and Josephine Donovan. *Animals and Women: Feminist Theoretical Explorations*. Durham, NC and London: Duke University Press, 1995.
Adams, William M. 'Nature and the Colonial Mind'. In *Decolonizing Nature: Strategies for Conservation in a Post-Colonial Era*, ed. William M. Adams and Martin Mulligan, 16–50. London: Earthscan, 2003.
_____. *Against Extinction: The Story of Conservation*. London: Earthscan, 2005.
Agamben, Giorgio. *The Open: Man and Animal*. Stanford: Stanford University Press, 2004.
Ahuja, Neel. 'Postcolonial Critique in a Multispecies World'. *PMLA* 124, no. 2 (March 2009): 556–63.
Akeley, Carl. 'Gorillas Real and Mythical'. *Natural History* 23, no. 5 (September/October 1923): 429–47.
_____. *In Brightest Africa*. London: Heinemann, 1924.
Akeley, Carl and L. J. Mary. *Lions, Gorillas and their Neighbours*. London: Stanley, Paul and Co., 1933.
Alderson, E. A. H. *Pink and Scarlet or Hunting as a School for Soldiering*. London: Heinemann, 1900.
Allen, David Elliston. *The Naturalist in Britain: A Social History*. London: Allen Lane, 1976.
Anderson, David and Richard Grove (eds). *Conservation in Africa: People, Policies and Practice*. Cambridge: Cambridge University Press, 1987.
Anderson, J. K. *Hunting in the Ancient World*. Berkeley: University of California Press, 1985.
Animal Studies Group. *Killing Animals*. Urbana and Chicago: University of Illinois Press, 2006.
Anon. *Some Remarks on Cruelty to Animals*. London: S. Low and Son, 1865.
Anthropological Review. 'Savage Africa'. Vol. 2, no. 2 (May 1864): 123–6.
Armstrong, Phillip. 'The Postcolonial Animal'. *Society and Animals* 10, no. 4 (2002): 413–19.
_____. '*Moby-Dick* and Compassion'. *Society and Animals* 12, no. 1 (2004): 19–38
_____. '"Leviathan is a Skein of Networks": Translations of Nature and Culture in *Moby-Dick*'. *English Literary History* (Winter 2004): 1039–63.
_____. 'What Animals Mean in *Moby-Dick*, For Example'. *Textual Practice* 19, no. 1 (2005): 93–111.
_____. *What Animals Mean in the Fiction of Modernity*. London and New York, Routledge, 2008.
Arnold, Guy. *Held Fast for England*. London: Hamish Hamilton, 1980.

Ashcroft, Bill, Garth Griffiths and Helen Tiffin. *The Empire Writes Back*, 2nd ed. London: Routledge, 2003.
Athenaeum. Review Article of du Chaillu's *Explorations*. 11 May 1861, 621–3.
———. 'The New Traveller's Tales'. 8 June 1861, 766.
———. 'M. Du Chaillu's Adventures'. 14 December 1861, 807
Baden-Powell, Robert. *The Matabele Campaign*. London: Methuen, 1896.
———. *Sport in War*. London: Heinemann, 1900.
———. *Pig-Sticking or Hog-Hunting*. London: Herbert Jenkins, 1924.
———. *Scouting for Boys*. Oxford: Oxford University Press, 2004 [1910].
Baker, Steve. *Picturing the Beast: Animals, Identity and Representation*. Manchester: Manchester University Press, 1993.
———. *The Postmodern Animal*. London: Reaktion, 2000.
Baldwin, W. C. *African Hunting: From Natal to the Zambesi*. London: John Bentley, 1863.
Ballantyne, R. M. *Red Eric*. London: Nelson, 1861.
———. *Gascoyne: The Sandalwood Trader*. London: Chambers, 1864.
———. *Lost in the Forest*. London: Nisbet and Co., 1869.
———. *Black Ivory*. London: Nisbet and Co., 1873.
———. *The Settler and the Savage*. London: Nisbet and Co., 1877.
———. *The Gorilla Hunters*. London: Nelson, 1878 [1861].
———. *Six Months at the Cape*. London: Nisbet and Co., 1879.
———. 'Hunting the Lions'. *Tales of Adventure: Wild Work in Strange Places*. London: Nisbet and Co., 1886 [1869].
———. *Blown to Bits*. London: Nisbet and Co., 1889 [1885].
———. *Personal Reminiscences*. London: Nisbet and Co., 1893.
———. *The Fugitives*. London: Nisbet and Co., 1899 [1887].
———. *The Coral Island*. London: Penguin, 1995 [1857].
———. 'The Defence and Relief of Lucknow'. Unpublished manuscript, Beinecke Manuscript Library, University of Yale (1859).
Baratay, Eric and Elisabeth Hardouin-Fugier. *Zoo: A History of Zoological Gardens in the West*. London: Reaktion, 1998.
Baudrillard, Jean. *Simulacra and Simulation*, trans. Sheila Faria Glazer. Ann Arbor: University of Michigan Press, 1994.
Beer, Gillian. *Darwin's Plots: Evolutionary Narratives in Darwin, George Eliot and Nineteenth-Century Fiction*. Cambridge: Cambridge University Press, 2000 [1983].
Beinart, William. 'Empire, Hunting and Ecological Change in Southern and Central Africa'. *Past and Present* 128 (August 1990): 162–86.
Beinart, William and Peter Coates. *Environment and History: The Taming of Nature in the USA and South Africa*. London and New York: Routledge, 1995.
Beinart, William and Lotte Hughes. *Environment and Empire*. Oxford: Oxford University Press, 2007.
Bennett, Tony. *The Birth of the Museum: History, Theory, Politics*. London: Routledge, 1995.
Beresford Ellis, Peter. *H. Rider Haggard: A Voice from the Infinite*. London: Routledge, 1978.
Berger, John. *About Looking*. London: Writers and Readers Publishing Cooperation, 1980.
Bernstein, Susan D. 'Ape Anxiety: Sensation Fiction, Evolution and the Genre Question'. *Victorian Culture* 39, no. 4 (2006): 383–97.
Berry Edward. *Shakespeare and the Hunt: A Cultural and Social Study*. Cambridge: Cambridge University Press, 2001.
Bhabha, Homi. *The Location of Culture*. London: Routledge, 1994.

Bilig, Michael. 'Commodity Fetishism and Repression'. *Theory and Psychology* 9, no. 3 (1999): 313–29.
Bishop, Rebecca. 'Journeys to the Urban Exotic: Embodiment and the Zoo-Going Gaze'. *Humanities Research* 11, no. 1 (2004): 106–24.
Bisset, Major-General. *Sport and War, or Recollections of Fighting and Hunting in South Africa from the Years 1834–1867*. London: John Murray, 1875.
Bivona, Daniel. *Desire and Contradiction: Imperial Visions and Domestic Debates in Victorian Literature*. Manchester: Manchester University Press, 1990.
_____. *British Imperial Literature 1870–1940: Writing and the Administration of Empire*. Cambridge: Cambridge University Press, 1998.
_____. 'Human Thighs and Susceptible Apes: Self-Implicating Category Confusion in Victorian Discourse on West Africa'. *Nineteenth Century Prose* 32, no. 2 (Fall 2005): 81–107.
Booth, William. *In Darkest England and the Way Out*. London: Salvation Army, 1890.
Bradley, Mary Hastings. *On the Gorilla Trail*. London and New York: D. Appleton and Co., 1922.
Brantlinger, Patrick. 'Victorians and Africans: The Genealogy of the Myth of the Dark Continent'. In *'Race', Writing and Difference*, ed. Henry Louis Gates Jr, 185–222. Chicago: University of Chicago Press, 1985.
_____. *Rule of Darkness: British Literature and Imperialism, 1830–1914*. Ithaca, NY: Cornell University Press, 1988.
Bristow, Joseph. *Empire Boys: Adventures in a Man's World*. London: HarperCollins, 1991.
Brown, Charles S. and Ted Toadvine. *Eco-Phenomenology: Back to the Earth Itself*. New York: State University of New York Press, 2003.
Browne, Janet. *Darwin: The Power of Place*. London: Jonathan Cape, 2002.
_____. *Darwin's Origin of Species: A Biography*. London: Atlantic Books, 2006.
Browne, Montagu. *Artistic and Scientific Taxidermy and Modelling*. London: Adam and Charles Black, 1896.
Buchan, John. *The African Colony*. Edinburgh and London: Blackwood and Sons, 1903.
_____ (ed.) *Great Hours in Sport*. London: Nelson, 1921.
_____. *The Half-Hearted*. London: Nelson, 1922 [1900].
_____. *A Lodge in the Wilderness*. London: Nelson, 1922 [1906].
_____. *The Watcher in the Threshold*. London: Nelson, 1931 [1902].
_____. *Comments and Characters*. London: Nelson, 1940.
_____. *The Long Traverse*. London: Hodder and Staughton, 1941.
_____. *The Prince of the Captivity*. London: Nelson, 1947 [1933].
_____. *The Runagates Club*. London: Nelson, 1952 [1928].
_____. *Memory Hold-the-Door*. London: Hodder and Staughton, 1952 [1940].
_____. 'The Grove of Ashtaroth'. *The Best Short Stories: Volume 1*, 99–126. London: Grafton, 1980 [1910].
_____. *The Three Hostages*. London: Penguin, 1981 [1924].
_____. *Witch Wood*. Oxford: Oxford University Press, 1990 [1927].
_____. *John MacNab*. Oxford: Oxford University Press, 1994 [1925].
_____. *Huntingtower*. Oxford: Oxford University Press, 1996 [1922].
_____. *The Leithen Stories*. Edinburgh: Canongate, 2000.
_____. *Prester John*. York: House of Stratus, 2001 [1910].
Bucher, Henry H. 'Canonization by Repetition: Paul du Chaillu in Historiography'. *Revue Francaise d'Histoire d'Outre-Mer* 66 (1979): 15–32.

Buckland, F. T. 'The Naturalist'. *Field*. 2 March 1861, 179.
_____. 'The Naturalist'. *Field*. 27 April 1861, 357.
Buell, Lawrence. *The Future of Environmental Criticism: Environmental Crisis and Literary Imagination*. Oxford: Blackwell, 2005.
Bunn, David. 'Embodying Africa: Woman and Romance in Colonial Fiction'. *English in Africa* 15, no. 1 (May 1998): 1–28.
Burbridge, Ben. *Gorilla: Tracking and Capturing the Ape-Man of Africa*. London, Bombay and Sydney: George Harper and Co., 1928.
Burton, Lt.-Col. R. W. 'A Bibliography of Big Game Hunting and Shooting in India and the East'. *Journal of the Bombay Natural History Society* 49, no. 2 (1950).
Calarco, Matthew. 'Deconstruction is Not Vegetarianism: Humanism, Subjectivity and Animal Ethics'. *Continental Philosophy Review* 37, no. 2 (2004): 175–201.
_____. *Zoographies: The Question of the Animal from Heidegger to Derrida*. New York: Columbia University Press, 2008.
Cartmill, Matt. *A View to a Death in the Morning: Hunting and Nature Through History*. Cambridge, MA: Harvard University Press, 1993.
Casid, Jill H. *Sowing Empire: Landscape and Colonization*. Minneapolis: University of Minnesota Press, 2005.
Cavalieri, Paola. *The Animal Question: Why Nonhuman Animals Deserve Human Rights*. Oxford: Oxford University Press, 2003.
Cavell, Stanley et al. *Philosophy and Animal Life*. New York: Columbia University Press, 2008.
Chambers, Paul. *Jumbo: The Greatest Elephant in the World*. London: Andre Deutsch, 2007.
Chambers, Robert. *Vestiges of the Natural History of Creation*. London: Churchill, 1844.
Chancellor, John. *Audubon: A Biography*. London: Weidenfield and Nicolson, 1978.
Cheng, Dorothy, L. and Robert M. Seyforth. *How Monkeys See the World: Inside the Mind of Another Species*. Chicago: University of Chicago Press, 1990.
Childs, Peter and Patrick Williams. *An Introduction to Post-Colonial Theory*. Hemel Hempstead: Prentice Hall, 1997.
Chrisman, Laura. *Rereading the Imperial Romance*. Oxford: Oxford University Press, 2000.
Christopher, A. J. *Colonial Africa*. Totoma: Barnes and Noble, 1984.
Cilano, Caro and Elizabeth DeLoughrey. 'Against Authenticity: Global Knowledge and Postcolonial Ecocriticism'. *Interdisciplinary Studies in Literature and Environment* 14, no. 1 (2007): 71–88.
Clark, T. J. *The Painting of Modern Life*. London: Thames and Hudson, 1985.
Clodd, Edward. *Memories*. London: Watts and Co., 1926.
Coetzee, J. M. *The Lives of Animals*. Princeton: Princeton University Press, 1999.
Cohen, Morton. *Rider Haggard: His Life and Works*. London: Macmillan, 1968.
Cohen, William A. and Ryan Johnson (eds). *Filth: Dirt, Disgust and Modern Life*. Minneapolis: University of Minnesota Press, 2005.
Collard, Andree and Joyce Contrucci. *The Rape of the Wild*. London: Women's Press, 1988.
Conrad, Joseph. *The Secret Agent*. London: Penguin, 1963 [1907].
Corby, Raymond and Bert Theunissen. *Ape, Man, Apeman: Changing Views since 1600*. Leiden: Leiden University Press, 1995.
Cosslet, Tess. *Talking Animals in British Children's Fiction, 1780–1940*. Aldershot: Ashgate, 2006.
Crosby, Alfred W. *Ecological Imperialism: The Biological Expansion of Europe, 900–1900*. Cambridge: Cambridge University Press, 1986.

Cumming, Roualeyn Gordon. *Five Years of a Hunter's Life in the Far Interior of South Africa*. London: John Murray, 1850.
Czech, Kenneth. *An Annotated Bibliography of African Big Game Hunting, 1785–1950*. St Cloud: Land's Edge, 1999.
Danahay, Martin. 'Nature Red in Hoof and Paw: Domestic Animals and Violence in Victorian Art'. *Victorian Animal Dreams: Representations of Animals in Victorian Literature and Culture*, ed. Deborah Morse and Martin A. Danahay, 97–120. Aldershot: Ashgate, 2007.
Darier, Éric (ed.) *Discourses of the Environment*. Oxford: Blackwell, 1999.
Darwin, Charles. Letter to W. B. Tegetmeier, 28 May 1861. The Darwin Correspondence Project. http://www.darwinproject.ac.uk/darwinletters/calendar/entry-3164.html (accessed 2 January 2009).
_____. Letter to Asa Gray, 11 December 1861. The Darwin Correspondence Project. http://www.darwinproject.ac.uk/darwinletters/calendar/entry-3342.html (accessed 27 December 2008).
_____. *The Descent of Man and Selection in Relation to Sex*. London: John Murray, 1898 [1871].
_____. *The Autobiography of Charles Darwin*. London: Collins, 1958 [1876].
_____. *The Origin of Species*. London: Penguin, 1982 [1859].
Dawson, Graham. *Soldier Heroes: British Adventure, Empire and the Imagining of Masculinities*. London: Routledge, 1994.
Deep Ecology Platform. http://www.deepecology.org/platform.htm (accessed 2 January 2009).
De Grazia, David. *Animal Rights: A Very Short Introduction*. Oxford: Oxford University Press, 2002.
Derrida, Jacques. '"Eating Well", or The Calculation of the Subject: An Interview with Jacques Derrida'. In *Who Comes After the Subject*, ed. Eduardo Cadava, Peter Connor and Jean-Luc Nancy, 96–119. London: Routledge, 1991.
_____. 'The Animal That Therefore I Am (More to Follow)', trans. David Wills. *Critical Inquiry* 28 (Winter 2002): 370–418.
_____. 'Violence Against Animals'. In *For What Tomorrow… A Dialogue*, trans. Jeff Fort. Stanford: Stanford University Press, 2004.
Desmond, Adrian. *Huxley: The Devil's Disciple*. London: Michael Joseph, 1994.
Dixson, A. F. *The Natural History of the Gorilla*. London: Weidenfield and Nicolson, 1981.
Donald, Diana. 'Pangs Watched in Perpetuity: Sir Edwin Landseer's Pictures of Dying Deer and the Ethos of Victorian Sportsmanship'. In *Killing Animals*, The Animal Studies Group, 50–68. Urbana and Chicago: University of Illinois Press, 2006.
_____. *Picturing Animals in Britain, 1750–1850*. New Haven: Yale University Press, 2007.
Dorré, Gina M. *Victorian Fiction and the Cult of the Horse*. Aldershot: Ashgate, 2006.
Douglas, Mary. *Purity and Danger: An Analysis of the Concepts of Pollution and Taboo*. London: Routledge, 1991 [1966].
Drayton, Richard. *Nature's Government: Science, Imperial Britain and the 'Improvement' of the World*. New Haven and London: Yale University Press, 2000.
Drotner, Kirsten. *English Children and New Magazines, 1751–1945*. New Haven and London: York University Press, 1988.
Dryden, Linda. *Joseph Conrad and the Imperial Romance*. Basingstoke: Macmillan, 2000.
Du Chaillu, Paul. *Explorations and Adventures in Equatorial Africa*. London: John Murray, 1861.

_____. 'The New Traveller's Tales'. *Athenaeum*. 25 May 1861, 694–5.
_____. *A Journey to Ashongoland*. London: John Murray, 1867.
_____. *Stories of the Gorilla Country*. London: Sampson Low, 1868.
_____. *Wild Life Under the Equator*. London: Sampson Low, 1869.
_____. *Lost in the Jungle*. London: Sampson Low, 1870.
_____. *The World of the Great Forest*. London: John Murray, 1901.
_____. *King Mombo*. London: John Murray, 1902.
_____. *In African Forest and Jungle*. London: John Murray, 1903.
_____. Unpublished letters. Natural History Museum, London.
Dunae, Patrick A. 'Penny Dreadfuls: Late Nineteenth Century Boys' Literature and Crime'. *Victorian Studies* 22, no. 2 (1979): 133–50.
_____. 'Boys' Literature and the Idea of Empire: 1870–1914'. *Victorian Studies* 24, no. 1 (Autumn 1980): 105–21.
Dworkin, Andrea. *Pornography: Men Possessing Women*. London: The Women's Press, 1981.
Eby, Cecil Degrotte. *The Road to Armageddon: The Martial Spirit in English Popular Literature, 1870–1914*. Durham, NC and London: Duke University Press, 1987.
Elder, Glen, Jennifer Wolch and Jody Emel. '*La Pratique Sauvage*: Race, Place and the Human/Animal Divide'. In *Animal Geographies: Place, Politics and Identity in the Nature-Culture Borderlands*, ed. Jennifer Wolch and Jody Emel, 72–90. London and New York: Verso, 1997.
Eldredge, Niles. *Darwin: Discovering the Tree of Life*. New York: Norton, 2005.
Eldridge, C. C. *The Imperial Experience: From Carlyle to Forster*. Basingstoke: Macmillan, 1996.
Ellegard, Alvar. *Darwin and the General Reader*. Gothenburg: University of Gothenburg Press, 1958.
Etherington, Norman. *Rider Haggard*. Boston: Twayne Publishing, 1984.
Farber, Paul Lawrence. *Finding Order in Nature: The Naturalist Tradition from Linnaeus to E. O. Wilson*. Baltimore: John Hopkins University Press, 2000.
Fenn, G. Manville. *Nat the Naturalist*. London: Blackie: 1882.
_____. *Glynn Severn's Schooldays*. London and Edinburgh: Chambers, 1904.
_____. *G. A. Henty: The Story of an Active Life*. Glasgow: Blackie and Sons, 1911.
Ferguson, Christine. 'Footnotes on *Trilby*: The Human Foot as Evolutionary Icon in Late Victorian Culture'. *Nineteenth Century Contexts* 28, no. 2 (June 2006): 127–44.
Field. 'The Library'. 11 May 1861, 396.
_____. 'The Gorillas in *The Field* Window'. 3 August 1861, 101.
Fitzgerald, William G. 'Animal Furniture'. *Strand*. 12 May 1896, 273–80.
Flower, W. H. *Essays on Museums and Other Subjects Connected with Natural History*. London: Macmillan, 1898.
Foucault, Michel. 'Of Other Spaces'. *Diacritics* 16 (Spring 1986): 22–7.
_____. *The Order of Things*. London: Routledge, 1989 [1966].
_____. 'Interview With Michel Foucault'. In *Power: Essential Works, Volume 3*, trans. Robert Hurley et al. London: Penguin, 1994 [1978].
Franey, Laura, E. *Victorian Travel Writing and Imperial Violence: British Writing on Africa, 1855–1902*. Basingstoke: Palgrave, 2003.
Fraser, Robert. *Victorian Quest Romance: Stevenson, Haggard, Kipling and Conan Doyle*. Plymouth: Northcote House, 1998.
Freedgood, Elaine. *Victorian Writing About Risk*. Cambridge: Cambridge University Press, 2000.
Freud, Sigmund. *Civilisation and its Discontents*, trans. Joan Riviere. London: Hogarth Press, 1979 [1930].

Friends of the Earth. http://www.foe.co.uk/index.html (last accessed 2 January 2009).
Frost, Christopher. *A History of British Taxidermy*. Lavenham: Lavenham Press, 1987.
Frye, Northrop. *Anatomy of Criticism*. Princeton: Princeton University Press, 1957.
_____. *The Secular Scripture: A Study of the Structure of Romance*. Cambridge, MA: Harvard University Press, 1976.
Fuchs, Barbara. *Romance*. London: Routledge, 2004.
Fudge, Erica. *Perceiving Animals: Humans and Beasts in Early Modern English Culture*. Basingstoke: Macmillan, 2000.
_____. *Animal*. London: Reaktion, 2002.
_____. 'A Left-Handed Blow: Writing the History of Animals'. *Representing Animals*, ed. Nigel Rothfels, 3–18. Bloomington and Indianapolis: Indiana University Press, 2002.
Fudge, Erica, Susan Wiseman and Ruth Bilbert (eds). *Beasts, Bodies and Natural Philosophy in the Early Modern Period*. Basingstoke: Macmillan, 1999.
Gadgil, Madhav and Ramachandra Guha. *This Fissured Land: An Ecological History of India*. Delhi: Oxford University Press, 1992.
Gandhi, Leela. *Postcolonial Theory: A Critical Introduction*. Edinburgh: Edinburgh University Press, 1998.
Gardener's Chronicle. 'Review of the *Explorations*'. 29 June 1861, 602.
Garner R. L. *Gorillas and Chimpanzees*. London: Osgood, McIlvane and Co., 1896.
Garrard, Greg. *Ecocriticism*. London: Routledge, 2004.
Gates, Barbara T. (ed.) *In Nature's Name: An Anthology of Women's Writing and Illustration*. Chicago and London: University of Chicago Press, 2002.
_____. 'Why Natural History?' *Victorian Literature and Culture* 35, no. 2 (2007): 539–49.
Gates, Henry, Louis Jr (ed.) *'Race', Writing and Difference*. Chicago: University of Chicago Press, 1985.
Gatti, Attilio. *The King of the Gorillas*. New York: Doubleday, Doran and Co., 1932.
Geographicus. 'The Gorilla Region of Africa'. *Times*. 3 March 1861, 12.
Gersdorf, Catrin and Sylvia Mayer. *Nature in Literary and Cultural Studies: Transatlantic Conversation in Ecocriticism*. Amsterdam: Rodopi, 2006.
Gifford, Terry. *Pastoral*. London: Routledge, 1999.
Girouard, Mark. *Alfred Waterhouse and the Natural History Museum*. New Haven and London: Yale University Press, 1989.
Gissing, George. *The Whirlpool*. Cranbury: Associated University Presses, 1977 [1897].
Gladstone, William. *Mr Gladstone on the Teaching of Natural History as a Feature of School Education*. No publication details, 1879.
Glotfelty, Cheryll. 'Introduction: Literary Studies in an Age of Environmental Crisis.' In *The Ecocriticism Reader: Landmarks in Literary Ecology*, ed. Cheryll Glotfelty and Harold Fromm, xv–xxxvii. London: University of Georgia Press, 1996.
Goodall, Jane R. *Performance and Evolution in the Age of Darwin: Out of the Natural Order*. London and New York: Routledge, 2002.
Gosse, Phillip Henry. *The Romance of Natural History*. London: Nisbet and Co., 1861.
Gott, Ted. '"It's Lovely to be a Gorilla Sometimes": The Art and Influence of Emmanuel Fremiet, Gorilla Sculptor'. *Melbourne Art Journal* 9/10 (2006/2007): 198–219.
Grant, Ben. '"Interior Explorations": Paul Belloni du Chaillu's Dream Book'. *Journal of European Studies* 38, no. 4 (2008): 407–19.
Gray, J. E. 'Zoological Notes on Perusing M. du Chaillu's "Adventures in Equatorial Africa"'. *Annals and Magazine of Natural History* 7 (1861): 60–65, 463–70.
_____. 'On the Habits of the Gorilla and Other Tailless Long-Armed Apes'. *Proceedings of the London Zoological Society* (1861): 212–13.

———. 'Observations on Mr. Du Chaillu's papers on the "New Species of Mammals" Discovered by him in West Equatorial Africa'. *Proceedings of the London Zoological Society* (1861): 273–8.
———. 'The New Traveller's Tales'. *Athenaeum*. 18 May 1861, 662–3.
———. 'M. du Chaillu's African Discoveries'. *Times*. 24 May 1861, 10.
———. 'Dr Gray of the British Museum on M. Du Chaillu's Book'. *Morning Advertiser*. 24 May 1861, 4.
———. 'The Gorilla'. *Athenaeum*. 21 September 1861, 373–4.
———. 'The Gorilla'. *Athenaeum*. 12 October 1861, 479.
Gray, Stephen. *South African Literature: An Introduction*. Cape Town: David Phillips, 1979.
Gregory, William K. and Henry C. Raven. *In Quest of Gorillas*. New Bedford: Darwin Press, 1937.
Green, Martin. *Dreams of Adventure: Deeds of Empire*. London: Routledge and Kegan Paul, 1980.
Green, Susie. *Tiger*. London: Reaktion, 2006.
Griffin, Donald R. *Animal Thinking*. Cambridge, MA: Harvard University Press, 1984.
Grove, Richard H. *Green Imperialism: Colonial Expansion, Tropical Island Edens and the Origins of Environmentalism, 1600–1860*. Cambridge: Cambridge University Press, 1995.
Grove, Richard H., Vinita Damodarn and Satpal Sangwan. *Nature and the Orient*. Delhi: Oxford University Press, 1998.
Guha, Ramachandra. 'Radical American Environmentalism and Wilderness Preservation: A Third World Critique'. *Environmental Ethics* 11, no. 1 (1989): 71–83.
———. *Environmentalism: A Global History*. Harrow: Longman, 2000.
Haggard, Rider H. *Eric Brighteyes*. New York: P. F. Collier, 1888.
———. *Maiwa's Revenge*. London: Longmans, 1888.
———. *Rural England*. London: Longmans, 1902.
———. *The Poor and the Land*. London: Longmans, 1905.
———. *Regeneration*. London: Longmans, 1910.
———. *The Mahatma and the Hare: A Dream Story*. London: Longman, Green and Co., 1911.
———. *The Ivory Child*. London: Hutchinson, 1916.
———. *Marie*. London: Cassell and Co., 1916 [1912].
———. *The Holy Flower*. London: Ward, Lock and Co., 1917.
———. *Ayesha: The Return of She*. London: Ward, Lock and Co., 1918 [1905].
———. *Heu-Heu*. London: Hutchinson, 1923.
———. *Nada the Lily*. London: Collins, 1957 [1892].
———. *Child of Storm*. London: MacDonald, 1958 [1913].
———. *Allan's Wife*. London, MacDonald, 1963 [1889].
———. *She*. Oxford: Oxford University Press, 1991 [1887].
———. *Allan Quartermain*. Ware: Wordsworth Classics, 1994 [1887].
———. *Diary of an African Journey*. London: Hurst and Co., 2000 [1914].
———. *King Solomon's Mines*, ed. Gerald Monsmon. Peterborough, ON: Broadview Press, 2002 [1885].
———. 'A Zulu War-Dance'. Appendix B3 in *King Solomon's Mines*, ed. Gerald Monsmon, 255–68. Peterborough, ON: Broadview Press, 2002 [1885].
———. 'About Fiction'. Appendix B4 in *King Solomon's Mines*, ed. Gerald Monsmon, 269–73. Peterborough, ON: Broadview Press, 2002 [1885].
Haley, Bruce. *The Healthy Body and Victorian Culture*. Cambridge, MA: Harvard University Press, 1978.

Halliday, Stephen. *The Great Stink of London: Sir Joseph Bazelgette and the Cleansing of the Victorian Metropolis*. Stroud: Sutton, 1999.
Ham, Jennifer and Matthew Senior. *Animal Acts: Configuring the Human in Western History*. London and New York: Routledge, 1997.
Hammond, Dorothy and Alta Jablow. *The Africa That Never Was*. New York: Twayne, 1970.
Haraway, Donna. *Primate Visions: Gender, Race and Nature in the World of Modern Science*. London and New York: Verso, 1989.
_____. *Simians, Cyborgs and Women: The Reinvention of Nature*. London: Free Association Books, 1991.
Harris, Capt. William Cornwallis. *The Wild Sports of South Africa*. London: John Murray, 1839.
Henning, Michelle. 'Anthropomorphic Taxidermy and the Death of Nature: The Curious Art of Hermann Ploucquet, Walter Potter and Charles Waterton'. *Victorian Literature and Culture* 35, no. 2 (2007): 663–79.
Henty, G. A. *The Tiger of Mysore*. London: Blackie, 1896.
_____. *Rujub the Juggler*. New York: Mershon, 1901 [1893].
_____. *Through Three Campaigns*. London: Blackie, 1903.
_____. *In Times of Peril*. Bungay: R. Clay and Sons, 1933 [1880].
_____. 'By Sheer Pluck'. In *The G. A. Henty Omnibus Book*. London: Blackie, n.d. [1885].
Himmelfarb, Gertrude. *Victorian Minds*. London: Weidenfield and Nicolson, 1968 [1952].
Hooper, Glenn. *Landscape and Empire, 1770–2000*. Aldershot: Ashgate, 2005.
Howarth, William. 'Some Principles of Ecocriticism'. In *The Ecocriticism Reader: Landmarks in Literary Ecology*, ed. Cheryll Glotfelty and Harold Fromm, 69–91. London: University of Georgia Press, 1996.
Huddart, David. *Homi K. Bhabha*. London: Routledge, 2008.
Huggan, Graham. '"Greening" Postcolonialism: Ecocritical Perspectives'. *Modern Fiction Studies* 50, no. 3 (Fall 2004): 701–33.
Huggan, Graham and Helen Tiffin. *Postcolonial Ecocriticism: Literature, Animals, Environment*. London: Routledge, 2010.
Hulme, Peter. *Colonial Encounters: Europe and the Native Caribbean, 1492–1797*. London: Routledge, 1992.
Huxley, Thomas H. 'Darwin on the Origin of Species'. *Times*. 26 December 1859, 8.
_____. 'Professor Huxley on Man's Place in Nature'. *Edinburgh Review* (April 1863): 548–69.
_____. *Lay Sermons, Addresses and Reviews*. London: Macmillan, 1870.
_____. *Man's Place in Nature and Other Anthropological Essays*. London: Macmillan, 1894 [1863].
Iglesia, Maria Angeles Toda. 'Deadly Marriages: Masculinity and the Pleasures of Violence in H. R. Haggard's Romances of Adventure'. In *Dressing up for War: Transformations of Gender and Genre in the Discourse and Literature of War*, ed. Aranzazu Usandizaga and Andrew Monnickendam. Amsterdam: Rodopi, 2001.
Ingold, Tim. *What is an Animal?* London: Unwin, 1988.
Irvine, Robert. 'Separate Accounts: Class and Colonization in the Early Stories of R. M. Ballantyne'. *Journal of Victorian Culture* 12, no. 2 (2007): 238–61.
Irwin, R. A. (ed.) *Letters of Charles Waterton of Walton Hall*. London: Rockcliff, 1955.
James, Erin. 'Review of Graham Huggan and Helen Tiffin'. *Green Letters* (2011): 113.
Jamieson, Dale. 'Against Zoos'. In Peter Singer (ed.), *In Defence of Animals: The Second Wave*. Oxford: Blackwell, 2006.
JanMohamed, Abdul R. 'The Economy of Manichean Allegory: The Function of Racial Difference in Colonialist Literature'. *Critical Inquiry* 12, no. 1 (Autumn 1985): 59–87.

Janson, H. W. *Ape and Ape Lore in the Middle Ages and Renaissance*. London: University of London, 1952.
Jasanoff, Maya. *Edge of Empire: Lives, Culture, and Conquest in the East, 1750–1850*. New York: Knopf, 2005.
Jeffries, Richard. *After London*. Oxford: Oxford University Press, 1980 [1885].
Jensen, J. Veron. *Thomas Henry Huxley: Communicating for Science*. Newark, DE: University of Delaware Press, 1991.
Johns, B. G. 'The Literature of the Streets'. *Edinburgh Review* 165 (1887): 40–65.
Johnson, Martin. *Congorilla*. New York: Brewer, Warren and Putnam, 1931.
Jones, Jeanette Eileen. '"Gorilla Trails in Paradise": Carl Akeley, Mary Bradley and the American Search for the Missing Link'. *Journal of American Culture* 29, no. 3 (2006): 321–36.
Jones, R. W. 'The Sight of Creatures Strange to Our Clime: London Zoo and the Consumption of the Exotic'. *Journal of Victorian Culture* 2, no. 1 (1997): 275–94.
Kafka, Franz. 'A Report to an Academy'. In *Explain To Me Some Stories of Kafka*, ed. Angel Flores. New York: Gordian Press, 1983 [1917].
Kalof, Linda, Amy Fitzgerald and Lori Baralt. 'Animals, Women and Weapons: Blurred Sexual Boundaries in the Discourse of Sport Hunting'. *Society and Animals* 12, no. 3 (2004): 237–51.
Kappeler, Susanne. *The Pornography of Representation*. Cambridge: Polity Press, 1988.
Katz, Wendy, R. *Rider Haggard and the Fiction of Empire*. Cambridge: Cambridge University Press, 1987.
Kean, Hilda. A*nimal Rights: Political and Social Change in Britain Since 1800*. London: Reaktion, 1998.
Keating, Peter. *The Haunted Study: A Social History of the English Novel 1875–1914*. London: Secker and Warburg, 1989.
Kenyon-Jones, Christine. *Kindred Brutes: Animals in Romantic Period Writing*. Aldershot: Ashgate, 2001.
Kerridge, Richard and Neil Sammells (eds). *Writing the Environment: Ecocriticism and Literature*. London: Zed Books, 1998.
Kingsley, Charles. *The Water Babies*. London: Dent and Sons, 1971 [1863].
Kingston, W. H. G. *In the Wilds of Africa*. London: Nelson, 1871.
Kipling, Rudyard. *The Jungle Books*. London: Penguin, 1987 [1894; 1895].
_____. *Puck of Pook's Hill and Rewards and Fairies*. Oxford: Oxford University Press, 1993 [1910].
Kirby, F. Vaughan. *In Haunts of Wild Game*. Edinburgh and London: Blackwood's, 1896.
Koenigsberger, Kurt. *The Novel and the Menagerie: Totality, Englishness and Empire*. Columbus: Ohio State University Press, 2007.
Koerner, Lisbet. 'Carl Linnaeus In His Time and Place'. In *Cultures of Natural History*, ed. N. Jardine, J. A. Secord and E. C. Spary, 145–62. Cambridge: Cambridge University Press, 1996.
Kristeva, Julia. *Powers of Horror: An Essay on Abjection*, trans. Leon S. Roudiez. New York: Columbia University Press, 1982.
Kruse, Juanita. *John Buchan and the Idea of Empire*. Lewiston, NY: E. Mellen Press, 1989.
Lamont, James. 'The Gorilla Controversy'. *Morning Advertiser*. 9 July 1861, 4.
Lang, Andrew. 'Realism and Romance'. *Contemporary Review* 52 (1887): 685–93.
Law, Graham. 'The Romace of Empire: John Buchan's Early Writings'. *Humanitas* 31 (February 1993): 1–13.

Lawlor, Leonard. *This Is Not Sufficient*. New York: Columbia University Press, 2007.
_____. '"Animals Have no Hand": An Essay on Animality in Derrida'. *New Continental Review* 7, no. 2 (2007): 43–69.
Leighton, Mary Elizabeth and Lisa Surridge. 'The Empire Bites Back: The Racialised Crocodile of the Nineteenth Century'. In *Victorian Animal Dreams: Representations of Animals in Victorian Literature and Culture*, ed. Deborah Morse and Martin A. Danahay, 249–70. Aldershot: Ashgate, 2007.
Lévi-Strauss, Claude. *Totemism*, trans. Rodney Needham. Boston: Beacon Press, 1962.
Lewens, Tim. *Darwin*. London: Routledge, 2007.
Lewes, G. H. *Studies in Animal Life*. London: Smith, Elder and Co., 1862.
Lewis, C. S. 'On Stories'. In *Essays Presented to Charles Williams*, 90–106. Oxford: Oxford University Press, 1947.
_____. *English Literature in the Sixteenth Century (Excluding Drama)*. Oxford: Clarendon Press, 1954.
Lippit, Akira Mizuta. 'Magnetic Animal: Derrida, Wildlife, *Animetaphor*'. *Modern Language Notes* 113 (1998): 1111–25.
_____. *Electric Animal: Toward a Rhetoric of Wildlife*. Minneapolis: University of Minnesota Press, 2000.
Logan, Maweena Kossi. *Narrating Empire: G. A. Henty and the Fictions of Empire*. London and New York: Garland, 1999.
Loomba, Ania. *Colonialism/Postcolonialism*. London: Routledge, 1998.
London Illustrated News. 'The Gorilla'. Vol. 34 (1859): 348.
London, Jack. *People of the Abyss*. London, 1903.
Love, Glen A. *Practical Ecocriticism: Literature, Biology, and the Environment*. Charlottesville: University of Virginia Press, 2003.
Lovelock, James. *Gaia*. Oxford: Oxford University Press, 1987 [1979].
Low, Gail Ching-Liang. *White Skins, Black Masks: Representation and Colonialism*. London: Routledge, 1996.
Lownie, Andrew. *John Buchan: The Presbyterian Cavalier*. London: Pimlico, 1995.
Luke, Brian. 'Violent Love: Hunting, Heterosexuality and the Erotics of Man's Predation'. *Feminist Studies* 24, no. 3 (Fall 1998): 627–55.
Lundblad, Michael. 'From Animal to Animality Studies'. *PMLA* 124, no. 2 (March 2009): 496–502.
Lyall, Alfred C. 'Novels of Adventures and Manners'. *Quarterly Review* 179 (1894): 530–52.
MacDonald, George. *The Princess and the Goblin and The Princess and Curdie*. Oxford: Oxford University Press, 1990 [1883].
MacDonald, Kate (ed.) *Reassessing John Buchan: Beyond the Thirty-Nine Steps*. London: Pickering and Chatto, 2009.
MacGillivray, W. *Lives of Eminent Zoologists from Aristotle to Linnaeus*. Edinburgh: Oliver and Boyd, 1834.
MacIntyre, Alasdair. *Dependent Rational Animals: Why Human Beings Need the Virtues*. London: Duckworth, 1999.
MacKenzie, John M. *Propaganda and Empire*. Manchester: Manchester University Press, 1984.
_____. 'Chivalry, Social Darwinism and Ritualised Killing: The Hunting Ethos in Central Africa up to 1914'. In *Conservation in Africa: People Politics and Practice*, ed. David Anderson and Richard Grove. Cambridge: Cambridge University Press, 1987.
_____. *The Empire of Nature: Hunting, Conservation and British Imperialism*. Manchester: Manchester University Press, 1988.

———. *Empires of Nature and the Nature of Empires: Imperialism, Scotland and the Environment*. East Lothian: Tuckwell Press, 1997a.

———. 'Empire and the Ecological Apocalypse: The Historiography of the Imperial Environment'. In *Ecology and Empire: Environmental History of Settler Societies*, ed. Tom Griffiths and Libby Robin, 215–28. Edinburgh: Keele University Press, 1997b.

Malamud, Randy. *Reading Zoos: Representations of Animals in Captivity*. Basingstoke: Macmillan, 1998.

———. *Poetic Animals and Animal Souls*. Basingstoke: Palgrave, 2003.

Mandelstam, Joel. 'Du Chaillu's Stuffed Gorillas and the Savants from the British Museum'. *Notes and Records of the Royal Society of London* 48, no. 2 (1994): 227–45.

Mangan, J. A. and Callum McKenzie. 'Radical Conservatives: Middle Class Masculinity, the Shikar Club and Big-Game Hunting'. *European Sports History Review* 4 (2002): 185–209.

———. '"Pig-Sticking is the Greatest Fun": Martial Conditioning in the Hunting Fields of Empire'. *European Sports History Review* 5 (2003): 97–119.

Marzec, Robert P. *An Ecological and Postcolonial Study of Literature: From Daniel Defoe to Salman Rushdie*. Basingstoke: Palgrave, 2007.

Marx, Karl. *Capital*, vol. 1, trans. Ben Fowkes. London: Penguin, 1990 [1867].

Mason, A. E. W. *The Four Feathers*. London: Macmillan, 1903 [1902].

Masterman, C. F. G. *The Heart of Empire: Discussions of Problems of Modern City Life in England*. Brighton: Harvester Press, 1973 [1901].

McCook, Stuart. '"It May be Truth, But It is Not Evidence": Paul du Chaillu and the Legitimation of Evidence in the Field Sciences'. *Osiris* 11 (1996): 177–97.

McCracken, Donal P. *Gardens of Empire: Botanical Institutions of the Victorian British Empire*. London and Washington: Leicester University Press, 1997.

McKibben, Bill. *The End of Nature*. London: Penguin, 1990.

McLaughlin, Joseph. *Writing the Urban Jungle: Reading Empire in London from Doyle to Eliot*. London: University Press of Virginia, 2000.

McLintock, Anne. *Imperial Leather: Race, Gender and Sexuality in the Colonial Conquest*. London: Routledge, 1995.

———. 'Maidens, Maps and Mines: The Reinvention of Patriarchy in Colonial South Africa'. *South Atlantic Quarterly* 87 (Winter 1998): 147–92.

McLynn, Frank. *Hearts of Darkness: The European Exploration of Africa*. London: Pimlico, 1992.

Merrill, L. L. *The Romance of Victorian Natural History*. Oxford: Oxford University Press, 1989.

Midgley, Mary. *Animals and Why They Matter*. Athens, GA: University of Georgia Press, 1983.

———. *Beast and Man*. London and New York: Routledge, 1995 [1980].

Mill, J. S. *Three Essays on Religion*. London: Longmans, 1874.

Miller, John. 'Adventures in the Volcano's Throat: Tropical Landscape and Bodily Horror in R. M. Ballantyne's *Blown to Bits*'. *Victorian Review* 34, no. 1 (Spring 2008): 115–30.

Miller, William Ian. *The Anatomy of Disgust*. Cambridge, MASS: Harvard University Press, 1997.

Mitman, Gregg. 'When Nature Went to the Zoo: Vision and Power in the Art and Science of Natural History'. *Osiris* 11 (1996): 117–43.

Mivart, St George. *Man and Apes: An Exposition of Structural Resemblances and Differences Bearing Upon Questions of Affinity and Origin*. London: Robert Hardwicke, 1873.

Monsman, Gerald. 'Of Diamonds and Deities: Social Anthropology and H. Rider Haggard's *King Solomon's Mines*'. *English Literature in Transition* 3 (2000): 280–96.
_____. 'H. Rider Haggard's *Nada the Lily*: A Triumph of Translation'. *English Literature in Transition* 47, no. 4 (2004): 371–98.
_____. *H. Rider Haggard on the Imperial Frontier: The Political and Literary Contexts of his African Romances*. Greensboro, NC: ELT Press, 2006.
Moore-Gilbert, Bart. *Postcolonial Theory: Contexts, Practices, Politics*. London: Verso, 1997.
Morning Advertiser. 23 May 1861, 4.
_____. 25 May 1861, 4.
_____. 'Letter from an "Old Traveller" on M. Du Chaillu's Work'. 29 May 1861.
_____. 1 June 1861, 3.
_____. 16 June 1861, 5.
_____. 'The Gorilla Controversy'. 3 July 1861, 4.
_____. 17 December 1861, 3.
Morse, Deborah and Martin A. Danahay. *Victorian Animal Dreams: Representations of Animals in Victorian Literature and Culture*. Aldershot: Ashgate, 2007.
Morton, Timothy. *The Ecological Thought*. Cambridge, MA: Harvard University Press, 2010.
Moss A. V. *Valiant Crusade*. London: Cassell, 1961.
Mukherjee, Upamanyu Pablo. *Postcolonial Environments: Nature, Culture and the Contemporary Indian Novel in English*. Basingstoke: Palgrave, 2010.
Mumford, Lewis, *The Culture of Cities*. London: Secker and Warburg, 1940.
Murray, John. 'The Gorilla War'. *Athenaeum*. 6 July 1861, 20.
Murphy, Patrick. 'Prolegomenon for an Ecofeminist Dialogics'. In *Feminism, Bakhtin and the Dialogic*, ed. Dale M. Bauer and S. J. McInstrey. Albany: State University of New York Press, 1991.
Nagel, Thomas. 'What Is It Like To Be a Bat'. *Philosophical Review* 83, no. 4 (October 1974): 435–50.
Nead, Lynda. *Victorian Babylon: People, Streets and Images in Nineteenth-Century London*. New Haven: Yale University Press, 2000.
Nixon, Rob. 'Environmentalism and Postcolonialism'. In *Postcolonial Studies and Beyond*, ed. Ania Loomba et al. Durham, NC and London: Duke University Press, 2005.
Noakes, Richard. 'The *BOP* and Late Victorian Juvenile Magazines'. In *Science in the Nineteenth Century Periodical: Reading the Magazine of Nature*, ed. Geoffrey Cantor et al. Cambridge: Cambridge University Press, 2004.
Nordau, Max. *Degeneration*. London: Heinemann, 1913 [1895].
Northcott, Michael S. *The Environment and Christian Ethics*. Cambridge: Cambridge University Press, 1998.
Norquay, Glenda (ed.) *R. L. Stevenson on Fiction: An Anthology of Literary and Critical Essays*. Edinburgh: Edinburgh University Press, 1999.
Noske, Barbara. *Beyond Boundaries: Humans and Animals*. Montreal: Black Rose Books, 1997.
Nyman, Jopi. *The Postcolonial Animal Tale from Kipling to Coetzee*. New Delhi: Atlantic, 2003.
O'Brien, Susie. 'Articulating a World of Difference: Ecocriticism, Postcolonialism and Globalization'. *Canadian Literature* 170–71 (2001): 140–58.
Ord, George. Unpublished letters to Charles Waterton. Library of the American Philosophical Society, Philadelphia.
Owen, Richard. 'Ostelogical Contributions to the Natural History of the Chimpanzee'. *Transactions of the Zoological Society of London* 3 (1848): 381–422.

———. *On the Classification and Geographical Distribution of the Mammalia*. London: John W. Parker and Son, 1859.
———. 'Darwin on the Origin of Species'. *Edinburgh Review* 11, no. 226 (April 1860): 487–532.
———. *On the Extent and Aims of a National Museum of Natural History*. London: Saunders, Otley and Co., 1862.
Owen, Rev. Richard. *The Life of Richard Owen*. London: John Murray, 1894.
Oxley, J. Macdonald. *The Specimen Hunters*. London: The Religious Tract Society, 1907.
Page, George. *Inside the Animal Mind*. New York: Broadway Books, 2001.
Paley, William. *Natural Theology*. London: The Christian Evidence Committee of the Society for Promoting Christian Knowledge, 1885 [1802].
Pandian, Anand, S. 'Predatory Care: The Imperial Hunt in Mughal and British India'. *Journal of Historical Sociology* 14, no. 1 (March 2001): 81–101.
Parry, Benita. *Post-Colonial Studies: A Materialist Critique*. London: Routledge, 2004.
Patterson, David K. 'Paul B. Du Chaillu and the Exploration of Gabon, 1855–1865'. *International Journal of African Historical Studies* 7, no. 4 (1974): 647–67.
Patton, Paul. 'Language, Power and the Training of Horses'. In *Zoontologies: The Question of the Animal*, ed. Cary Wolfe, 83–100. Minneapolis: University of Minnesota Press, 2003.
Phillips, Dana. *The Truth of Ecology: Nature, Culture and Literature in America*. New York: Oxford University Press, 2003.
Phillips, Richard. *Mapping Men and Empire: A Geography of Adventure*. London: Routledge, 1997.
Pick, Daniel. *Faces of Degeneration*. Cambridge: Cambridge University Press, 1989.
Plumwood, Val. *Feminism and the Mastery of Nature*. London: Routledge, 1993.
———. *Environmental Culture: The Ecological Crisis of Reason*. London: Routledge, 2002.
Pratt, Mary Louise. *Imperial Eyes: Travel Writing and Transculturation*. London: Routledge, 1992.
Pringle, Thomas. *Narrative of a Residence in South Africa*. Cape Town: C. Struik, 1966 [1835].
Proceedings of the Royal Geographical Society. 25 February 1861, 111.
Pulteney, Richard. *A General View of the Writings of Linnaeus*. London: R. Taylor and Co., 1805.
Punch. 'The British Lion's Vengeance on the Bengal Tiger'. 22 August 1857, 76–7.
———. 'Monkeyana'. 18 May 1861, 206.
———. 'The Lion of the Season'. 25 May 1861, 213.
———. 'The Latest From Africa'. 13 July 1861, 19.
Quayle, Eric. *Ballantyne the Brave: A Victorian Writer and His Family*. London: Hart-Davis, 1967.
———. *R. M. Ballantyne: A Bibliography of First Editions*. London: Dawson's of Pall Mall, 1968.
Quinn, Stephen Christopher. *Windows on Nature: The Great Habitat Dioramas of the American Museum of Natural History*. New York: Abrams, 2007.
Rangarajan, Mahesh. *India's Wildlife History*. Delhi: Permanent Black, 2001.
Reade, Winwood. *Savage Africa*. London: Smith, Elder and Co., 1863.
———. 'Notes on the Derbyan Eland, the African Elephant and the Gorilla'. *Proceedings of the London Zoological Society* (1863): 169–73.
Regan, Tom and Singer, Peter. *Animal Rights and Human Obligations*. New Jersey: Prentice Hall, 1989.

Reid, Captain Mayne. *The Plant Hunters*. London: J. and C. Brown and Co., 1858.
Richards, Jeffrey. 'Spreading the Gospel of Self-Help: G. A. Henty and Samuel Smiles'. *Journal of Popular Culture* 16, no. 2 (Fall 1982): 52–64.
Richards, Thomas. *The Commodity Culture of Victorian England: Advertising and Spectacle*. Stanford: Stanford University Press, 1990.
_____. *The Imperial Archive: Knowledge and the Fantasy of Empire*. London: Verso, 1993.
Ritvo, Harriet. 'Animal Pleasures: Popular Zoology in Eighteenth and Nineteenth-Century England'. *Harvard Library Bulletin* 33, no. 3 (Summer 1985): 239–79.
_____. *The Animal Estate: The English and Other Creatures*. Cambridge, MA: Harvard University Press, 1987.
_____. 'The Power of the Word: Scientific Nomenclature and the Spread of Empire'. *Victorian Newsletter* (Spring 1990): 5–8.
_____. *The Platypus and the Mermaid*. Cambridge, MA: Harvard University Press, 1997.
_____. 'Destroyers and Preservers: Big-Game in the Victorian Empire'. *History Today* 52 (January 2002): 33–7.
Rothfels, Nigel. *Savages and Beasts: The Birth of the Modern Zoo*. Baltimore and London: John Hopkins University Press, 2002.
Rudler, F. W. *On Natural History Museums: With Suggestions for the Formation of a Central Museum in Wales*. London: 1876.
Rupke, Nicolaas A. *Richard Owen: Victorian Naturalist*. New Haven: Yale University Press, 1994.
Ryan, James R. *Picturing Empire: Photography and the Visualisation of the British Empire*. London: Reaktion, 1997.
_____. 'Hunting with the Camera: Photography, Wildlife and Colonialism in Africa'. In *Animal Spaces, Beastly Places: New Geographies of Human Animal Relations*, ed. Chris Philo and Chris Wilbert. London: Routledge, 2000.
Said, Edward. *Orientalism*. London: Peregrine, 1985 [1978].
_____. *Culture and Imperialism*. London: Vintage, 1994 [1993].
Salmon, E. G. 'What the Working Classes Read'. *The Nineteenth Century* 20 (1886): 108–17.
_____. *Juvenile Literature As It Is*. London: Henry J. Drane, 1888.
Salmon Edward and Major A. A. Longden. *The Literature and Art of Empire*. London: Collins, 1924.
Salt, Henry S. *Seventy Years Among Savages*. London: Unwin, 1921.
_____ (ed.) *Killing for Sport*. London: G. Bell and Sons, 1915.
_____. *Animal Rights: Considered in Relation to Social Progress*. London: Centaur Press, 1980 [1894].
Sandison, Alan. *The Wheel of Empire*. London: Macmillan, 1967.
Sartre, Jean-Paul. *Being and Nothingness: An Essay on Phenomenological Ontology*, trans. Hazel E. Barnes. London: Methuen and Co., 1972 [1943].
Savage, Thomas and Jeffries Wyman. 'Notice of the External Characters and Habits of Trodlydytes Gorilla, A New Species of Orang from the Gaboon River'. *Boston Journal of Natural History* 5, no. 4 (December 1847): 417–42.
Scanlon, John. *On Garbage*. London: Reaktion, 2005.
Scarry, Elaine. *The Body in Pain: The Making and Unmaking of the World*. Oxford: Oxford University Press, 1985.
Scheick, William, J. 'Adolescent Pornography and Imperialism in Haggard's *King Solomon's Mines*'. *English Literature in Transition* 37, no. 2 (1994): 19–30.

Schell, Heather. 'Tiger Tales'. In *Victorian Animal Dreams: Representations of Animals in Victorian Literature and Culture*, ed. Deborah Morse and Martin A. Danahay, 229–48. Aldershot: Ashgate, 2007.

Scherren, Henry. *Popular History of Animals for Young People*. London: Cassell and Co., 1895.

_____. *The Zoological Society of London: A Sketch of its Foundation and Development*. London: Cassell and Co., 1905.

Scott, J. E. A. *A Bibliography of the Works of Sir Henry Rider Haggard*. Bishop's Stortford: Elkin Matthews, 1947.

Scruton, Roger. *On Hunting*. London: Random House, 1999

Selous, F. C. *A Hunter's Wanderings in Africa*. London: Richard Bentley, 1861.

_____. *Sport and Travel: East and West*. London: Longmans, 1900.

Sewell, Anna. *Black Beauty*. London: Collins, 1965 [1877].

Shakespear, Capt. H. *The Wild Sports of India*. London: Smith, Elder and Co., 1860.

Shakespeare, William. *Titus Andronicus*. London: The Arden Shakespeare, 1995 [c. 1590].

Shepard, Paul. 'Virtually Hunting Reality in the Forests of Simulacra'. In *Reinventing Nature: Responses to Postmodernism*, ed. M. E. Soulé and Gary Lease. Washington DC: Island Press, 1995.

_____. *The Others: How Animals Made Us Human*. Washington DC: Island Press, 1996.

Showalter, Elaine, *Sexual Anarchy*. London: Bloomsbury, 1991.

Shukin, Nicole. *Animal Capital: Rendering Life in Biopolitical Times*. Minneapolis: University of Minnesota Press, 2009.

Simmons, Laurence and Armstrong, Philip (eds). *Knowing Animals*. Leiden and Boston: Brill, 2007.

Simons, John. *Animal Rights and the Politics of Literary Representation*. Basingstoke: Palgrave, 2002.

Singer, Peter. *Animal Liberation*. New York: New York Review, 1975.

Smith, Craig. 'Every Man Kills the Thing He Loves: Empire, Homoerotics and Nationalism in John Buchan's *Prester John*'. *Novel: A Forum in Fiction* (Winter 1995): 173–200.

Smith, Janet Adam. *John Buchan: A Biography*. Oxford: Oxford University Press, 1995.

Soper, Kate. 'What is Nature'. In *The Green Studies Reader: From Romanticism to Ecocriticism*, ed. Laurence Coupe, 123–6. London and New York: Routledge, 2000.

Soulé, M. E. and Gary Lease (eds). *Reinventing Nature: Responses to Postmodernism*. Washington DC: Island Press, 1995.

Spiegel, Marjorie. *The Dreaded Comparison: Human and Animal Slavery*. New York: Mirror Books, 1996 [1988].

Spivak, Gayatri Chakravorty. 'Can the Subaltern Speak?' In *Marxism and the Interpretation of Culture*, ed. Cary Nelson and Laurence Grossley. Chicago: University of Illinois Press, 1988.

Spurgeon, Rev. C. H. 'The Gorilla and the Land He Inhabits'. A lecture given in the Metropolitan Tabernacle, 1 October 1861.

Spurr, David. *The Rhetoric of Empire: Colonial Discourse in Journalism, Travel Writing and Imperial Administration*. Durham, NC and London: Duke University Press, 1993.

Stebbing, E. P. *Jungle Byways in India*. London: John Lane, 1910.

_____. *Stalks in the Himalayas*. London: John Lane, 1912.

Steeves, H. Peter. *Animal Others: On Ethics, Ontology and Animal Life*. Albany: State University of New York Press, 1999.

Stevenson, R. L. 'A Humble Remonstrance'. In *Memories and Portraits*. London: Chatto and Windus, 1919.

_____. *Dr Jekyll and Mr Hyde*. Oxford: Oxford University Press, 1987 [1886].
Stiebel, Lindy. *Imagining Africa: Landscape in H. Rider Haggard's African Romances*. Westport: Greenwood Press, 2001.
Stigand, Capt. C. H. and D. D. Lyell. *Central African Game and its Spoor*. London: Horace Cox, 1906.
Storey, Harry. *Hunting and Shooting in Ceylon*. New Delhi and Madras: Asian Educational Services, 1998 [1906].
_____. *A Ceylonese Sportsman's Diary*. New Delhi and Madras: Asian Educational Services, 2000 [1921].
Storey, William, K. 'Big Cats and Imperialism: Lion and Tiger Hunting in Kenya and Northern India, 1898–1930'. *Journal of World History* 2, no. 2 (Fall 1991): 135–73.
Stott, Rebecca, 'Scaping the Body: Of Cannibal Mothers and Colonial Landscapes'. In *The New Woman in Fiction and Fact*, ed. Angelique Richardson. Basingstoke: Palgrave, 2001.
Street, Brian V. *The Savage in Literature: Representations of 'Primitive' Society in English Fiction, 1858–1920*. London: Routledge, 1975.
Sutcliffe, Antony (ed.) *Metropolis 1890–1940*. London: Alexander Press, 1984.
Swift, Jonathan. *Gulliver's Travels*. London: Penguin, 1984 [1726].
Tiffin, Helen. 'Unjust Relations: Post-Colonialism and the Species Boundary'. In *Compr(om)ising Post/Colonialism(s)*, ed. Greg Ratcliffe and Gerry Turcote. Sydney: Dangaroo Press, 2001.
Times. 'Royal Geographical Society'. 28 May 1861, 12.
Tolini, Michelle. '"Beetle Abominations" and Birds on Bonnets: Zoological Fantasy in Late-Nineteenth-Century Dress'. *Nineteenth-Century Art Worldwide* (2002). http://19thcartworldwide.org/spring_02/articles/toli_print.html (accessed 4 October 2009).
Twine, Richard. *Animals and Biotechnology: Ethics, Sustainability and Critical Animal Studies*. London: Earthscan, 2010.
Vaucaire, Michel. *Paul du Chaillu: Gorilla Hunter*, trans. Emily Pepper. London: Harper, 1930.
Vibert, Elizabeth. 'Real Men Hunt Buffalo: Masculinity, Race and Class in British Fur Traders' Narratives'. In *Cultures of Empire: Colonizers in Britain and the Empire in the Nineteenth and Twentieth Centuries*, ed. Catherine Hall. Manchester: Manchester University Press, 2000.
Wallace, A. R. *The Malay Archipelago*. London: Macmillan, 1877 [1869].
_____. 'Monkeys'. *Contemporary Review* 41 (1882): 417–30.
_____. *Studies Scientific and Social*, 2 vols. New York: Macmillan, 1900.
Waterton, Charles. *Essays on Natural History*. London: Longman, 1857.
_____. Letter to the *Gardener's Chronicle*. 30 March 1861, 288.
_____. Letter to the *Gardener's Chronicle*. 8 June 1861, 528, 552.
_____. Letter to the *Gardener's Chronicle*. 22 June 1861, 577.
_____. Waterton and Ord. Unpublished correspondence. Glasgow University Library.
Watts, Richard. 'Towards an Ecocritical Postcolonialism: Val Plumwood's *Environmental Culture* in dialogue with Patrick Chamoiseau'. *Journal of Postcolonial Writing* 44, no. 3 (September 2008): 251–61.
Wells, H. G. *The Time Machine*. London: Everyman, 1993 [1895].
White, Andrea. *Joseph Conrad and the Adventure Tradition*. Cambridge: Cambridge University Press, 1993.
White Jr, Lynn. 'The Historical Roots of our Environmental Crisis'. In *The Ecocriticism Reader: Landmarks in Literary Ecology*, ed. Cheryll Glotfelty and Harold Fromm. London: University of Georgia Press, 1996.

Wilson, E. O. *Biophilia*. Cambridge, MA: Harvard University Press, 1984.
Wills, Rev. Freeman. 'Recreating Evening Schools'. *The Nineteenth Century* 20 (1886): 130–38.
Wohl, Anthony S. *Endangered Lives: Public Health in Victorian Britain*. London: Dent, 1993.
Wolfe, Cary (ed.) *Zoontologies: The Question of the Animal*. Minneapolis: University of Minnesota Press, 2003.
_____. *Animal Rites: American Culture, The Discourse of Species and Posthumanist Theory*. Chicago: University of Chicago Press, 2003.
Wonders Karen. *Habitat Dioramas: Illusions of Wilderness in Museums of Natural History*. Uppsala: Uppsala University Press, 1993.
Wood, Rev. J. G. *The Illustrated Natural History*. London: Routledge, 1862.
_____. 'Modern Taxidermy'. *Cornhill Magazine* 7 (1863): 20–25.
_____. 'On Killing, Setting and Preserving Insects'. *Boy's Own Paper* 27, no. 1 (1879): 469.
_____. *Boy's Own Natural History*. London: Routledge, 1881.
_____. *The Dominion of Man*. London: Richard Bentley and Son, 1889.
Wright, Thomas. 'On a Possible Popular Culture'. *Contemporary Review* 40 (1881): 25–44.
Yerkes, Robert M. and Ada W. Yerkes. *The Great Apes: A Study of Anthropoid Life*. New Haven: Yale University Press, 1929.
Young, Robert J. C. *Colonial Desire: Hybridity in Theory, Culture and Race*. London: Routledge, 1995.
_____. *Postcolonialism: An Historical Introduction*. Oxford: Blackwell, 2001.
_____. *The Idea of English Ethnicity*. Oxford: Blackwell, 2008.
Youngs, Tim. *Travellers in Africa*. Manchester: Manchester University Press, 1994.
_____. 'White Apes at the Fin-de-Siècle'. In *Writing and Race*, ed. Tim Youngs. London and New York: Longmans, 1997.
Zgórniak, Marek, Narta Kapera and Mark Singer. 'Fremiet's *Gorillas*: Why Do They Carry Off Women?' *Artibus et Historiae* 27, no. 54 (2006): 219–37.

INDEX

'About Fiction' (Haggard) 29
Adams, Carol 54
Adams, William M. 12, 17
Adanson, Michel 64
Adorno, Theodor 13–14
African Colony, The (Buchan) 9, 33
Agamben, Giorgio 137
Ahuja, Neel 14–15, 18
Akeley, Carl 58–61, 63–4, 71, 124
albatross 49
Alderson, General E. A. 39
Alfred, Prince 8
Allan Quartermain (Haggard) 30, 160, 161, 166
Allan's Wife (Haggard) 9
alligator 79–81
American Museum of Natural History 58, 63
animal studies 3, 5–6, 15–18, 31, 36, 185–6
Animal Studies Group 3, 13, 167
animality studies 6
armadillo 62
Armstrong, Philip 5, 107, 188
Arnold, Guy 33
Ashanti War, The 21, 74
Athenaeum, The 100, 100, 111, 113, 115

baboon 1–2, 98, 127, 151
Baden-Powell, Robert 40, 70–73, 78, 81, 153–5
Bailey's Magazine 7
Baldwin, W. C. 7, 13, 167
Ballantyne, R. M.: and violence 1–3, 6–10, 19, 39, 165; and publication history 21, 69; and lack of critical attention 24; and romance 26–7, 170; and young readers 73, 86; and natural history 89; and the gorilla controversy 127, 129–48; and degeneration 151–2, 155–8, 160; and masculinity 172–82; and anthropomorphism 187
Baratay, Eric 61
Bazelgette, Sir Joseph 146–7, 151
Baudrillard, Jean 14, 57, 59
Beinart, William 11
Bennett, Edward 38
Bhabha, Homi 25, 107
Bilig, Michael 54
biodiversity 8, 10, 15, 17–18, 31, 32
Blake, William 37
blaubok 8
Blown to Bits (Ballantyne) 89, 127, 135, 139–41, 144–6, 152
Boer War, The 6, 34
Booth, William 150–51, 161
Boyd, Edward 166–7
Boy's Own Paper 34, 68–9, 71–4
Braddon, Sir Edward 39
Bristow, Joseph 33, 82
British Museum 63, 89, 103, 109, 110, 111, 113
Browne, Janet 106, 107
Browne, Thomas, 29
Buchan, John: and hunting 9–10, 45–6; and romance 19–20, 29–39, 183–4, 188; and criticism 24; and capitalism 27, 51–5, 92; and natural history 71; and masculinity 86, 94, 166, 168–9; and industrialisation 153–5, 157–62
Buckland, F. T. 102–3
Buell, Lawrence 18

buffalo 8, 164–5, 177
Buffon, Comte de 64
Burroughs, Edgar Rice 164
By Sheer Pluck (Henty) 21, 74–6, 79–83, 85–95, 133, 142

Canada 7, 154
Cartmill, Matt 167
Ceylon 9, 10, 39, 49, 52, 177
Chambers, Robert 2
Chrisman, Laura 92, 162–3
Cilano, Caro 16
Clodd, Edward 117
Collard, Andree 177
Contemporary Review, The 117
Contrucci, Joyce 177
Conrad, Joseph 24, 138, 150
Coral Island, The (Ballantyne) 6, 24, 127, 135
crocodiles 49, 80–81
critical animal studies 6, 185
Cumming, Roualeyn Gordon 7–9, 54, 175
Cuvier, Georges 61

Darwin, Charles: and survival of the fittest 66–7; and human identity 97–9, 131, 141; and the gorilla controversy, 104–5, 114; and colonialism 120, 171; and A. R. Wallace 126; and hygiene 143–4; and degeneration 148, 150
deep ecology 16
Defoe, Daniel 26
degeneration theory: and sanitation 21, 96, 146; and violence 45, 86; and literary form 72, 166; and species difference 148–58, 162–3, 169, 183; and class 160
DeLoughrey, Elizabeth 16
Derrida, Jacques 14, 18, 107, 138 186–7
Disraeli, Benjamin 98
Donald, Diana 3, 37, 53, 54
Doody, Margaret 27
Doyle, Arthur Conan 30
Drayton, Richard 62
Dr Jekyll and Mr Hyde (Stevenson) 150, 166
Dryden, Linda 25–6, 30–31

du Chaillu, Paul: and natural history and adventure writing 19, 21; and criticism 24; and the gorilla controversy 100–27, 149; and R. M. Ballantyne 129–31, 135, 137, 139; and *Punch* 143; and contamination 146–7, 151–3
du Maurier, George 142
Dumas, Alexandre 26
Dunae, Patrick 74
Dworkin, Andrea 170–71, 177

ecocriticism 3–6, 13, 15–18, 31, 159, 185–6
Egerton, Sir Philip Gray 113
elephants: and hunting 1–2, 7–8, 10, 39, 174; and commodification 46, 48–51; and natural history 61; in a magic lantern show 91; in national parks 120; and aggression 160
Ellis, Havelock 177
Evernden, Neil 30
Explorations and Adventures in Equatorial Africa (du Chaillu) 104–15, 119, 121, 123–6, 129, 137

Fan people 90–92
Fenn, G. M.: and G. A. Henty 19, 97, 100, 121, 132, 150, 152, 166, 172, 183; and natural history 21, 74–96, 180, 184; and criticism 24; and hygiene 135
Ferguson, Christine 142
Field, The 7, 102, 103, 110, 113
First World War 34, 46
Fitzgerald, William G. 49–51, 54
Flower, W. H. 62, 95
Foucault, Michel 59, 64–7, 70, 88, 95, 169
Freud, Sigmund 29, 97, 167
Friends of the Earth 15
Frye, Northrop 26–8, 35, 170, 172, 181
Fuchs, Barbara 26–7
Fudge, Erica 97, 147

Gardener's Chronicle, The 115, 125
Garrard, Greg 5, 159, 161
Gide, André 138
giraffe 49, 132

Gissing, George 153
Gladstone, William 70, 101
Glotfelty, Cheryl 4
Gorilla Hunters, The (Ballantyne): and violence 1–2, 39, 165, 177; and Ballantyne's reputation 6–7; and the gorilla controversy 127, 129–35, 139; and romance 21, 170; and masculinity 86, 172–5, 178–81; and anthropomorphism 187
gorillas: and species difference 21, 181, 183; and the gorilla controversy 96, 97–149; and degeneration theory 151–4; and dreams 170; and masculinity 175
Gosse, P. H. 68
Gray, Asa 143
Gray, John Edward 109–13, 115, 121
Green, Martin 23, 25–6, 29
Guha, Ramachandra 12

Haeckel, Ernst 16
Haggard, H. Rider: and violence 9, 21, 160–71, 176; and biography 19; and criticism 24; and romance 26–31; and natural history 92; and hygiene 116; and transformation 158, 184
Hagenbeck, Carl 60, 62
Half-Hearted, The (Buchan) 39
Halliday, Stephen 146
Ham, Jennifer 168
Hanno 102
Haraway, Donna 59, 88, 97, 98
Hardouin-Fugier, Elisabeth 61
Harris, William Cornwallis 7, 8
Henty, G. A.: and biography and career 19–21; and criticism 24; and romance 26; and the Indian 'Mutiny' 32–45; and commodity culture 48, 50, 53, 55, 180; and natural history 74–96, 172–3; and G. M. Fenn 97, 100, 121, 150, 152, 166, 183; and violence 132–3; and hygiene 142
hippocampus debate 99–100, 142
Houssa 79
Huggan, Graham 4–6, 12

Hughes, Lotte 11
Hulme, Peter 27
Hunting the Lions (Ballantyne) 7, 155, 174, 177
Huxley, T. H.: and taxonomy 67; and education 70; and Darwinism 98–101, 142; and the gorilla controversy 112, 114; and degeneration 156

In Brightest Africa (Akeley) 124
In Darkest Africa (Booth) 150
Indian 'Mutiny' 20, 32–46, 48–50
industrialisation: and degeneration 6, 153–7, 166; and environmental degradation 9–11, 17, 20; and romance 30, 86
intersectionalism 14–18

Johnson, Dr Samuel 28
Johns, B. G. 150–52
Jonson, Ben 177
Journey to Ashongoland (du Chaillu) 121

Kafka, Franz 116
Kangaroos 61
Kant, Immanuel 15
Kestner, Joseph A. 24
King Kong 125
King Solomon's Mines (Haggard): and Haggard criticism 24; and capitalism 27; and science 92; and masculinity 160 and empire 162; and violence 165, 175
Kingsley, Charles 145, 148, 154
Kingston, W. H. G. 25
Kipling, Rudyard 30, 37, 139, 164
Kirby, F. Vaughan 176–7, 179
Koerner, Lisbet 64
Krakatoa 89, 127, 139, 144–6
Kristeva, Julia 142

Lamont, James 104
Landseer, Edwin 37
Lang, Andrew 29–30, 31
Lankester, Edwin Ray 150
Le Corbusier 153
leopard 18, 40, 52, 80–81, 163–5, 176–7

Leopold, Aldo 16, 185
Lewis, C. S. 26, 34
lions: and hunting 9, 36–7, 39–40, 77, 168, 174, 177; and symbolism 42, 44; and taxidermy 52; and natural history 60; and masculinity 86, 156–8; as metaphor 101, 118–19, 163–5
Linné, Carl von 63–6, 137
Livingstone, Dr 7
Lodge in the Wilderness, A (Buchan): and imperialism 20–21, 32–8, 183; and violence, 41, 45–6, 86, 168; and commodity culture 51–3; and industrialisation 157–60
Logan, Mawuena Kossi 44
London Illustrated News 126
London, Jack 149–54, 156, 162, 188
London Standard, The 34
London Zoo 60, 62
Loomba, Ania 16
Lost in the Jungle (du Chaillu) 123
Lovelock, James 16
Low, Gail Ching-Liang 30, 154
Lundblad, Michael 6
Lyall, Alfred C. 23, 28
Lyell, D. D. 12, 160, 169

Maathai, Wangari 12
MacDonald, George 150
MacKenzie, John M.: and indigenous hunting 9; and imperial hunting 11, 35, 37–8, 165; and civilisation 53; and natural history 65, 96; and the erotics of hunting 172
Malay Archipelago, The (Wallace) 87–8, 126–8, 132
Mangan, J. A. 155
Manichaeism 15–16, 53, 55, 184
Marvin, Garry 167
Marryat, Captain 25
Masterman, C. F. G. 153
Marx, Karl 47, 50
McCook, Stuart 109, 114
McCracken, Donal 62
McKenzie, Callum 155
Memory Hold-the-Door (Buchan) 30–31
Mill, J. S. 141–2

Millais, J. G. 166
Milner, Lord Alfred 32
moa 9
Monsman, Gerald 24, 28, 163
More, Henry 98
Morning Advertiser, The 110–13, 115–16, 129
Morton, Timothy 16
Mughal Empire 9, 38
Mukherjee, Pablo 3, 5, 16
Murchison, Roderick 101, 113
Murray, John 104, 111, 112

Nada the Lily (Haggard) 21, 161–7, 176
Naess, Arne 16
Nat the Naturalist (Fenn) 21, 74–96, 135, 185
New Zealand 9
Nietzsche, Friedrich 37, 167–8
Nineteenth Century, The 152
Nixon, Rob 4
Noakes, Richard 68–9
Nordau, Max 150
Noske, Barbara 184, 186
nshiego mbouvé 135, 137–9

O'Brien, Susie 3, 12
orangutans 102–3, 117, 125–8, 132, 139, 142
Ord, George 112, 116–17
Order of Things, The (Foucault) 64, 67
ostrich 62
Ovid 181
Owen, Richard: and the natural history museum 61–3; and the gorilla controversy 98–101, 103, 105, 112–13, 125–6, 136, 142, 147

Pandian, Anand S. 38, 41, 63
parrots 51, 90, 91, 95
People of the Abyss, The (London) 149–54, 156, 162, 188
penny dreadful 68–70, 73, 85, 151–3, 166
Plumwood, Val 172, 184, 186
porcupine 66
postcolonial studies 3–6, 10–18, 23–5, 30, 107, 184–6
poststructuralism 4

Power-House, The (Buchan) 53
Prester John (Buchan) 24, 27, 33, 162
Price, Aubrey C. Rev 6
Prince of the Captivity, The (Buchan) 54
Pringle, Thomas 7
psychoanalysis 21, 28, 30, 170, 172
Punch 42, 44, 116, 118–19, 143

Quaggas 8, 10
Quinn, Stephen, Christopher 59, 88

Raffles, Sir Stamford 65
Rangarajan, Mahesh 8
Reade, Winwood 119–20, 125
Red Eric (Ballantyne) 21, 127, 135–9, 151
Regan, Tom 13
Reid, Captain Mayne 25, 73
Rhino 8, 177
Richards, Thomas 46–7
Ritvo, Harriet 60, 64–6, 72, 176
Royal Geographical Society 100, 101
Rudler, F. W. 80
Rueckert, William 4
Rujub the Juggler (Henty): and imperialism 20, 183; and the Indian 'Mutiny' 32–45; and commodity culture 48, 50, 53; and masculinity 76, 95, 173
Rupke, Nicolaas 100
Ryder, Richard 13

Said, Edward 3–4
Saint Hilaire, Geoffre 111
Salmon, E. G. 23–4, 34, 69, 73
Salt, Henry Stephens 72
Salvation Army 150, 161
Saro-Wiwa, Ken 12
Savage, Thomas 102–3, 141–2
Schell, Heather 72
Scott, Walter 26
Scouting for Boys (Baden-Powell) 70, 153
Scruton, Roger 167
Selous, Frederick Courteney 8
Senghor, Leopold 16
Settler and the Savage, The (Ballantyne) 2
Shakespear, Major H. 10, 155, 177
Shakespeare, William 172, 181
She (Haggard) 24

Shepstone, Sir Theophilus 162
Shukin, Nicole 47, 55
Sierra Leone 92
Singer, Peter 13
Six Months at the Cape (Ballantyne) 1
Snyder, Gary 184
Soper, Kate 4
South Africa: and hunting 2, 7–12, 158–9; and John Buchan 19, 159; and Boer War 34; and ostrich farming 62; and emigration 154–5; and Rider Haggard 162
South Seas 27
speciesism 13, 82
Spiegel, Marjorie 14–16
Spivak, Gayatri 66, 88
Spurgeon, Rev. C. H. 111–12, 143, 147, 151
Spurr, David 65, 138, 142, 178
Sportsman, The 7
Stables, Gordon 73
Stanley, H. M. 150
Stevenson, R. L. 24, 30, 133, 150, 166
Stigand, Captain C. H. 12, 160, 169
Strand Magazine 48–9
Storey, Harry 9, 10, 49–53, 55, 169, 177
Stories of the Gorilla Country (du Chaillu) 121, 124

taxidermy 21, 59–60, 88, 93–5, 131
Tegetmeier, W. G. 114
Thirty-Nine Steps, The (Buchan) 24
Thomson, Andrew, Rev. Dr 6
Tiffin, Helen 5, 6, 15
tigers: and hunting 8, 36–45, 76–7, 81, 177; conservation 12; and commodification 48; skins 90
Tolstoy, Leo 26
Twine, Richard 14
Tylor, E. B. 29
Tyson, Edward 102–3

veganism 185
Verne, Jules 73
Victoria, Queen 8, 72

Wallace, A. R. 87–9, 107, 117, 126–8
Ward, Rowland 51

Water Babies, The (Kingsley) 146, 154
Waterton, Charles 66, 103, 110, 112–17, 125–7, 147
warthog 9, 16
Watts, Richard 4
Wells, H. G. 154
White, Andrea 24, 28
Wilberforce, Samuel 98
Wild Life Under the Equator (du Chaillu) 122, 124
Wills, Rev. Freeman 152

Wolf 8, 164–5, 176
Wolfe, Cary 54
Wood, Rev. J. G. 71–2, 78
Wright, Frank Lloyd 153
Wyman, Jeffries 102–3, 141

Xenophon 39

zoocriticism 6
zoos 10, 18, 60–61, 63, 67
Zulus 162–6, 176

www.ingramcontent.com/pod-product-compliance
Lightning Source LLC
Chambersburg PA
CBHW021824300426
44114CB00009BA/318